nurturing
math curiosity

With Learners in Grades K–2

Chepina Rumsey & Jody Guarino

Copyright © 2024 by Solution Tree Press

Materials appearing here are copyrighted. With one exception, all rights are reserved. Readers may reproduce only those pages marked "Reproducible." Otherwise, no part of this book may be reproduced or transmitted in any form or by any means (electronic, photocopying, recording, or otherwise) without prior written permission of the publisher.

555 North Morton Street
Bloomington, IN 47404
800.733.6786 (toll free) / 812.336.7700
FAX: 812.336.7790

email: info@SolutionTree.com
SolutionTree.com

Visit **go.SolutionTree.com/mathematics** to download the free reproducibles in this book.

Printed in the United States of America

Library of Congress Cataloging-in-Publication Data

Names: Rumsey, Chepina, author. | Guarino, Jody, author.
Title: Nurturing math curiosity with learners in grades K-2 / Chepina
  Rumsey, Jody Guarino.
Description: Bloomington, IN : Solution Tree Press, 2024. | Includes
  bibliographical references and index.
Identifiers: LCCN 2024003795 (print) | LCCN 2024003796 (ebook) | ISBN
  9781960574367 (paperback) | ISBN 9781960574374 (ebook)
Subjects: LCSH: Mathematics--Study and teaching (Kindergarten) |
  Mathematics--Study and teaching (Elementary) | Motivation in education.
Classification: LCC QA135.6 .R85 2024 (print) | LCC QA135.6 (ebook) | DDC
  372.7--dc23/eng/20240222
LC record available at https://lccn.loc.gov/2024003795
LC ebook record available at https://lccn.loc.gov/2024003796

Solution Tree
Jeffrey C. Jones, CEO
Edmund M. Ackerman, President

Solution Tree Press
President and Publisher: Douglas M. Rife
Associate Publishers: Todd Brakke and Kendra Slayton
Editorial Director: Laurel Hecker
Art Director: Rian Anderson
Copy Chief: Jessi Finn
Senior Production Editor: Sarah Foster
Copy Editor: Jessica Starr
Proofreader: Jessi Finn
Text and Cover Designer: Julie Csizmadia
Acquisitions Editors: Carol Collins and Hilary Goff
Content Development Specialist: Amy Rubenstein
Associate Editors: Sarah Ludwig and Elijah Oates
Editorial Assistant: Anne Marie Watkins

GROWING THE MATHEMATICIAN IN EVERY STUDENT COLLECTION

Consulting Editors: Cathy L. Seeley and Jennifer M. Bay-Williams

No student should feel they're "just not good at math" or "can't do math"!

Growing the Mathematician in Every Student is a collection of books that brings a joyful positivity to a wide range of topics in mathematics learning and teaching. Written by leading educators who believe that every student can become a mathematical thinker and doer, the collection showcases effective teaching practices that have been shown to promote students' growth across a blend of proficiencies, including conceptual development, computational fluency, problem-solving skills, and mathematical thinking. These engaging books offer preK–12 teachers and those who support them inspiration as well as accessible, on-the-ground strategies that bridge theory and research to the classroom.

Consulting Editors

Cathy L. Seeley, PhD, has been a teacher, a district mathematics coordinator, and a state mathematics director for Texas public schools, with a lifelong commitment to helping every student become a mathematical thinker and problem solver. From 1999 to 2001, she taught in Burkina Faso as a Peace Corps volunteer. Upon her return to the United States, she served as president of the National Council of Teachers of Mathematics (NCTM) from 2004 to 2006 before going back to her position as senior fellow for the Dana Center at The University of Texas. Her books include *Faster Isn't Smarter* and its partner volume, *Smarter Than We Think*, as well as two short books copublished by ASCD, NCTM, and NCSM: (1) *Making Sense of Math* and (2) *Building a Math-Positive Culture*. Cathy is a consulting author for McGraw Hill's *Reveal Math* secondary textbook series.

Jennifer M. Bay-Williams, PhD, a professor at the University of Louisville since 2006, teaches courses related to mathematics instruction and frequently works in elementary schools to support mathematics teaching. Prior to arriving at the University of Louisville, she taught in Kansas, Missouri, and Peru. A prolific author, popular speaker, and internationally respected mathematics educator, Jenny has focused her work on ways to ensure every student understands mathematics and develops a positive mathematics identity. Her books on fluency and on mathematics coaching are bestsellers, as is her textbook *Elementary and Middle School Mathematics: Teaching Developmentally*. Highlights of her service contributions over the past twenty years include serving as president of the Association of Mathematics Teacher Education, serving on the board of directors for the National Council of Teachers of Mathematics and TODOS: Mathematics for ALL, and serving on the education advisory board for Mathkind Global.

Acknowledgments

When we first met in 2013, we had no idea that we'd be writing a book together! Unexpectedly, we met as consultants who were hired to create a professional development series with a team of educators from across the United States related to upper-elementary school fraction concepts. In a chance conversation while presenting our fraction work at a conference, we discovered our shared curiosity for exploring mathematical argumentation in the primary grades. This timely conversation launched a collaboration between two like-minded educators from California and Iowa!

Throughout the journey, we have been fortunate to learn alongside people from many schools, districts, and states, including curious children, dedicated teachers, and supportive administrators. We especially want to thank John Drake, Jeremy Cavallaro, Jon Wiebers, Christina Cho, Rachael Adams Gildea, Bethany Lockhart Johnson, Sara Manseau, and Michelle Sperling.

We wrote articles to share our work, but we had too many ideas to put in shorter pieces. We playfully said that we should write a book together, and it didn't take long for that playful thought to become a serious goal. It was a five-year journey to find just the right home for our book; along the way we learned so much from each person we worked with, especially Kassia Wedekind, Jamie Cross, Carol Collins, Amy Rubenstein, Sarah Foster, and the entire Solution Tree team. We appreciate Carol for believing in our idea and finding the right publisher, and Amy for supporting us as we talked through early drafts of this book. We are grateful to Sarah for all her thoughtful insights and encouragement as we navigated writing our first book.

So much of our thinking has been informed by our experiences and conversations with friends, colleagues, and mentors. We thrive on learning with and from all of our former students and from Christine Allen, Jen Austin, Jeff Barrett, Sharon Barry, Jennie Beltramini, Joan Case, Vanessa Cerrahoglu, Jonathan Alberto Cervantes Barraza, Shelbi Cole, Phil Daro, John Dossey, Saad El-Zanati, Megan Franke, Elena Gacek, Lynsey Gibbons, Kristin Gray, Valerie Henry, Allison Hintz, Vicki Jacobs, Nick Johnson, Tiffany Kane, Elham Kazemi, Rachel Lambert, Cindy Langrall, Jiwon Lee, Tami Martin, Sherri Martinie, Bill McCallum, Linda Plattner, Rossella Santagata, Marie Sykes, Beth van Es, Myuriel von Aspen, Ian Whitacre, Leslie Whitaker, Cathery Yeh, and Jason Zimba.

Finally, the book would not be what it is without the support of our friends and families—especially Brian, Joe, Griselda, Frank, and Connie—and inspiration from our children. Nick, Presley, Peyton, Jackie, and Emily, your playfulness, curiosity, and wonder at the world are an inspiration every day.

Solution Tree Press would like to thank the following reviewers:

Lauren Aragon
Instructional Specialist for Innovation
 & Development
Pasadena Independent School District
Houston, Texas

John D. Ewald
Education Consultant
Frederick, Maryland

Janet Nuzzie
District Intervention Specialist,
 K–12 Mathematics
Pasadena ISD
Pasadena, Texas

Katie Saunders
Elementary/Middle School Teacher
Anglophone School District West
Fredericton, New Brunswick, Canada

Rea Smith
Math Facilitator
Fairview Elementary
Rogers, Arkansas

Visit **go.SolutionTree.com/mathematics**
to download the free reproducibles in this book.

Table of Contents

Reproducibles are in italics.

ABOUT THE AUTHORS — xvii

INTRODUCTION — 1

How Do We Get Started Together? 2

PART I: Nurturing Our Classroom Community and Growing Our Teacher Toolbox — 7

CHAPTER 1 — 9

Establishing the Foundation for Mathematical Argumentation

Teaching Mathematicians in Grades K–2 13

Understanding Layers of Mathematical Argumentation 14

Unpacking Layers of Argumentation in the Classroom Vignettes 17

Exploring Consecutive Sums 18

Questions for Further Reflection 26

Chapter 1 Summary 26

Chapter 1 Application Guide 27

CHAPTER 2 — 29
Nurturing a Classroom Community

- Creating a Playful Environment 31
- Setting Classroom Norms for Mathematics 35
- Using Talk Moves 37
- Using Physical Classroom Space 41
- Questions for Further Reflection 42
- Chapter 2 Summary 42
- *Chapter 2 Application Guide* 43

CHAPTER 3 — 45
Growing Our Teacher Toolbox

- Tools for Planning 46
- Tools for Representing Mathematical Ideas 48
- Tools for Communicating 53
- Questions for Further Reflection 60
- Chapter 3 Summary 61
- *Chapter 3 Application Guide* 62

CHAPTER 4 — 65
Connecting the Classroom Environment and Teacher Toolbox Through Routines

- Using Instructional Routines 66
- Exploring Number of the Day Instructional Routine 69
- Exploring Choral Counting Instructional Routine 74
- Exploring True or False Instructional Routine 83
- Making Connections to Classroom Community and Teacher Toolbox 90
- Questions for Further Reflection 90
- Chapter 4 Summary 91
- *Chapter 4 Application Guide* 92

PART II: Growing the Layers of Argumentation — 95

CHAPTER 5 — 97
Exploring the First Layer: Notice, Wonder, and Beyond

- Understanding Notice and Wonder 101
- Connecting Notice and Wonder to Consecutive Sums 103

Table of Contents

Using Tasks for Noticing and Wondering 105

Noticing and Wondering and the Number of the Day Routine 110

Questions for Further Reflection 112

Chapter 5 Summary 113

Chapter 5 Application Guide 114

CHAPTER 6 — 117

Exploring the Second Layer: Conjecturing

Understanding Conjecturing 123

Connecting Conjecturing to Consecutive Sums 124

Looking at More Examples of K–2 Conjectures 130

Using Tasks for Conjecturing 132

Continuing With the Number of the Day Instructional Routine 134

Questions for Further Reflection 136

Chapter 6 Summary 136

Chapter 6 Application Guide 137

CHAPTER 7 — 139

Exploring the Third Layer: Justifying

Understanding Justifying 143

Connecting Justifying to Consecutive Sums 143

Learning Ways That Students Justify 144

Using Tasks for Justifying 151

Continuing With the Number of the Day Routine 156

Questions for Further Reflection 157

Chapter 7 Summary 157

Chapter 7 Application Guide 158

CHAPTER 8 — 161

Exploring the Fourth Layer: Extending

Understanding Extending 164

Connecting Extending to Consecutive Sums 168

Using Tasks for Extending 168

Questions for Further Reflection 172

Chapter 8 Summary 173

Chapter 8 Application Guide 174

PART III: Growing More Mathematical Ideas — 175

CHAPTER 9 — 177
Finding Opportunities for Argumentation

Discovering Opportunities 177
Questions for Further Reflection 189
Chapter 9 Summary 189
Chapter 9 Application Guide 190

CHAPTER 10 — 193
Using Children's Literature to Engage in Argumentation

Making Connections to Mathematical Argumentation 199
Planning Read-Alouds 199
Questions for Further Reflection 203
Chapter 10 Summary 203
Chapter 10 Application Guide 204

EPILOGUE — 207

APPENDIX A — 211
Instructional Routine Planning Template

Instructional Routine Planning Template 212
Choral Counting Example 217
Number of the Day Example 222
Number of the Day Example With Annotations 227
True or False Example 232

APPENDIX B — 239
Mathematical Ideas Across Chapters

Mathematical Ideas Across Chapters 240

REFERENCES AND RESOURCES — 243

INDEX — 249

About the Authors

 **Chepina Rumsey, PhD,** is an associate professor of mathematics education at the University of Northern Iowa (UNI) in Cedar Falls, Iowa. She is a former elementary school teacher who loves learning alongside her students and integrating subject areas. At UNI, she supports elementary and early childhood majors as they prepare to teach mathematics in their own future classrooms. Chepina focuses her research on mathematical argumentation and learning mathematics in elementary classrooms through exploration and building on students' natural curiosity and wonder.

In addition to teaching, Chepina leads professional development initiatives in many states, supporting K–5 teachers as they integrate best practices related to mathematical argumentation, problem solving, early algebraic thinking, and number sense in their classrooms. She presents at state, national, and international conferences to share ideas and learn from others. Chepina also contributes as a consultant for curriculum development companies to write lessons and review materials.

Chepina's research has been published in *Cognition and Instruction*, *Mathematics Teacher: Learning and Teaching PK–12*, *Journal of Mathematical Behavior*, *School Science and Mathematics, Teaching Children Mathematics, The Reading Teacher*, and a chapter in *Conceptions and Consequences of Mathematical Argumentation, Justification, and Proof.*

Chepina received a bachelor of arts in mathematics and a bachelor of science in elementary education from Keene State College in Keene, New Hampshire, a master's degree in mathematics from Illinois State University, and a PhD in mathematics education from Illinois State University.

Jody Guarino, EdD, is manager of the Teaching, Learning and Instructional Leadership Collaborative, where she supports teaching and learning within coherent instructional systems at the Orange County Department of Education. She engages with teachers and instructional leaders to support professional learning, teacher collaboration, classroom content, and instructional leader coaching in the areas of elementary mathematics and English language arts. She is also a School of Education senior lecturer at the University of California, Irvine (UCI). In her work at UCI, Jody has the privilege of learning alongside scholars, teacher educators, and graduate students to understand and support adult and student learning.

Jody has spent more than thirty years in education, working with early childhood through graduate students. Her work and identity have been heavily influenced by the Cognitively Guided Instruction community, including researchers, mathematics teacher educators, teachers, and students. She has been a classroom teacher, district mentor, teacher on special assignment, and administrator. Working at district, county, state, and national levels, Jody has developed and implemented research-based professional learning in mathematics, assessment, and early literacy with preservice and in-service teachers across the United States, as well as supported districts in designing and enacting multiyear improvement initiatives. She has been involved in several research projects about understanding how teachers can learn from mathematics teaching, investigating video use to support teacher learning, understanding the affordances of paired-collaborative clinical placements, exploring professional learning that supports discourse and argumentation in elementary classrooms, and understanding schoolwide improvement initiatives. Jody has written articles for *Mathematics Teacher: Learning and Teaching PK–12, Teaching Children Mathematics, The Learning Professional, Professional Development in Education, Issues in Teacher Education*, and *ZDM - International Journal on Mathematics Education*.

Jody received a bachelor's degree in sociology and communications from the University of Southern California, a master's degree in curriculum and instruction from California State University, Fullerton, and a doctorate in education leadership from Azusa Pacific University.

To learn more about Jody's work, visit her website (https://education.uci.edu/lecturer-guarino-j.html) or follow @jody_guarino on X (formerly Twitter).

To learn more about the book, follow @mathcuriosityK2 on X (formerly Twitter).

To book Chepina Rumsey or Jody Guarino for professional development, contact pd@SolutionTree.com.

Introduction

Have you ever listened in awe to a K–2 student's ideas as they made connections and thought of something in a new way? Have your students amazed you with ideas about numbers and patterns, seeing something you hadn't thought of before or may have taken for granted? As former teachers and current mathematics teacher educators, we wondered about K–2 students' thinking and how we could nurture students' reasoning through mathematical argumentation by building on what children naturally do: curiously wonder about their world. We are passionate about this topic because we want to develop students' confidence and conceptual understanding at an early age, and we see this book as a way of building a strong foundation rooted in reasoning and curiosity. We know that:

Children enter this world as emergent mathematicians, naturally curious, and trying to make sense of their mathematical environment. When children are curious and *wonder*, they ask questions, helping them to feel confident when doing mathematics. Each and every child must be afforded opportunities to not only feel confident as doers of mathematics but also to experience *joy* and see *beauty* in their mathematical discoveries. (Huinker, 2020, p. 17)

Our first goal of this book is to support you as you integrate exploration and mathematical argumentation in grades K–2. We imagine you are a current or future K–2 teacher who wants to build exploration, curiosity, and argumentation in your classroom. This book will provide explicit examples of what this looks like in action. Additionally, if you are a

K–2 instructional coach, co-teacher, or administrator, this book will be valuable as you support K–2 teachers.

Young children bring so much to our classrooms with their curiosity, desire to explain what they see in the world, and ideas about how things work. Mathematical argumentation is about nurturing students as they explore, notice patterns, curiously wonder, ask questions, conjecture, and justify. As we explore alongside students to understand their thinking, it can also change how we think about mathematics! Our second goal is to potentially help you grow as a mathematician as you explore mathematics content in new ways.

We are grateful to the K–5 teachers who explored this idea with us during professional learning. This book shares what we learned while investigating alongside teachers and students, specifically in grades K–2. The activities, student work, and vignettes are based on our findings in the professional learning projects we have led with teachers.

All the teachers you'll meet in this book were part of our professional learning projects. While we were the facilitators who brought an agenda, readings, and coaching, we all entered the experience eager to explore and learn together. Three of the teachers (Bethany, Rachael, and Christina) were part of a two-year professional learning project at a single school and were in their first or second year of teaching when we started. For that two-year project, we met with the teachers monthly to explore argumentation, plan activities together to use in their classrooms, look at video of each other's classrooms, and analyze students' thinking. Other teachers you'll meet were part of another one-year professional development project involving forty teachers across multiple schools.

Michelle and Sara are teachers from the second project, which also met monthly using a similar model and structure to our previous project. Throughout the book, we'll use real names for Bethany, Rachael, Christina, Sara, and Michelle, but the other teachers and all the students that you'll meet have pseudonyms to keep their identities confidential. Throughout the book, you will also read "Teacher Voices" sections, which are taken from their reflective journals and are used with their permission.

We are so grateful for the collective learning we experienced through these projects and are excited to extend the collaboration with readers in this format. We look forward to continuing the conversation and exploring with you.

How Do We Get Started Together?

In this book, we will set you up for success by sharing every aspect necessary to nurture math curiosity in young students.

Part 1: Nurturing Our Classroom Community and Growing Our Teacher Toolbox— We begin by investigating how classroom communities, teacher tools, and instructional strategies nurture a foundation for curiosity and mathematical argumentation. Unpacking these ideas can be helpful for argumentation and other aspects of teaching! In chapter 1, we build a foundation for the book by unpacking examples of mathematical argumentation and offering specific definitions to guide discussion. In chapter 2, we explore essential elements of classroom environments that nurture argumentation. We share the importance of classroom norms, using space to support sense-making and collaboration, supporting language development, and ensuring each student has a voice. In chapter 3, we identify and develop tools we find essential in argumentation, including those for planning, representing mathematical ideas, and communicating. Then, in chapter 4, we'll connect the environment (chapter 2) and teacher toolbox (chapter 3) as we describe instructional routines that lend themselves to argumentation.

Part 2: Growing the Layers of Argumentation—*Mathematical argumentation* is a way for curious mathematicians to explore and build a deep understanding of mathematics. When students engage in mathematical argumentation, they communicate their ideas, listen to those of others, and make connections. In part 2, chapters 5 through 8, we explore the four layers of mathematical argumentation—noticing and wondering, conjecturing, justifying, and extending—that establish the foundation for our work. We'll also follow one classroom lesson throughout all four chapters to unpack each layer using the Number of the Day instructional routine.

Part 3: Growing More Mathematical Ideas—In part 3, we tie together all ideas from preceding parts as we explore early mathematics concepts, such as composing and decomposing operations, properties, and more! Chapter 9 describes hidden opportunities to include mathematical argumentation within curriculum materials and tasks. Chapter 10 offers opportunities to connect with children's literature. In the epilogue, we reflect on what we as educators gain with mathematical argumentation and invite the reader to consider how to continue learning and growing with others!

Throughout the book, we present classroom vignettes to help you see what mathematical argumentation looks and sounds like in K–2 classrooms. We offer some background for each vignette and discuss alternative teacher moves or questions. When we do this, it's not to criticize the teacher's work in the vignette. It's to reflect and acknowledge that there is much to think about, and teachers can take alternative pathways during meaningful discussions.

To help you grow your mathematical wonder, each chapter features a section called Your Turn, which invites you to explore related mathematics. Sometimes, this section prepares you to look at a classroom vignette with your own knowledge activated. Other times, Your Turn extends an idea, allowing you to relate better to the chapter topics as a learner. Other features in each chapter include Pause and Ponder to help you think about what you've read so far, as well as Questions for Further Reflection and an Application Guide that provide prompts to help you connect what you learned in the chapter to your classroom.

Also included is appendix A to guide you through using the layers of argumentation in instructional routines, such as choral counting, Number of the Day, and true or false. We also include a link to a video where we explain how to use color in your class records. Note that many of the figures and reproducibles here are available in full color at **go.SolutionTree.com/mathematics**. Appendix B gives you an overview of the mathematical ideas across all chapters.

We hope the features included throughout the book will help readers reflect and create a vision for what mathematical argumentation will look like in their own classrooms.

Additionally, the features support a potential book study, where Your Turn, Pause and Ponder, Application Guide, and Questions for Further Reflection can be used to guide group discussions.

PART 1:

Nurturing Our Classroom Community and Growing Our Teacher Toolbox

CHAPTER 1

Establishing the Foundation for Mathematical Argumentation

As we build our vision of what's possible with young mathematicians, let's start by exploring a task with kindergartners where they decompose tens. While the task might not initially seem related, we discuss how decomposing tens is connected to argumentation and how we can begin to nurture argumentation and wonder in our classrooms. After that, we explore a vignette regarding second graders conjecturing about even numbers. Then, we unpack the layers of mathematical argumentation in both vignettes. Finally, we explore consecutive sums.

CLASSROOM VIGNETTE: DECOMPOSING TENS IN A KINDERGARTEN CLASSROOM

In Bethany's kindergarten classroom, students were solving the following story problem involving decomposing 10: *Mrs. Guarino has 10 rabbits in her backyard. Sometimes, the rabbits are in the hutch, and sometimes, out on the grass. Show the different ways the rabbits can be in the hutch and on the grass.*

Some students worked with counters, moving them on and off an image of a hutch. Other students drew circles, each circle representing a rabbit, with a line separating two groups of rabbits to signify those in the hutch and those on the grass. Students engaged in all kinds of work related to this problem using concrete tools, pictures, and numbers. As Bethany walked around, she came to Ava, who said, "I think there are eleven different ways that the rabbits can be in and out of the hutch. I think I have all the ways. I didn't write the equal yet, but I think I have all the ways." See figure 1.1 for Ava's work.

1 + 9   6 + 4
2 + 8   7 + 3
3 + 7   8 + 2
4 + 6   9 + 1
5 + 5   10 + 0
              0 + 10

there are 11

Figure 1.1: Ava's solution to the rabbit story problem.

Bethany: How do you know you have all the ways?

Ava: I think I have all the ways, and I have all the ways backward.

Bethany: What do you mean?

Ava: When I look at all this, I have 3 plus 7 (points to expression) and 7 plus 3 (points to expression).

Ava stood up and walked over to the chart hanging on the classroom wall that showed decomposing 5 from a previous lesson.

Ava: I noticed that it's the regular number, but one more. Like, if I have 6, there are seven different ways.

Bethany: Do you think that works for every number?

Ava: I think it works for all the numbers to 20.

Ava and her classmates in Bethany's kindergarten class had been developing fluency in decomposing 5. They worked with their teacher to create a chart hanging on the wall, close to where Ava was sitting as she worked on the rabbit problem (see figure 1.2).

Ava noticed there are six ways to make 5, which led her to make the connection to the current problem and wonder if there are eleven ways to make 10. Ava recorded the eleven ways to make 10, and she did so quite systematically. She verbalized that she also found "all the ways backward," perhaps a prelude to thinking about the commutative property.

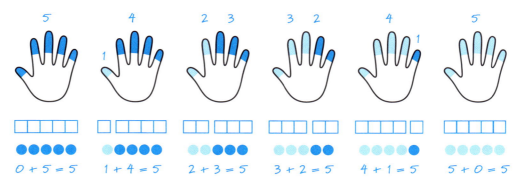

Source: © 2023 Bethany Lockhart. Used with permission.

Figure 1.2: Classroom chart showing the decomposition of 5.

Visit go.SolutionTree.com/mathematics for a free, full-color reproducible version of this figure.

If we pay close attention to Ava's explanation, we also notice that she's made a *conjecture*, a general statement that she thinks might be true for other numbers. She said, "I noticed that it's the regular number, but one more. Like if I have 6, there are seven different ways." She then conjectured that this rule would work for any number up to 20, a large quantity she is familiar with. In a kindergarten way, she is discovering that for any whole number n, there are $n + 1$ ways to add two whole numbers to get a sum of n.

Not all students thought like Ava! Many moved counters around and wrote expressions in systematic and unsystematic ways. With all the different ideas and strategies present in the classroom during a task like this, it is easy to miss the mathematical argumentation that is happening. In this book, we'll help you see the argumentation that is already happening in classrooms and the potential for future argumentation in tasks and activities. When students engage in mathematical argumentation, they look for patterns, communicate about their ideas, listen to those of others, and make connections as they notice and wonder, conjecture, justify, and extend. Ava did a lot of these in this short example. We will revisit this kindergarten lesson where you can see the amazing thinking and reasoning of young mathematicians. We are excited to unpack and discuss many important parts of this example in later chapters.

Throughout this book, we will support you in integrating mathematical argumentation in your classroom and guide you to grow by showing you mathematics in ways that you might not have explored before. To join young students in curiosity and wonder, which comes naturally to them, we need to nurture that in ourselves. Like mathematics education consultant Helen J. Williams (2022), we believe that "doing mathematics is part of being human. Each and every learner is entitled to a broad and deep experience of mathematics that connects with their existing knowledge and understanding and helps them to flourish" (p. 8). Let's continue to build that in ourselves, too!

As mentioned in the introduction (page 1), the following "Your Turn" invites you to grow your mathematical wonder by taking a learner's perspective. Let's look again at Ava's conjecture.

nurturing math curiosity

YOUR TURN
AVA'S CONJECTURE

To restate Ava's conjecture in a mathematically precise way, she said that for any whole number, n, there are $n + 1$ ways to add two whole numbers to get a sum of n. She was exploring how many ways there are to get a sum of 10 in the context of rabbits inside and outside of the hutch. Explore with some different numbers to help unpack the conjecture.

- How many ways are there to add two whole numbers to get a sum of 7?

- What patterns do you notice in your examples?

- What's the first number that works for this conjecture? Will it work for numbers beyond 20?

- How can you convince someone that this will always work?

Teaching Mathematicians in Grades K–2

You might wonder why Ava's conjecture is so fascinating to us and why we began our journey together here. Through our own work as elementary teachers and teacher educators, we have seen a lot going on in the minds of K–2 mathematicians. They are often curious about their world, notice patterns, and ask questions, just like Ava. They are wired to learn new information, explore with hands-on tools, and make sense of the world around them, all while developing their language and social skills.

Teachers hear a range of communication in K–2 mathematics classes. For example, we have listened to students discussing a solution, a procedure, a strategy, a classmate's idea, a question, an observation, a connection to another idea, a rule, and so on. While there is value in the different ways of communicating, it is important to provide opportunities for students to develop their conceptual understanding through higher levels of discussion and mathematical argumentation at all grade levels. What does that mean? As educators, we strive to foster deep mathematical discussions within K–2 lessons to build a strong foundation that includes well-developed conceptual understanding and communication skills. We want to nurture a strong mathematical identity and give all students a voice in the classroom, creating an environment where all students flourish.

We also want to provide opportunities beyond stating procedures and focusing on answers. Similarly, mathematics education researchers Susan Jo Russell, Deborah Schifter, and Virginia Bastable (2011) write:

Children spend much time in mathematics solving individual problems. But the core of the discipline of mathematics is looking *across* multiple examples to find patterns, notice underlying structure, form conjectures around mathematical relationships, and, eventually, articulate and prove general statements. (p. 2)

As stated in the introduction, we explored the idea of communicating about the "core of the discipline of mathematics" through mathematical argumentation with K–2 teachers and their students. As we spent time in their classrooms, we saw many examples of K–2 students engaging as a community of learners, exploring and communicating deep mathematics much like Ava in the opening vignette.

Understanding Layers of Mathematical Argumentation

The amazing student thinking heard in Ava's conjecture relates back to mathematical argumentation. In the vignettes we share in this book, students are communicating about the "core of the discipline of mathematics" (Russell, Schifter, & Bastable, 2011, p. 2) by noticing patterns, making conjectures, justifying, and extending their ideas in new ways. In our research (Rumsey, Guarino, Gildea, Cho, & Lockhart, 2019; Rumsey, Guarino, & Sperling, 2023), we observe mathematical argumentation in the primary classroom as it grows through the following four layers.

1. **Noticing and wondering:** Making observations and asking curious questions

2. **Conjecturing:** Making general statements about the observations

3. **Justifying:** Convincing others and explaining why a conjecture is true or false

4. **Extending:** Making connections beyond the current conjecture, and noticing and wondering with the new ideas in mind

These layers emerged as we worked with K–2 teachers and students, and we find that it's easier to break mathematical argumentation into smaller parts rather than tackling it all at once. Other researchers also find that mathematical argumentation breaks down into distinct parts. Schifter and Russell (2020) developed a "model of five phases that separate different points of focus in the complex process of formulating and proving such generalizations: (1) noticing patterns, (2) articulating conjectures, (3) representing with specific examples, (4) creating representation-based arguments, and (5) comparing and contrasting operations" (p. 15). Mathematics educators Traci Higgins, Susan Jo Russell, and Deborah Schifter (2022) find "four key dimensions of student conjecturing that apply to the context of generalizing about the behavior of the arithmetic operations" (p. 188) for students in grades 2 through 5. Mathematics education researchers Jennifer Knudsen, Harriette S. Stevens, Teresa Lara-Meloy, Hee-Joon Kim, and Nicole Shechtman (2017) write that with middle school students there is a four-part model of mathematical argumentation: (1) generating cases, (2) conjecturing, (3) justifying, and (4) concluding. While the models and terminology are not the same, these examples show that there are interrelated components of argumentation. Our hope is that breaking down each of the layers we found in K–2 classrooms will support you in nurturing mathematical argumentation in your own classroom.

By growing layers of mathematical argumentation within your classroom, you build a strong foundation for students while nurturing skills beyond the mathematics classroom. In addition, you create a classroom culture where learning is shared, everyone's voice is valued, and students communicate clearly. Exploring, conjecturing, justifying, communicating, and considering other people's ideas are important skills to develop, not only in mathematics, but also in all other subjects, such as English language arts and science.

We describe the four layers in chapters 5 through 8 (pages 97–174), so that you can see the distinctions between them and nurture them organically in your own classroom. The layers of argumentation don't happen in isolation. Sometimes, students will flow between layers on their own; other times, you'll need to nudge them into a new layer with questions. Mathematician Francis Su (2020) writes that we can "think of exploration as a continuous cycle, passing from one phase to the other and back again" (p. 57). When we get to the fourth layer, we will have new things to notice and wonder that are built on the previous conjecture and exploration. We can modify conjectures and ideas, lingering longer on the context and continuing to explore. Before continuing on, let's read how first-grade teacher Rachael and second-grade teacher Christina describe mathematical argumentation.

TEACHER VOICES

WHAT IS MATHEMATICAL ARGUMENTATION?

"I would describe argumentation as the language used in mathematics, whether it be oral or written communication. This includes discourse between the students and the teacher, the students and their peers, or even articulating an idea or concept. Making a *noticing* about a mathematical concept is the first step in argumentation, but then the students learn to take that idea, speak about that idea to refine it, then support their thinking through words (oral or written) or pictures and come to some sort of generalization or conjecture about a mathematical concept." (Rachael, grade 1 teacher)

"Argumentation, for me, is allowing students to come up with noticings and synthesize their questions and observations into claims. They would take these claims and find evidence to support if their claims are true or not and then be able to articulate evidence to others, so their audience can understand their ideas. Articulating ideas can come in many different representations and forms." (Christina, grade 2 teacher)

CLASSROOM VIGNETTE: SECOND GRADERS CONJECTURE ABOUT EVEN NUMBERS

One of the big questions when we started the professional development project was, What does mathematical argumentation look like in grades K–2? As we began working with teachers, we all wondered what they could do to encourage mathematical argumentation, what students sounded like when they communicated in this way, and what class activities looked like. Let's look in another classroom to dig into some of the characteristics of mathematical argumentation with young mathematicians.

In Christina's second-grade classroom, students solved the following word problem: *Eli had 16 stickers. He gave 8 stickers to his sister. How many stickers does Eli have now?*

While this story problem initially seems unrelated to mathematical argumentation, students had been working on conjecturing throughout the school year, so it was not a surprise when a student wanted to discuss the problem more generally after solving it. The students regularly looked for and made sense of patterns and structures within our number system, operations, and mathematical concepts. Regarding the 16 and 8 in the word problem, Javi said, "I have a conjecture. All doubles equal even numbers." Christina invited students to write Javi's conjecture in their journals and take ten minutes to explore it.

Jordan: On addition, doubles always are equal.

Asher: It's true with addition because an even number is a number that you can split into two parts that are the same. And I tested it with simple numbers.

60 + 60 = 120

8 + 8 = 16

4 + 4 = 8

10 + 10 = 20

20 + 20 = 40

22 + 22 = 44

35 + 35 = 70

18 + 18 = 36

And, then I did 13 + 13 = 26, 6 + 6 = 12, and 12 + 12 = 24.

As he solved a subtraction word problem, Javi noticed there were two 8s: 8 stickers that Eli gave to his sister and 8 that he had left. Javi connected the work they'd been doing to understand odd and even numbers. He conjectured that, "All doubles equal even numbers." Javi and his classmates then tested his conjecture. Even though working through several examples isn't enough to justify that a conjecture is always true, it's a good way to explore the idea and build up an intuition about what's happening in the conjecture. Students examined addition—a familiar operation—and a series of other number sets. Through the discussion that followed, and specifically Jordan and Asher's exploration of the conjecture, Javi refined his conjecture to state, "When we add doubles, the answer will be even." This modification was a result of students conjecturing, justifying, sharing, modifying, and extending ideas, and it is more precise than the original conjecture.

PAUSE AND PONDER

VIGNETTES

- What do you notice about the two vignettes (pages 9 and 15) we've shared so far?

- What are students noticing and conjecturing? How do they begin to justify their ideas and share them with others?

- What do you wish you could ask the students to learn more about their thinking?

- How are the vignettes connected to things you have heard in your classroom?

Unpacking Layers of Argumentation in the Classroom Vignettes

Dropping into Bethany's kindergarten classroom (page 9) and Christina's second-grade classroom (page 15), we can start to see ways that K–2 mathematicians playfully and curiously engage in mathematics, and we can see the layers of mathematical argumentation.

For example, in Bethany's class, Ava *noticed* patterns in the expressions, gathered information, and *conjectured* that the number of ways a number can be decomposed will be one more than the number itself. Ava shared this idea and thought about which numbers this conjecture worked for, *extending* her idea. Christina's second-grade students worked on a *conjecture*—thought about operations and odd and even numbers through the lens of doubles. The students refined and modified the conjecture as they discovered that doubles, when added together, always equal even numbers. The students did not only state the conjectures; they began to *justify* and share with the whole class to modify their ideas and make them more precise. In these two classrooms, we've seen layers of mathematical argumentation already emerging! Table 1.1 shows the vignettes with explicit examples of the four layers.

Table 1.1: Argumentation in the Classroom Vignettes

Layer of argumentation	Where argumentation emerged in *Classroom Vignette: Decomposing Tens in a Kindergarten Classroom*	Where argumentation emerged in *Classroom Vignette: Second Graders Conjecture About Even Numbers*
Noticing and wondering	• Observed patterns between addends • Collected information about the pattern	• Noticed patterns within doubles • Made connections between doubles and even numbers
Conjecturing	• Pushed an observation to a generalization about all numbers: the total number of ways a number can be decomposed will be one more than the number itself	• Conjectured that "all doubles equal even numbers"
Justifying	• Explained the idea to a teacher and peers • Looked for evidence in the classroom on past public records	• Explained the conjecture and why it works to the class using evidence and reasoning
Extending	• Thought about what numbers the conjecture works for	• Noticed that even numbers can be decomposed in many ways, not just into doubles • Modified and refined the conjecture through a discussion with classmates

Exploring Consecutive Sums

This book is not just about growing wonder and curiosity in your students; it is about growing as teachers, so you can meet students where they are. Curiously exploring is an important component of learning at all levels (Piaget, 1952) as we create cognitive schemas and assimilate and accommodate new information (Piaget, 1977). We learn when we make strong connections between new information and previously known information. Learning is not about discrete facts but about growing a well-connected web of knowledge (Piaget, 1977; Van de Walle, Karp, & Bay-Williams, 2013). To help you grow your wonder and curiosity, we will explore consecutive sums in "Your Turn: Explore Consecutive Sums," and we will revisit this task throughout the book.

YOUR TURN
EXPLORE CONSECUTIVE SUMS

Let's explore consecutive sums. This task is for you to explore as a learner rather than to teach to your K–2 students. The consecutive sums task is well known among mathematicians who study number theory and can be used in upper-elementary grades through graduate-level mathematics courses. Su (2020) writes, "Doing math properly is engaging in a kind of play: having fun with ideas that emerge when you explore patterns, and cultivating wonder about how things work" (p. 50). This task is your opportunity to explore and play with some mathematical ideas.

Look at the following equations. Notice that some numbers (like 9, 13, and 18) can be expressed as the sum of a string of consecutive positive numbers (NRICH Project, n.d.). In other words, they can be written as an addition equation and the numbers being added together go in order.

9 = 2 + 3 + 4

13 = 6 + 7

18 = 3 + 4 + 5 + 6

Instructions: Set a timer and spend 10–15 minutes exploring what you notice and wonder. The following are some ideas to think about if you need support getting started.

- Try examples and write your own equations.

nurturing math curiosity

- **Make a table or a chart to organize your thoughts.**

  _____
  _____
  _____
  _____
  _____
  _____
  _____
  _____
  _____

- **Draw pictures or diagrams.**

- **Notice patterns.**

  _____
  _____
  _____
  _____
  _____
  _____
  _____
  _____
  _____

- **Make your thinking visible.**

  _____
  _____
  _____
  _____
  _____
  _____
  _____
  _____
  _____

Establishing the Foundation for Mathematical Argumentation

1. I notice . . .

2. I wonder . . .

If you are reading this as part of a book study, share your ideas with others and look for ways that your ideas are similar, different, and connected. In figure 1.3 (page 22), we provide samples of what other teachers noticed and wondered. Choose some of the work shown in the figure, make sense of the other teachers' ideas, make notes on the pages, and make connections to what you came up with. How are some of the samples related to your ideas? Is there something you hadn't thought of that you find interesting? How is the work organized? Was it helpful to make patterns more apparent? What patterns do you notice in the equations?

$3 + 4 = \underline{7}$ ↘ +5
$3 + 4 + 5 = \underline{12}$ ↘ +6
$3 + 4 + 5 + 6 = \underline{18}$ ↘ +7
$3 + 4 + 5 + 6 + 7 = \underline{25}$ ↘ +8
$3 + 4 + 5 + 6 + 7 + 8 = \underline{33}$ ↘ +9
$3 + 4 + 5 + 6 + 7 + 8 + 9 = \underline{42}$ ↘ +10
$3 + 4 + 5 + 6 + 7 + 8 + 9 + 10 = \underline{52}$

When you add 4 consecutive whole numbers is it always even?

$1 + 2 + 3 + 4 = \underline{10}$ ↘ +4
$2 + 3 + 4 + 5 = \underline{14}$ ↘ +4
$3 + 4 + 5 + 6 = \underline{18}$ ↘ +4
$4 + 5 + 6 + 7 = \underline{22}$ ↘ +4
$5 + 6 + 7 + 8 = \underline{26}$ ↘ +4
$6 + 7 + 8 + 9 = \underline{30}$

Going up by 4

$9 = 4 + 5$
$9 = 2 + 3 + 4$

Two ways to get 9.
Do others have 2 or more ways?

$1 = 0 + 1?$ Does this count?
$2 =$
$3 = 1 + 2$
$4 =$
$5 = 2 + 3$ Can every number be written this way?
$6 = 1 + 2 + 3$
$7 = 3 + 4$
$8 =$
$9 = 2 + 3 + 4; \ 4 + 5$
$10 = 1 + 2 + 3 + 4$
$11 = 5 + 6$
$12 = 3 + 4 + 5$
$13 = 6 + 7$
$14 = 2 + 3 + 4 + 5$
$15 = 4 + 5 + 6; \ 7 + 8$
$16 =$

$2 + 3 + 4 + 5 = 14$
    7
    7

$1 + 2 + 3 + 4 + 5 + 6 = 21$
    7
    7
    7

$18 = 3 + 4 + 5 + 6$
    9
    9

③ $1+2$ ⑥ $1+2+3$

⑩ $1+2+3+4$ ⑮ $1+2+3+4+5$

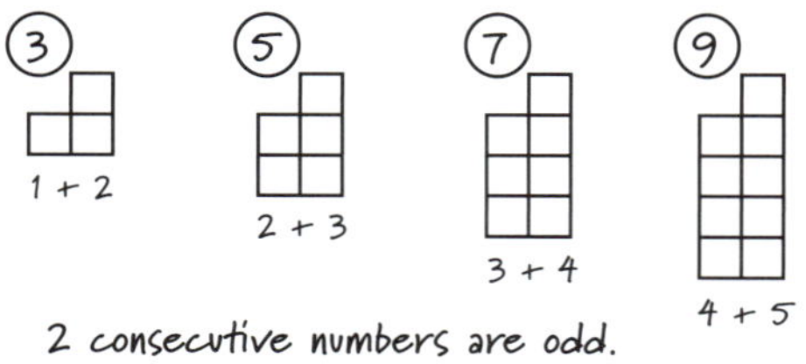

③ $1+2$ ⑤ $2+3$ ⑦ $3+4$ ⑨ $4+5$

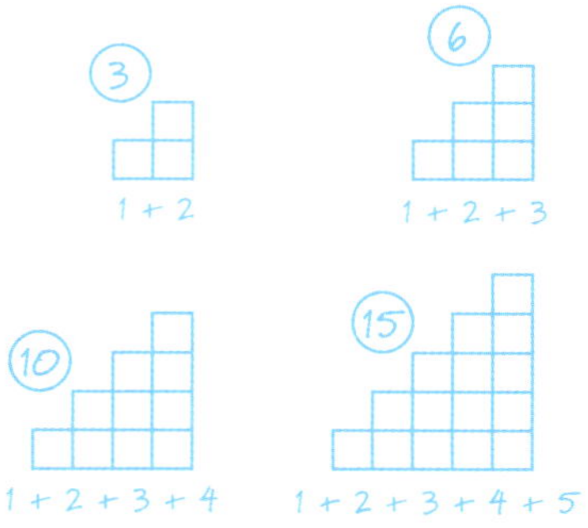

2 consecutive numbers are odd.

Establishing the Foundation for Mathematical Argumentation

2 ADDENDS	3 ADDENDS	4 ADDENDS
1 + 2 = 3)+2	1 + 2 + 3 = 6)+3	1 + 2 + 3 + 4 = 10)+4
2 + 3 = 5)+2	2 + 3 + 4 = 9)+3	2 + 3 + 4 + 5 = 14)+4
3 + 4 = 7)+2	3 + 4 + 5 = 12)+3	3 + 4 + 5 + 6 = 18)+4
4 + 5 = 9	4 + 5 + 6 = 15	4 + 5 + 6 + 7 = 22
5 + 6 = 11	5 + 6 + 7 = 18	5 + 6 + 7 + 8 = 26
6 + 7 = 13	6 + 7 + 8 = 21	6 + 7 + 8 + 9 = 30
7 + 8 = 15	7 + 8 + 9 = 24	7 + 8 + 9 + 10 = 34
8 + 9 = 17	8 + 9 + 10 = 27	8 + 9 + 10 + 11 = 38
9 + 10 = 19	9 + 10 + 11 = 30	9 + 10 + 11 + 12 = 42
These are all odd. They go up by 2.	Sums are even, odd, even. Sums are multiples of 3.	Sums are all even. Go up by 4.

Figure 1.3: Examples of teachers' explorations.

The following wonderings emerged as we discussed this problem with other teachers.

- Can all numbers be made of consecutive sums?
- Is there an algorithm or rule for which numbers have a sum of consecutive numbers?
- Is there a way to figure out how many equations are possible for a given number?
- Is there a pattern related to even and odd numbers?
- Is there a pattern related to prime and composite numbers?
- What happens when you include negative numbers as the addends?
- Why doesn't it work for 2, 4, 8, and 16?
- How can we figure out if a sum has two, three, or four consecutive number addends?
- Are strings of three consecutive positive numbers always a multiple of 3? Why is it that a string of four consecutive positive numbers isn't always a multiple of 4?

Now that you have seen other ideas, revisit your wonderings in the "Your Turn: Explore Consecutive Sums" (page 19). What did you notice and wonder while you were exploring? Pick one to investigate further or pick something that interests you from the samples in figure 1.3 and think about it using some of the following prompts.

- How will the pattern continue? Does that work for all numbers? What numbers does it work for?
- Is that observation always true? When will it be true? When is it not true?
- Can you draw a visual representation to show the pattern? Can you use a tool to show the pattern?
- What do you believe might always be true about _____? Is that true always, sometimes, or never? How do you know?

WRITE YOUR OWN CONJECTURE

Write a conjecture—a statement that you think might always be true—about the idea that interests you.

How could you convince someone that the conjecture is true? Use objects, pictures, numbers, or words to justify why your conjecture is true.

Are there words that could make the conjecture more precise? How can we rewrite your conjecture to make it more precise and understandable to other people?

What else do you think might be true now that we've explored this conjecture? How does this idea extend to other numbers?

This may seem like a simple task, but there is a lot to think about! Slowing down to explore a problem takes practice. We tend to be in a hurry as adults, so it can be hard to enter a task with the curiosity and wonder of a young student. As part of this book, we hope we can nurture the curiosity and wonder in you, too!

What new ideas did you learn through the exploration of consecutive sums? How did it connect to your previous knowledge? Jot down your answers to the questions in the columns in figure 1.4. We will come back to this figure as we continue reflecting throughout the book.

Questions	Your Responses
Noticing and Wondering • What was challenging about noticing? What was challenging about wondering? • What patterns were you drawn to? • What peer observations and wonderings surprised you? • How did it feel to wonder?	
Conjecturing • What questions helped push your wonderings into a generalized conjecture? • What was challenging?	
Justifying • What are your go-to ways of convincing someone else? • What was challenging about convincing someone else?	
Extending • What other ideas are you drawn to? Where does your brain want to go next? • What connections can you make to other mathematical ideas?	

Figure 1.4: Reflecting on your experience with consecutive sums.

Questions for Further Reflection

The following questions will help you synthesize your learning by reflecting on chapter 1.

- What inspired you within this chapter?
- What did the chapter leave you wondering?
- As you reflect on the chapter, what opportunities does argumentation offer your students?
- What does argumentation offer you as a teacher?

Chapter 1 Summary

In this chapter, we shared our observations of what argumentation looks like with young mathematicians through two classroom vignettes. We discussed the four layers of argumentation and nurtured your curiosity through the consecutive sums task. We are glad you are beginning this journey with us. Use "Chapter 1 Application Guide" to help you integrate this chapter's ideas into your classroom. Next, in chapter 2, we'll discuss exploring a classroom community.

Chapter 1 Application Guide

Use the following application guide to connect these ideas to your classroom.

Chapter 1 Topics	Connect to Your Classroom
K–2 Mathematicians	• Spend time listening to your students' ideas with open curiosity. • Model curiosity by asking questions, noticing patterns, and wondering out loud.
Layers of Mathematical Argumentation	• Notice where the layers of argumentation might emerge in the mathematical content that you are currently working on. You don't need to do anything with it, just notice it!

CHAPTER 2

Nurturing a Classroom Community

We mentioned in chapter 1 that mathematical argumentation is about nurturing students as they explore, notice patterns, wonder, ask questions, conjecture, and justify. Chapter 1 included vignettes that give a sense of what students are capable of and the kinds of ideas that they share when given an opportunity. As teachers and learners, we know that the environment has a profound impact on learning. We've felt it as students, and we strive to create an environment that is welcoming for our students and is a place for brains to sparkle and grow. Williams (2022) writes, "Mathematics exists in and builds on the environment we provide and the relationships we foster with our learners" (p. 15). Therefore, we will share ideas we find beneficial while nurturing a new sense of mathematical wonder in our students. In this chapter, we discuss a playful mathematical environment, classroom norms for mathematics, connections to speaking and listening, ways to incorporate talk moves, and how to organize the physical space in our classroom.

First, to make our perspective clear, we share the guiding principles behind our work and our teaching. Then, we describe some specific strategies that you can incorporate, not just during mathematics time but in your classroom learning environment. The following guiding principles have influenced our teaching in all settings and have contributed positively to the learning environments.

- Students bring curiosity, wonder, and intuitive knowledge to our classrooms.

- Everyone in the community has important ideas to contribute.
- Students' partial understandings should be recognized and celebrated.
- Teachers should build students' identities as mathematicians and support all students to grow and be mathematical knowers.
- We can all learn from each other, and it is important to value the knowledge and ideas within the community.
- Students need opportunities to learn how to communicate, both to speak with others and listen.
- Teachers impact the classroom environment, student learning, and students' identities in a powerful way.
- Teachers constantly make important decisions in the discretionary spaces of the classroom.

These guiding principles help us focus our attention on the content, students, our role as teacher, and the classroom community. What we will share in this chapter relates back to these principles, which guide our work.

PAUSE AND PONDER
YOUR GUIDING PRINCIPLES

- What guiding principles do you have?

- How do your guiding principles impact the environment you nurture in your classroom?

Creating a Playful Environment

In *Catalyzing Change in Early Childhood and Elementary Mathematics,* author and mathematics education professor DeAnn Huinker (2020) calls "for the creation of mathematically powerful learning environments that provide space for wondering and asking questions, allowing children to experience the joy of mathematical understanding, and fostering an appreciation for the beauty of mathematics" (p. 18). Curiosity is an important part of learning and is a socio-emotional characteristic that researchers recognize as necessary for early learning (Shah, Weeks, Richards, & Kaciroti, 2018). Researchers Prachi E. Shah, Heidi M. Weeks, Blair Richards, and Niko Kaciroti (2018) used a representative sample of the United States to study the relationship between curiosity and achievement, finding that "curiosity was significantly associated with academic achievement in kindergarten" (p. 384) for both mathematics and reading. But what do wonder and curiosity look like in a classroom, and how do we include more exploratory and playful opportunities in the established environment? Not every opportunity in a K–2 classroom must be playful or exploratory, but the goal is to nurture opportunities when they make sense and add to lessons in a meaningful way.

We envision curiosity and wonder thriving in a playful environment, but let's be specific about what we mean by play and playful. There are lots of ways to play and many benefits from playing with mathematics. However, the guidance and engagement of adults has a crucial role in the playful experience and the mathematical learning that emerges from it (Downton, MacDonald, Cheeseman, Russo, & McChesney, 2020). Williams (2022) writes that:

> Play and playfulness provide space and time for learners to think and play with the ideas we are teaching them. Moreover, being playful and allowing plenty of space for children's own ideas helps them realise their potential as mathematicians and models respect for the ideas of others—adults and peers alike. (p. 10)

A playful experience can be enhanced when teachers provide "artful guidance and challenging activities" (Seo & Ginsburg, 2004, p. 103). When teachers, who know the goals and general direction of the lesson, curiously engage in exploration with students, they can strategically build from students' ideas. For example, in chapter 1 (page 9), Ava and her kindergarten classmates investigated how many rabbits could be in the hutch or on the grass as they worked with number pairs that make 10. Some students came up with one pair of numbers, others came up with multiple pairs, and Ava concluded that she found them all. Once students had time for exploration, Bethany invited everyone back together, and they shared the combinations they found. As each student shared, Bethany carefully recorded that student's idea on a public record, often following up with a question like, "Did anyone find another way the rabbits can be in the hutch or on the grass?" or "How will we know that we have all the ways?" The teacher's charting and questioning is an example of *artful guidance*, as she nudged students from solving a story problem to seeing structure and using reasoning to consider how they would know they found all combinations of 10. Like Williams (2022), we use the word *playful*:

> To emphasise that, even if it is the adult that has initiated the mathematics, it is possible to grant the learner agency in what plays out after that. A key characteristic of play is that the experience is self-directed. Being playful combines play and guidance. We can utilise the motivation and creativity that children bring to their free play with a Vygotskian recognition that children's learning can be expanded when sensitively supported by an adult. (p. 8)

This is what we saw in the opening classroom vignette with Ava; she received a task to find ways 10 bunnies could be in a hutch or on the grass, and she began to wonder if she had all the ways. Bethany then extended her wondering, posing additional questions. The question, "Do you think that works for every number?" led Ava to make a conjecture and move toward a generalization—all rooted in Ava's playing with mathematics.

We use the word *playful* throughout this book, and we imagine a *playful environment* having some of the following characteristics.

- Teachers are curious and ask questions.
- Teachers encourage curiosity and questions from students.
- Teachers provide opportunities for students to *play with mathematics* (Williams, 2022). Teachers introduce a mathematical concept and provide time for students to explore the idea, deciding for themselves what to explore.
- Teachers dedicate time to the exploration of student ideas.
- Students are motivated to keep exploring, sometimes even beyond the lesson block.
- Teachers value creativity.
- Teachers encourage all students to share and value ideas.

Let's look at some examples of our guiding principles and playfulness in action. As we share another kindergarten vignette, make observations about the classroom community and how new knowledge is created and shared using the following prompts.

- What do you notice about how the students interact with the task and each other?
- How is the classroom similar and different to your classroom or ones you've been in?

CLASSROOM VIGNETTE: DIEGO'S KINDERGARTEN CONJECTURE

Kindergarten teacher Sara and her students spent much of the year working on counting, composing and decomposing numbers, and working with operations (Guarino & Manseau, 2023). They had worked with teen numbers and understood that numbers can be composed of a ten and ones; for example, 14 is composed of 1 ten and 4 ones. On this day, students were subtracting 10 from teen numbers and using ten-frames to represent their thinking.

Jason noticed, "When you take 10 away, you can just cross out one ten-frame; you don't even need to count." Sara and her students engaged in Jason's idea, trying out his method with each of the teen numbers on the worksheet: 15 – 10, 16 – 10, and 17 – 10. Sara placed each ten-frame on a sheet of paper that was large enough for all the students to see. Students started by representing the teen number and then crossed out a ten, as Jason had suggested. We published this work in the National Council of Teachers of Mathematics' (NCTM) *Mathematics Teacher: Learning and Teaching PK–12* journal, and you can see specific examples in that article (Guarino & Manseau, 2023).

Knowing that this conjecture worked with 15 – 10, 16 – 10, and 17 – 10, the teacher encouraged students to consider if this conjecture would work for other numbers and invited them to share examples. Diego leaned over to Jody (who was in the classroom observing the lesson) and whispered, "Jason's strategy works with other numbers, too. You could subtract 2 tens or more." On the back of his paper, he wrote "21, 22, and 23" explaining that a ten can be removed from each of these numbers, too. He added, "I told Jason, and he said it won't work. So, I agree with him, it won't work." Since everyone in the classroom community has important ideas to contribute, Jody suggested they test Diego's new conjecture to create an opportunity for him to realize that it was true and worth thinking more about. The lesson concluded, and students were dismissed to recess without a chance to bring Diego's conjecture to the whole group.

Diego had listened carefully to Jason's conjecture and extended it to additional numbers, moving beyond the teen numbers the class had been working with and into the next decade. He generated some numbers that worked with his extended conjecture, listed them on his paper, and shared them with a peer. Then, he appealed to Jason as the authority; when Jason told him it wouldn't work, Diego crossed out his idea. One form of justification we'll learn about in chapter 7 (page 144) is appealing to authority (Kazemi & Hintz, 2014), but why did Diego view Jason as the authority and immediately withdraw his own ideas? How was Jason positioned in the classroom? How was Diego positioned in the classroom? Thinking about Diego and the important contribution he made to the classroom community, we decided to revisit his idea as a class the next day. Diego used his curiosity and wonder, and we wanted all the students to have a chance to learn from him.

The following day, mathematics began by revisiting the conjecture the class had worked on the prior day to tap into the shared experience. Then, they investigated Diego's conjecture. Since Diego initially shared his idea with Jody in the previous lesson, she started by bringing his idea to the whole classroom community.

Jody: Diego, yesterday you were thinking about other numbers this conjecture could work with. Do you remember what number you were thinking about?

Diego: 30.

Jody: And what was your conjecture, Diego?

Diego: You can cross out two or more tens.

Jody: Diego said you can cross out two or more tens. Turn and talk to a partner. What do you think about that idea?

With a visual representation of three ten-frames on the board, students discussed Diego's conjecture with their partners. As students shared their ideas about Diego's conjecture, he walked to the front of the room with a smile on his face. He walked over and grabbed the pointer. Jody called the students back together, and Diego, taking over the teacher role, asked, "Who wants to share an idea?" Through his facial expressions and actions, it was evident that Diego saw himself as a contributor to the classroom community. The class's work stemmed from his idea—an idea he had previously discredited when Jason told him it would not work.

We drop back into the conversation, as Diego poses his question.

Diego: Who wants to share an idea?

Luka (walking to the board and pointing to the ten-frames): You can take away two tens.

Jody: Should we try that?

Students: Yes!

Jody (crosses out the two ten-frames): Does that work?

Maria: You took away 20. That's 30, so there's 10 left. It worked!

Jody: So, let's go back to Diego's conjecture. Does that always work? When does it work to cross out two or more tens?

Jody added the question, "When does it work to cross out two or more tens?" to the board. Then, she asked, "Does anyone have a number we could test this with?" Diego called on students with raised hands to share examples. As students called out ideas, they were written on the board to later test.

In addition to connecting to our guiding principles and the idea of playfully exploring, this interaction shows student identity within the classroom community and how students see themselves and each other as thinkers and doers of mathematics. It's essential to consider our role as teachers in strengthening student identities as we think about our classroom communities. Researchers and mathematics educators Despina Stylianou and Maria Blanton (2018) write:

> True development of mathematical practices happens when students feel confident enough to participate at the center, not the periphery, of mathematical activity. For that to occur, our classes have to be spaces where children are members of a community—a place where ideas are shared, celebrated, built on, tweaked, and, ultimately, owned by all. (p. 54)

How can we include these ideas in our own classrooms? We saw Diego discredit his own idea when Jason said it wouldn't work. What if we had dismissed this and moved on? How would Diego feel about his ideas? Instead, we followed up on his ideas, positioning him as a mathematical thinker in a classroom community as we considered his conjecture and numbers it would work with. We witnessed firsthand what this did for Diego. He came to the front of the room, smiled, and invited peers to share other numbers; he saw himself as a contributor to the classroom community and others saw him the same way. Mathematics educators Julia Aguirre, Karen Mayfield-Ingram, and Danny Bernard Martin (2013) say, "We believe that *how* students experience mathematics in their classrooms shapes their views of mathematics and themselves as mathematics learners and doers" (p. 19). Our goal is to create and nurture classroom learning communities where all students thrive and are invited to explore, ask questions, and share ideas.

Setting Classroom Norms for Mathematics

We saw in the vignette that Diego had an idea worth sharing but was hesitant about it once another student said it didn't work. Luckily, an adult was there to hear the brilliance of his thinking and bring it to the whole class's attention, highlighting his ideas and showing everyone that he has ideas worth sharing and learning from. Let's talk about what we can do to promote the idea that all students have ideas worth sharing and that we can learn from everyone in our classroom community.

Norms are different from classroom rules. Rather than thinking about rules, which are more about compliance, norms get us to think about community building. *Norms* are a way of thinking about how to participate in a classroom community of learners and what it means to learn mathematics together. In addition, norms are established whether or not we are intentional about it. So, if we do nothing, we can't be strategic about what we want to foster in our classroom. Several mathematics educators have lists of norms to foster in mathematics class, including Jo Boaler (2022), Signe Kastberg and R. Scott Frye (2013), and Elham Kazemi and Allison Hintz (2014). All teachers won't have the same norms, and that's OK. According to mathematics educators Erna Yackel and Paul Cobb (1996), "Norms are not predetermined criteria introduced into the classroom from the outside. Instead, these normative understandings are continually regenerated and modified by the students and the teacher through their interactions" (p. 475).

With your guidance, norms will be established, revisited, and revised as the year goes on, but you can begin by intentionally considering your goals for your classroom community. Figure 2.1 shows some ideas that we have seen work well in our own classrooms and in classrooms we have visited where a playful environment is being nurtured. We've listed them as statements written from the perspective of a student about what it means to be part of the classroom community, what it means to do mathematics, how we learn, and who can share ideas.

What It Means to Be Part of Our Learning Community

1. We are curious explorers who ask questions (of mathematics and each other).
2. We learn from our mistakes and keep trying when things are challenging.
3. Everyone has important ideas to share, and we can learn from each other. We learn when we make connections between ideas.
4. We share our ideas and listen to other people to understand their ideas. If we have a question or suggestion, we can give feedback respectfully.

Figure 2.1: Sample classroom norms.

One way to develop norms with your students is to pose a guiding question. For example, "How do we want our mathematics class to be?" Teachers can invite students to share ideas that teachers write down as students share them. Sometimes, we might offer follow-up questions to further clarify student ideas. For example, everyone should listen while a student shares. A teacher might ask, "Why is it important to listen to each other? How does it make you feel when people listen to your ideas?" These ideas can be revisited and added to for multiple days, showing students that the classroom is a community where everyone has a voice—this concept is important enough to dedicate time to it. A final step in norm development can be to group related ideas into themes and generate a norm to match each theme, resulting in a list similar to our previous ideas.

We know that "discussion increases students' engagement, helps them take responsibility for their learning, [and] prompts higher-level thinking" (Kelly, Ogden, & Moses, 2019, p. 31). Yet, speaking and listening are skills that need to be nurtured and practiced. In Year 1 of the project, Bethany noted that an important skill she wanted to foster included "building students' stamina for listening and responding to each other." Using the word *stamina* seemed like an important observation, and it made us wonder how we can foster speaking and listening during mathematics lessons in a way that allows students to grow those communication skills.

Students need explicit instruction in communication, including modeling speaking and listening skills, such as facing the speaker, listening without distractions, and asking questions to clarify. We agree that "in mathematics, this curiosity takes the form of questioning. Students are encouraged to demonstrate the value of peer solutions by asking thoughtful questions about the problem-solving process and solutions" (Kastberg & Frye, 2013, p. 32). Taking time at the beginning of the school year is worth the effort to have things go smoothly later in the year.

CLASSROOM VIGNETTE: KINDERGARTNERS TURN AND TALK

Bethany started the year with her kindergarten students by introducing them to turn and talks. She often posed a question and gave students private think time (one minute to ponder their answer to a question or prompt). Then, she asked students to turn and talk. Students faced their preassigned partner; one student shared while the other listened, and then they switched. Bethany saw this as a beginning step. As she listened to student interactions, she noticed that students followed the instructions, looked at their partners, and shared their thinking, but it was rare to see multiple exchanges. The turn and talks didn't sound conversational.

As Bethany considered strategies for supporting student talk, she noticed Savannah and Gina sometimes posed a follow-up question or commented on something their partner said. Bethany decided to pair Savannah with Gina, wondering if they would engage in more conversational discourse, and if so, how she might leverage their discussion to unpack what a conversation might look and sound like. In this instance, Bethany identified a challenge and hypothesized moves to solve it.

Later in the day, Bethany and her students were counting by twos chorally, beginning with 1. Students counted "1, 3, 5, 7." Bethany paused and asked, "What number do you think comes next?"

Bethany: Turn and talk to your partner.

Savannah: I think 9 is next.

Gina: Why do you think 9?

Savannah: Because each time we skip a number. So, if we skip 8, 9 is next.

Bethany: Gina, I noticed that you listened to Savannah and then asked her a question. I wondered the same thing. How did she know it was 9? Asking a question is a great way to understand your partner's thinking.

In that moment, Bethany attended to their interaction, positioning Gina as competent, calling out the specific move she made and what it offered. She continued cultivating this new pairing, and the interactions became more conversational. Her next step was to leverage their interactions to create a vision of what a conversation with multiple exchanges could look and sound like. Bethany asked Savannah and Gina if she could record a turn and talk. She recorded an interaction using the camera on her phone. Later in the day, she brought the class together on the carpet. She shared with students that they would watch a video of a turn and talk, setting the lens for what to attend to.

Bethany: Earlier today, I recorded Savannah and Gina during a turn and talk. We're going to watch the video one time and then I'm going to ask you to share what you saw and heard. I will write down what you share. Then, we'll watch the video again; let's see if you notice some of the things other people noticed that are on the chart or we can add new things to the chart.

This gave students an opportunity to witness a conversation and identify moves they could use in their own turn and talks. It also provided a space to talk about some of the moves and why they might be important. For example, students noticed Savannah and Gina "kept talking." Bethany probed, "What were they talking about?" This elicited that the talk was grounded in the topic, and you can learn from listening to your partner. We know how important speaking and listening are within argumentation, and we also know they are things that teachers need to attend to. As stated earlier, creating space for students to speak and listen, and supporting them to do so, is important in nurturing a classroom community.

Using Talk Moves

The turn and talks Bethany's students engaged in are an example of *talk moves*. Talk moves provide teachers and students with strategies for engaging in productive discussions, which contribute to students' cognitive, affective, and social learning. In some classrooms, talk is predominantly between teacher and students; our goal is for communication to be between teacher and students, students and teacher, and students and students. We value a safe, risk-free environment where all voices are heard and students and their ideas are respected. Talk moves support this type of classroom culture, which we may not have experienced as elementary students.

From a speaker lens, talk moves can provide structure as we articulate our thinking. Sharing our ideas can be challenging; we need to speak at a volume that others can hear and use understandable words and sentence structure, all while we're learning and grappling to make sense of ideas ourselves. Turn and talks, or *think-pair-shares*, can create space for learners to practice what they want to say, putting their thoughts into words. Listeners can ask the speaker to restate what they said, providing them an opportunity to use different words, making sure those words are comprehensible. They might also add on to our ideas, signaling that they've listened and value our ideas enough to engage in them. Talk moves can be a helpful tool for listeners as we think about the goal of listening: to understand. If something is unclear, we might ask clarifying questions or revoice an idea, "So you're saying . . ." Revoicing can provide access to an idea being shared.

We know from the work of teacher educators Megan Franke, Nick Johnson, Angela Turrou, and others who research Cognitively Guided Instruction that student achievement increases when students engage in the ideas of others (Webb et al., 2019). According to mathematics educators Thomas P. Carpenter, Elizabeth Fennema, Megan Loef Franke, Linda Levi, and Susan Empson (2014), "Engaging with other students' mathematical ideas is one of the best ways to support students to generate insights into mathematical relationships and develop more sophisticated strategies" (p. 153). Talk moves support students to attend to, understand, and think about others' ideas. By using talk moves, students can focus on the details of others' thinking, compare their thoughts with what others share, and add to other students' ideas. This is evident in the earlier vignette as Diego engages in and adds on to Jason's conjecture, building on the idea that you can take away a ten from teen numbers to the idea that two or more tens can be removed from larger quantities.

We first learned of talk moves from authors Suzanne H. Chapin, Catherine O'Connor, and Nancy Canavan Anderson (2009) in their book, *Classroom Discussions: Using Math Talk to Help Students Learn*. As we started using talk moves in our own classrooms, we noticed the opportunities talk moves offered all our students, including English learners and students with disabilities. Ideas were easier to follow and engage in. Often in conversations, if you miss an idea being shared, you might not fully hear or process it, so it's hard to make sense of what's happening or join in. With talk moves, ideas are revoiced, repeated, and added to. Through these moves, we found more time was spent on sharing ideas and there were multiple entry points to participate and engage in ideas.

In table 2.1, we share talk moves (Chapin, O'Connor, & Anderson, 2009; Kazemi & Hintz, 2014) we've used in our classrooms and experienced in the classrooms of teachers we've worked with. We include the talk move, what it offers teachers (T) and students (S) from a lens of exploration and argumentation, and references to what it might sound like in some of the vignettes shared in this book. The italic parts in the third column help highlight the part of the statement that includes the talk move.

Table 2.1: Talk Moves

Talk move	What it offers students (S) and teachers (T) from the lens of argumentation	What it might sound like in the classroom (from earlier vignettes)
Partner talk or think-pair-share	(S) An opportunity to process and articulate thinking, formulate and share ideas, and hear ideas of others (T) A way to hear student ideas and perspectives	"Jason said you can take a ten away from teen numbers. *Turn and talk* to a partner. Why does this work?"
Revoice	(S) An opportunity to clarify understanding of what was said	"*So, you're saying* you can take away a ten when you subtract from a teen number, and you don't even need to count?"
Repeat	(S) An opportunity to reengage or understand an important idea (T) A way to draw student attention to an important idea that was shared	"*Diego said* you can take away a ten, or more than 1 ten, from some numbers."
Add on	(S) An opportunity to engage and deepen others' ideas (T) A way ideas shared can be extended	"*I want to add on to* Diego's thinking. I think you can take away 2 tens from any number over 20."
Give an example	(S) An opportunity to make sense of an idea shared and generate a related example (T) A way ideas offer insight into student thinking and can be further investigated	"*Does anyone have a number* we could test this with?"
Revise	(S) An opportunity to revise their thinking based on new information (T) A way to help students understand that new information should be considered, and students can change their ideas	"Seeing the ten-frames crossed out, *I want to revise my thinking*. I agree with Diego; you can take more than 1 ten away from some numbers."

While the context of this book is mathematical argumentation, talk moves have a life far beyond that. Talk moves support students and teachers in productive communication in general. In the past, speaking and listening were more behavioral; we were expected to speak and listen to others, with little to no support in learning how, and we were evaluated on this. Now, there are resources that identify specific skills for listening and speaking. According to the English language arts standards (National Governors Association [NGA] Center for Best Practices & Council of Chief State School Officers [CCSSO], 2010a), across grades K–2, students "participate in collaborative conversations . . . with peers and adults in small and larger groups" and gain skills in speaking and listening. They also "follow agreed-upon rules for discussions" and "add drawings or other visual displays to descriptions" (NGA & CCSSO, 2010a). In table 2.2 (page 40), we include related K–2 standards from the Common Core State Standards for English language arts (CCSS ELA) to show how the standards build across grades.

Table 2.2: Speaking and Listening Across Grades K–2

Kindergarten	First Grade	Second Grade
• "Continue a conversation through multiple exchanges."	• "Build on others' talk in conversations by responding to the comments of others through multiple exchanges."	• "Build on others' talk in conversations by linking their comments to the remarks of others."
• Clarify by asking questions. • Answer questions about the details of what was shared.	• "Ask questions to clear up any confusion about the topics and texts under discussion." • Clarify by asking questions. • Answer questions about the details of what was shared.	• "Ask for clarification and further explanation." • Recount key ideas or details about what was shared. • "Ask and answer questions about what a speaker says in order to clarify comprehension, gather additional information, or deepen understanding of a topic or issue."

Source for standard: NGA & CCSSO, 2010a.

TEACHER VOICES
COMMUNICATION

"Students are able to question and explain reasoning when they have practice to do so." (Christina, grade 2 teacher)

"I need to give the students more time to talk. They had several turn and talk moments, but they were pretty short. It was nice to see the students excited to have a-ha moments." (Bethany, grade K teacher)

"Students are able to understand other people's ideas, restate what their peers are saying, ask a question for clarification, make a comment to disagree or agree with their thinking, and share their ideas in a clear and meaningful way for their peers to be able to understand." (Christina, grade 2 teacher)

"Students have been practicing using their voice in the classroom, as this is built from Day 1 in our morning meetings. Each child's voice is heard each day, and their classmates' responsibility is to listen. This short activity that we have done daily has made a large impact on the way students listen to each other during mathematics lessons. Silent signals give students who do not have the floor a chance to make a connection or share their thinking. This has also made a large impact in our classroom discussions." (Rachael, grade 1 teacher)

Nurturing a Classroom Community

Using Physical Classroom Space

We can also think about the physical classroom space and how we can adjust it to nurture the classroom community. We have noticed some characteristics of classroom spaces that nurture a playful exploration and community discussion. The following are three strategies we've noted in classrooms and why they are beneficial.

1. A large open space for students to sit on the floor for some of the conversation is helpful for discussions. There's a community feeling when everyone is sitting together, on the same level. This space is free from distraction, with attention given to the ideas shared and people sharing them. We've been in some classrooms where students physically turn while someone shares an idea, attending to the speaker. We want to create spaces where students feel listened to and heard. We find proximity is helpful because students can hear each other and attend to one another's thinking.

2. Having a classroom space to gather on the floor seems to be a common feature for discussions, but also having a gathering place for public records has been helpful. When we say *public record*, we mean large chart paper where ideas are recorded and explored—we'll explore public records more in chapter 3 (page 51). Having a place where these records are kept and referred to can be a powerful tool. We have seen young children going up to the past months' public records to make connections to the current conjecture or idea. We have also seen children showing their parents during open houses that the mathematics ideas are *still* up on the wall, being preserved for future discussions. These can be layered on a bulletin board or continually added to an anchor chart.

3. In addition to preserving public records, having a dedicated wall space for working conjectures can be useful. We have seen these used as a place to put ideas that need to be acknowledged but not discussed in the moment. All students have great ideas to share, but teachers often can't get to all of them in one lesson. When a student shares something that their teacher wants to acknowledge but needs to think about first, or put to the side for another time, it can be added to a conjecture wall.

We have also seen bulletin boards that include mathematics language for students to refer to—see Rumsey, Guarino, Gildea, and colleagues (2019, p. 212) for an example. Precise language and language frames can be included for children to refer to during conversations. One teacher wrote:

I have been focusing on building the language students use during math lessons. I have created my "language of the discipline" wall in my classroom again, and I have added quite a few definitions and sentence frames. We have defined addition, subtraction, and the equal sign. Along with these definitions are the symbols used for these words. (Rachael, grade 1 teacher)

Questions for Further Reflection

The following questions will help you synthesize your learning by reflecting on chapter 2.

- What do you notice about students' speaking and listening in your classroom?
- What norms would be helpful in your classroom?
- What are your thoughts about the two vignettes shared in this chapter ("Diego's Kindergarten Conjecture" and "Kindergartners Turn and Talk")? How did the teachers build students' identities as mathematical knowers?
- What talk moves do you want to work on with your students? How will you introduce the talk moves? How will you support students to use them?
- How does your classroom space encourage community and playful exploration? What modifications might you make?

Chapter 2 Summary

We've shared ideas about nurturing a playful classroom community where teachers establish norms to grow a space where students learn together. While this book is about mathematical argumentation, these ideas are beneficial in all mathematics classes, even if the focus isn't on argumentation for the particular lesson.

- We are curious explorers who ask questions.
- We learn from our mistakes and keep trying when things are challenging.
- Everyone has important ideas to contribute, and we can learn from each other. We learn when we make connections between ideas.
- We share our ideas and listen to other people to understand their ideas. If we have a question or suggestion, we can give feedback respectfully.

The "Chapter 2 Application Guide" can help you connect the ideas in this chapter to your classroom. In chapter 3, we'll build on these norms as we grow our teacher toolbox and consider what teachers can do to help build a playful classroom community. We'll give tools for planning, representing mathematical ideas, and communicating that you can add to what you are already doing.

Chapter 2 Application Guide

Use the following application guide to connect these ideas to your classroom.

Chapter 2 Topics	Connect to Your Classroom
A Playful Environment	• Find an opportunity this week related to content you are learning about for your students to play with mathematics. Provide 10–15 minutes for students to explore an idea, deciding for themselves what to explore.
Nurturing a Community of Learners	• Notice who is talking during class in different subject areas and groupings. Keep a journal for a week to observe patterns.
Classroom Norms for Mathematics	• Write out norms that you want to encourage in your classroom.
Talk Moves	• Choose a talk move from table 2.1 (page 39) to practice in the coming week and plan when you will incorporate it into your lesson.
Physical Classroom Space	• Create a conjecture wall to place ideas written on sticky notes that can't be discussed at the moment. Model this by adding your own ideas to the conjecture wall and encouraging others to add theirs. • Create a place in the classroom to store and display public records so that students can refer to them to connect to prior learning.

CHAPTER 3

Growing Our Teacher Toolbox

What we do as teachers impacts the classroom environment, student learning, and students' identities in powerful ways, and teachers are constantly making important decisions in the discretionary spaces of the classroom. Researchers and mathematics education organizations have recognized the important types of teacher knowledge (Ball, Hill, & Bass, 2005) and the following eight effective teaching and learning practices that teachers use in their classrooms:

1. Establish mathematics goals to focus learning
2. Implement tasks that promote reasoning and problem solving
3. Use and connect mathematical representation
4. Facilitate meaningful mathematical discourse
5. Pose purposeful questions
6. Build procedural fluency from conceptual understanding
7. Support productive struggle in learning mathematics
8. Elicit and use evidence of student thinking (NCTM, 2014, p. 10)

We want to illuminate the background work that teachers are doing to set the stage for an environment that nurtures argumentation, because it's powerful work that allows the rest to take root. This chapter includes the following topics, offering helpful tools from our work as we supported teachers in creating playful environments that encourage exploration and discussion.

- **Tools for planning:** We'll share a template with planning suggestions.
- **Tools for representing mathematical ideas:** We'll share considerations for using physical and visual representations.
- **Tools for communicating:** We'll share ideas for using hand signals, asking questions, and supporting precise language.

Tools for Planning

In our experience as classroom teachers and working with teachers, we've seen how thoughtful planning can positively impact the student experience. Planning is a balance between being prepared with a coherent storyline for the lesson that matches the goals and being flexible to pivot as student ideas are shared. Similarly, Williams (2022) says that teaching needs to be both *responsive* and *intentional*. What does it look like to be responsive and intentional as we integrate more opportunities for exploration and argumentation? While they might seem like opposites, can being more intentional help us also be more responsive? We know that teachers plan and prepare for lessons in various ways. Careful planning leads to a smoother, more intentional enactment. Being responsive and listening to students and their ideas is at the center of teaching. It's important to stay open to the ideas students bring up within the enactment of the instructional routines we discuss in chapter 4 (page 65), even if they are different from the ideas you anticipated or lead the discussion in a different way than you had envisioned. We can't plan everything, but we can be intentional about a lot, which will open our ability to respond to curious surprises.

Some lessons and topics lend themselves more to argumentation and exploration, and we will highlight what makes certain topics more suited throughout this book. It is not something you must include every day in every lesson; however, the more you intentionally include argumentation, the more it will naturally emerge in your classroom. As we add argumentation opportunities into lessons, we can ask ourselves the following questions.

- Which lessons lend themselves to argumentation and explorative opportunities?
- How can we include opportunities for students to notice and wonder?
- Are there tools that might be helpful for students to visualize the patterns and procedures?
- What patterns extend beyond the examples shown in the lesson? What ideas are generalizable?
- How does this content connect to past lessons and build a foundation for future lessons?
- Are there class conjectures that we can build on?

The "Instructional Routine Planning Template" in figure 3.1 is designed to help with planning activities that include the four layers of argumentation. The template's initial page can be used to make content connections for an instructional routine, list

Growing Our Teacher Toolbox

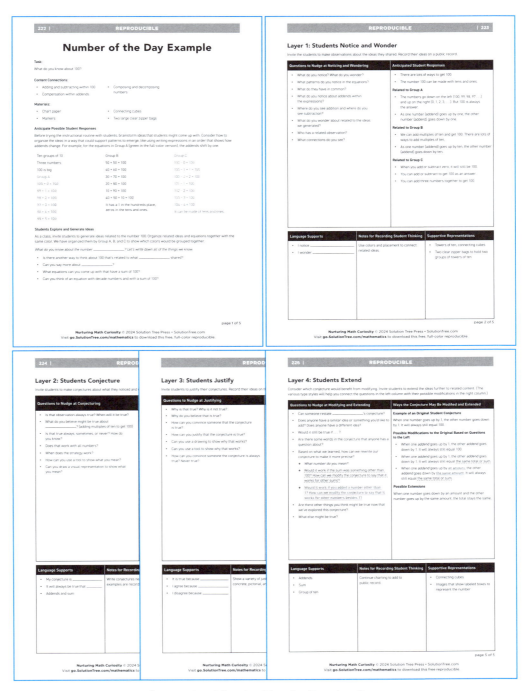

Figure 3.1: Example of the "Instructional Routine Planning Template."

required materials, anticipate student responses, and create questions to help students participate in the routine and generate ideas. The initial page is followed by one page for each layer of argumentation. The reproducible for this template is in appendix A (page 211). The appendix also includes examples of the template that follow some of the classroom vignettes.

Using the template to see how the numbers play out and to anticipate what students might do is a valuable planning component. We can be intentional about the numbers and predict as much as possible, but student thinking can lead in different directions. By making some predictions in advance, we can be ready to respond to the surprises that inevitably come along. Some questions to help anticipate what may happen during a lesson include the following.

- How might students respond?
- What ideas might emerge?
- How do those ideas connect to the learning goal?
- What questions might prompt more connections and allow us to generate related ideas?

Anticipating student thinking is helpful in considering ideas you want to further explore and thinking about questions you might pose to nudge toward important mathematical ideas that build to your goal. For example, Josephine asked her first graders, "Is there an equation that is related to Rafael's idea, 100 + 0 = 100?" She did this to generate more ideas that would connect to her goal. As equations were shared, she strategically recorded them in an order that would make the patterns emerge, no matter what order they were shared in. Josephine was intentional about how the equations were written, and she planned that aspect in advance of the lesson to highlight the patterns. We'll see this vignette explored in part 2 (page 95).

The planning template in appendix A (page 211) also has other features to help us be intentional about communication (for example, questions and language frames and representing mathematical ideas. We list many possible questions so that you can choose what would fit the lesson; not all questions will be used every time!

Tools for Representing Mathematical Ideas

As teachers, we create opportunities to make mathematical patterns, structure, and ideas more visible, and we do this using various visual and physical representations that work well for our students. In our case, these are curious young mathematicians making sense of numbers and operations. We know that "effective teaching of mathematics engages students in making connections among mathematical representations to deepen understanding of mathematics concepts and procedures and as tools for problem solving" (NCTM, 2014, p. 24).

We use the term *representations* to mean the concrete, pictorial, and abstract visuals that illuminate the structure of mathematics. As NCTM (2014) puts it, "Students' understanding is deepened through discussion of similarities among representations that reveal underlying mathematical structures or essential features of mathematical ideas" (p. 26). Research shows the power that representations have for learning, especially as multiple representations are connected, internalized, and discussed. It can be difficult because, as researchers Deborah Loewenberg Ball, Heather C. Hill, and Hyman Bass (2005) state, "The teacher has to think from the learner's perspective and to consider what it takes to understand a mathematical idea for someone seeing it for the first time" (p. 21).

Simply showing a representation without making sense of it as a community of learners is not enough to empower meaning or sense-making (Ball, 1992). As teachers, we must bridge what we know about mathematics (beyond grade-level content) with what the students are learning. On top of that, we need to consider how to use those representations for exploration and argumentation.

As we plan lessons, we can be intentional about what representations we'll use to show student thinking and the mathematical ideas of the activity during class discussions. For example, with kindergartners exploring 10 as the Number of the Day, a ten-frame would be beneficial to include in the discussion if students don't already mention it. Students might also share ten fingers as they add observations about the number 10. Depending on our goal for the lesson, we may want to be intentional about introducing certain representations that we think will help students make connections and generalizations. We can have the ideas planned and still be responsive to the ideas that students share.

USING VISUAL AND PHYSICAL REPRESENTATIONS

Visual and physical representations are ideal for playfully exploring, and it's essential that they are reliable and accurately represent the structure of the mathematical ideas explored. It's also vital to incorporate representations into all layers of argumentation, from noticing and wondering to extending. As teachers, we need to help illuminate the mathematics revealed in the representation. We can explore the representations in advance to see how we can bridge where the students are and where they are going to ensure that what we see in the representation as adults is also visible to students. Related to numbers and operations, two-color counters, connecting cubes, base ten blocks, ten-frames, and number lines are powerful representations for young students, as long as we allow opportunities for discussion and meaningful connections. To give you some ideas of how these representations are used in this book, figure 3.2 provides an example of the tool being used, possible generalizable ideas, and connections to related vignettes and activities in this book.

Representation (Tool)	Related K–2 Generalizable Ideas	Connections to Vignettes and Your Turns
Two-Color Counters	• Counting • Decomposing • Adding and subtracting	Ava conjectures about the ways to make 10 in "Classroom Vignette: Decomposing Tens in a Kindergarten Classroom" (page 9).

Figure 3.2: Connections between representations and generalizable ideas.

continued →

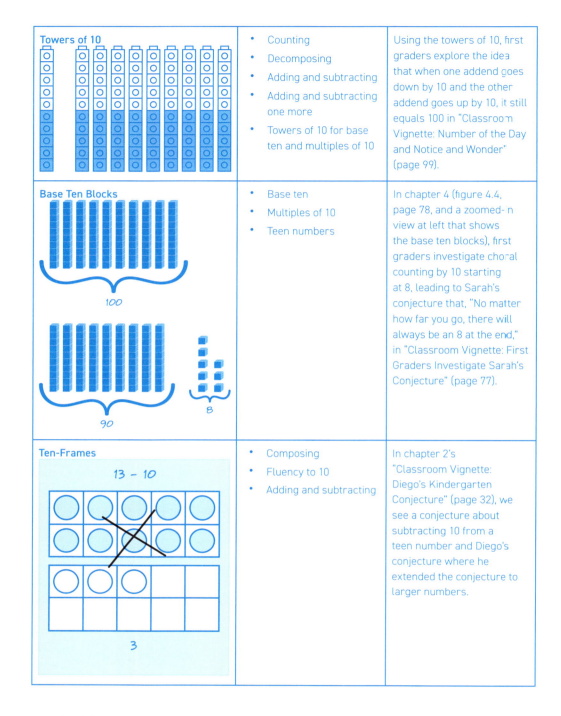

The following is a list of questions to consider as you choose which representations to use.

- What mathematics might students see in this representation?
- What do I hope that students see with the representation?
- What does this representation offer that would be hidden otherwise?
- How can I help my students see the mathematics in this representation?

- How does the representation show the meaning of the operation?
- How can the representation help us generalize beyond specific examples?

We want to be intentional about what tools we invite students to explore. We'll keep integrating representations in the vignettes and activities that we share in this book. We also want to think about how we record student ideas—how we both represent their ideas and extend them. As we are planning, it's important to consider how we'll record to make patterns and ideas more visible in what we call a public record. Let's explore how to record ideas and representations in ways that make student thinking and patterns visible.

USING PUBLIC RECORDS

Considering how ideas will be recorded and saved is another important part of nurturing a classroom community. We have seen amazing pictorial representations of student work by teachers we have worked with, and we learned from them. In our lessons and activities, having a plan of how to represent ideas allows for more intentional choices about placement and colors and fewer in-the-moment decisions. It's not to say that you'll never look back at a representation and think that you could have made it better, but it happens less often and less drastically when you've planned it in advance than when you've improvised in the moment.

TEACHER VOICES
PLANNING THE CHART

"Our math lessons have turned into whole class discussions around math concepts, where all students are seeing and noticing patterns and making conjectures. I have found it helpful to draw out what I would like the chart to look like for that lesson ahead of time; that way, I can see how to easily organize student thinking in a way that ultimately benefits the students." (Rachael, grade 1 teacher)

For example, when Bethany (from Ava's conjecture in chapter 1, page 9) planned how to represent the ways to make 5 early in the year, she wrote out how she was going to record the combinations students came up with as they engaged in various activities. For example, when students had five cubes and arranged them in different configurations to make 5, she represented each configuration with the cubes in order: 0 and 5, 1 and 4, 2 and 3, 3 and 2, 4 and 1, and 5 and 0. Another day, as students used two-color counters, spilling them from a cup and counting how many red and how many yellow counters were showing, these observations were also added to the public record, following the same structure. She planned details that included the color and placement of potential ideas. The public record here was revisited and added to across several days and then hung on the classroom wall, becoming both a learning artifact and a tool students could continue to use (see figure 3.3, page 52).

nurturing math curiosity

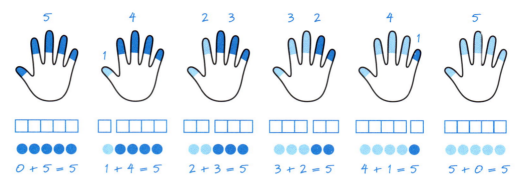

Source: © 2023 Bethany Lockhart. Used with permission.
Figure 3.3: Public record showing ways to make 5.

Visit go.SolutionTree.com/mathematics for a free, full-color reproducible version of this figure.

As Ava said in the opening vignette there is "one more way than the number," so the power of the public record became apparent when she hypothesized there are eleven ways to make 10 and walked over to the public record to explain her thinking. Ava drew on prior experience that she saw as related to the current work while she figured out how many bunnies could be on the grass or in the hutch.

It's OK if things don't go perfectly, but having notes on how to record and improve the process can free up your mental energy so you can focus on students, not the recording. Think about which ideas you want to highlight and how you can use colors and position to make those ideas stand out. For example, if several equations all have an addend of 0, consider writing them on the same area of the public record in the same color. If you have a choral count and notice that the ones place stays the same the whole time, consider making the ones place the same color across numbers. Even though you can't predict all the ideas that students will share, it will be helpful to anticipate some of the ideas related to your goals and how you can color coordinate and position them. Color coding has been a powerful tool in our work.

We find that considering the following questions during the planning phase will lead to a smoother, more strategic enactment.

- How will student ideas be recorded and made explicit?
- Will similar ideas be grouped together, or color coded to make patterns more visible?
- As students share connections, how will those be annotated?
- How can color coding be used to highlight connections?
- How will students be given credit for their contributions?
- How will you list student contributions as they're shared?
- How will you group related ideas?

- Is there a way to group ideas together to support a particular position (true or false) or conjecture?
- Would it make sense to record everything in the same color or record student ideas in a different color than the equation or task itself?

Tools for Communicating

Just as with representations, communicating happens throughout argumentation, at all layers of the exploration. Deep mathematical learning occurs through multiple modes of communication: gesture, movement, tools, and both written and spoken language. Together these modes of communication play important roles in supporting mathematical development for all children (Turrou, Johnson, & Franke, 2021, p. vii). The norms and talk moves discussed in chapter 2 (page 37) lay the foundation of speaking and listening, and we add on to that foundation here. In our own classrooms and classrooms that we have visited through our professional development work coaching teachers, we have seen powerful teacher questioning, language frames that support students' language, and co-constructed public records that nurture an environment of curiosity and exploration. Teachers' decisions and roles are instrumental if we want to nurture a playful environment and support the norms mentioned in chapter 2. What should we be doing as teachers to make that happen? We'll explore hand signals, questions, supporting precise student language, language frames, and group structures to encourage conversations in the following sections.

USING HAND SIGNALS

Using dedicated hand signals during discussions can be a helpful way to simultaneously communicate and expand what it means to participate in a discussion. This nonverbal communication helps us know that people are listening. We've seen a thumbs-up used to communicate that students have an idea or more fingers to show multiple ideas. Teachers get feedback about if students had enough time for a task, while students don't feel pressured that peers' hands are raised while they are still thinking. We have also seen hand signals to show agreement with peers or a question. Consider the feeling of validation when an idea is shared and other students signal agreement. Without speaking the words, you know other people are thinking the same thing. Rachael, in her first year of teaching, noted in her journal that:

I find myself driven by student thinking, recording exactly what students say, but also wanting students to build off of each other. I feel like students have gotten used to listening to each other, and having silent signals for them to communicate with offers input and connections without disrupting the person who is talking. (Personal communication, Rachael, grade 1 teacher)

nurturing math curiosity

PAUSE AND PONDER
HAND SIGNALS

- Are there hand signals that you use but hadn't thought to include during mathematics lessons?

- What benefits do you see with this nonverbal communication strategy?

- How can you introduce and use hand signals with your students?

ASKING QUESTIONS

We know that "effective mathematics teaching relies on questions that encourage students to explain and reflect on their thinking as an essential component of meaningful mathematical discourse" (NCTM, 2014, p. 35). Asking questions throughout the exploration, during all layers of argumentation, supports students as they make sense of the mathematics and supports teachers to make sense of the students' thinking. The questions teachers pose can support students to be more specific, elaborate on the details of their thinking, and make connections to important mathematical ideas (Franke et al., 2009). While some questions emerge naturally in response to students' thinking, other questions can be intentionally planned. The following are some of the questions that we find helpful, organized by layer. We'll see these questions again later in the book as we dive into the "Instructional Routine Planning Template" (page 211) more thoroughly.

Questions to nudge at noticing and wondering

- What do you notice? What do you wonder?
- What patterns do you see? Will that pattern continue?
- What do the equations have in common?
- How do the equations relate to other observations?
- Who has a related observation?
- Where do you see connections?

Questions to nudge at conjecturing

- Is that observation always true? When will it be true?
- What do you believe to always be true about _____?
- How will the pattern continue?
- Is that true always, sometimes, or never? How do you know?
- Can you draw a visual representation to show what you mean? What does each part of your representation show and how does it connect to the conjecture?
- How can you use a tool to show what you mean?

Questions to nudge at justifying

- Why do you believe that to be true?
- Can you draw a picture to show why that works?
- Can you use tools to show why that works?
- How can you convince someone the conjecture is always true? Never true?
- Why is that true? Why is it not true?

Questions to nudge at extending

- Can someone restate _____'s conjecture?
- Does anyone have a similar idea or something you'd like to add?

- Does anyone have a different idea?
- Are there some words in the conjecture that anyone has a question about?
- How can we rewrite our conjecture to make it more precise?
- Are there other things you think might be true now that we've explored this conjecture?
- What else might be true?

TEACHER VOICES
QUESTIONS

"We use a lot of questioning throughout our lessons, but I want to make sure our questions are open ended enough so we can get a variety of different ideas. When our questions are too specific, it narrows down what students share." (Rachael, grade 1 teacher)

SUPPORTING PRECISE STUDENT LANGUAGE

Let's consider ways to support student language since we know it is a powerful ingredient for learning. Thinking about precise language is part of lesson planning and can make it more impactful. We can think about the lesson's goal and how precise language can be used in the routine to support that goal. We also need to consider what precise language will support learning and how that can give deeper access to the content. According to Ball, Hill, and Bass (2005):

> Teachers must constantly make judgments about how to define terms and whether to permit informal language or introduce and use technical vocabulary, grammar, and syntax. When might imprecise or ambiguous language be pedagogically preferable and when might it threaten the development of correct understanding? (p. 21)

CLASSROOM VIGNETTE: SUBTRACTION WITH GRADE 1

In this vignette, we share a first-grade lesson where we saw the power of precise language for argumentation as students explored subtraction and the strategy of decomposing. Specifically, our goal was to position students to make sense of the decomposing strategy as we used mathematical argumentation to build procedural fluency with conceptual understanding (Rumsey, Guarino, & Sperling, 2023). For example, with expressions like 17 – 8, we can decompose the 8 into 7 and 1 to help us mentally visualize the subtraction in two steps, as shown in figure 3.4.

$$17 - 7 = 10$$
$$10 - 1 = 9$$
$$7 + 1 = 8$$

Figure 3.4: Decomposing 8 into 7 and 1 to subtract 17 − 8.

Visit go.SolutionTree.com/mathematics for a free, full-color reproducible version of this figure.

That is helpful because if we imagine 17 as 1 ten and 7 ones, there are not enough ones in the ones place to take away 8 (see figure 3.5).

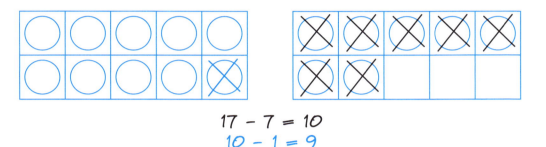

$$17 - 7 = 10$$
$$10 - 1 = 9$$

Figure 3.5: Pictorial representation of decomposing to solve 17 − 8.

Visit go.SolutionTree.com/mathematics for a free, full-color reproducible version of this figure.

We can cross off all 7 from the ten-frame on the right and then one more from the full ten-frame on the left. If we cross off using coordinating colors, then the seven Xs could be in red to match the equation 17 − 7 = 10. The one X would be in blue to match the equation 10 − 1 = 9. The color coding helps to make the connection between parts of the process. To see the color coding, you can download the full-color version of figure 3.5 (visit **go.SolutionTree.com/mathematics**).

Looking at multiple examples and representations helped students to curiously notice and wonder about the strategy and begin to make conjectures. One pair of conjectures that we explored was:

- If the second number is big, decompose.
- If the second number is small, you don't need to decompose.

Several issues of precision came up with the original conjectures as students tried to discuss the ideas, including the following.

- Which number are we talking about? In the example of 17 − 8, is the *second number* the digit 7 in 17 or the 8?
- What does it mean to be big? The number is big compared to what?

Because the class started to get lost in the conjectures' language and it was difficult to tell if the students were all talking about the same numbers, the teacher introduced the words *minuend* and *subtrahend* (see figure 3.6, page 58). By asking questions and pushing students to be more precise, the class discussion was able to go further because it wasn't getting bogged down by confusing language.

Figure 3.6: Minuend and subtrahend.

SUBTRACTION CONJECTURE

The class conjecture was: *"If the subtrahend is bigger than the ones place of the minuend, decomposing is helpful."* Look back at figure 3.6 to refresh on the terminology. Come up with some examples that fit with the conditions of that conjecture to help you make sense of what the conjecture is saying.

Another subtraction strategy that we wanted to feature for 17 – 8 also had two steps but differed from the one we used.

10 – 8 = 2

7 + 2 = 9

Compare it to this strategy that we described in the lesson:

17 – 7 = 10

10 – 1 = 9

- How are they alike and different? Where do the minuend and subtrahend go?

- Use the same representation to find the value of the expression using both strategies to highlight the differences and similarities.

- Why does one have subtraction and addition and the other just has subtraction?

With those new words and an exploration of what it means to be a big or small number, the class conjectures were modified to the following.

- If the subtrahend is bigger than the ones place of the minuend, decomposing is helpful.
- If the subtrahend is smaller than the ones place of the minuend, decomposing is not needed.

The precise language was instrumental in implementing argumentation because the class's shared understanding allowed for deeper understanding of the conjectures being discussed. You can read more about that specific lesson sequence in our article published in *Mathematics Teacher: Learning and Teaching PK–12* (Rumsey, Guarino, & Sperling, 2023).

USING LANGUAGE FRAMES

Regarding the language of the lesson, sentence frames or stems can be helpful for students to participate in exploration of mathematical concepts. Sometimes students want to participate but don't yet have the language to enter the conversation. Language frames or sentence starters offer support for how to listen and talk with each other (Ross, Fisher, & Frey, 2009; Rumsey & Langrall, 2016). Students need explicit instruction and modeling to gain certain social listening and speaking skills as educators. Educators Donna Ross and colleagues (2009) note that "language frames are effective tools, but students require teacher modeling of these tools to build their capacity for holding meaningful discussions" (p. 29). Rachael, a first-grade teacher who uses sentence frames, observes that by the middle of the school year, "students are beginning to relate their thinking to one another, as well as build off of each other. The sentence frames that we use help the students to organize their thinking to be able to successfully communicate their ideas."

When selecting a language frame, Rachael says:

I pick which sentence frames will be most beneficial, and I also model what that sounds like. I remind students how important it is to take turns and listen to each other; that way, the conversation does not repeat too much, and the conversation has depth.

In each example of the "Instructional Routine Planning Template" (page 211), we'll include language supports and precise language to consider. See figure 3.7 for language frame examples.

Language Frames

I notice _____

I wonder _____

I know _____

I have a different idea: _____

I can represent the number _____ as _____.

_____ is similar to _____ because _____

I see a connection between _____

I have a question about _____

Figure 3.7: Language frames.

USING GROUP STRUCTURES TO ENCOURAGE CONVERSATION

We discussed talk moves in chapter 2 and considered the use of questioning and language supports in this chapter. Now, let's think about ways to create opportunities for students to participate in conversations. The grouping and engagement structures we create in our classrooms are important to consider. Do students have private think time to process and make sense of ideas on their own? How do we know when we're giving students enough time? What opportunities do students have to share ideas with a partner and practice their use of language in a safe space? Listen and respond to the ideas of others? Slide their voices in to be heard or invite others into conversations? Thinking back to Diego's experience (page 32), he and his classmates were asked to consider a peer's conjecture, given private think time to make sense, and given time to turn and talk, sharing their ideas and hearing ideas of others. Had these opportunities not been part of the lesson, Diego may not have come up with his ideas or shared them with Jason and Jody, which advanced all of the students' thinking in the class.

Questions for Further Reflection

The following questions will help you synthesize your learning by reflecting on chapter 3.

- What mathematical ideas do you teach that might lend themselves to argumentation?
- What representations are your students familiar with?
- What tools do your students access and how do they access them?
- How are public records used in your classroom? How might you use a public record in an upcoming lesson?
- What does student talk sound like in your classroom?

- Whose voices are heard? Whose voices are not heard?
- What opportunities do the students in your classroom have to talk with partners before engaging in a larger discussion?
- How are *all* students supported to participate in discussions?

Chapter 3 Summary

We've shared a variety of tools for the teacher toolbox that enhance opportunities for teachers and students to engage in argumentation. By providing students with access to tools and resources and being intentional about what questions we ask and how we represent students' mathematical ideas, we can open doors for them to participate, communicate, and make meaning in deep ways. The "Chapter 3 Application Guide" (page 62) can help you connect the ideas in chapter 3 to your classroom. In chapter 4, we will connect chapter 2 (the classroom environment) and chapter 3 (the teacher toolbox) with instructional routines that lend themselves to argumentation.

Chapter 3 Application Guide

Use the following application guide to connect these ideas to your classroom.

Chapter 3 Topics	Connect to Your Classroom
Tools for Planning	• Look at appendix A (page 211) and seek connections to the first three chapters. • Write one way that you are intentional in your lessons and one way that you are responsive in your lessons.
Tools for Representing Mathematical Ideas	• Look around your classroom and make an inventory of the tools that can be used to represent mathematical ideas in upcoming mathematics topics. Use figure 3.2 (page 49) to jumpstart your thinking.
Public Records	• Draw out a public record for an upcoming lesson showing how you will write three to five related student ideas during a short, large group debriefing.
Tools for Communicating	• Ask the students, "What do you notice?" and "What do you wonder?" in a lesson this week and listen to their ideas. • List some precise language that you want to highlight in an upcoming lesson.

CHAPTER 4

Connecting the Classroom Environment and Teacher Toolbox Through Routines

We have been growing our classroom community and teacher toolbox in part 1 (page 7). In chapter 2 (page 29), we shared ideas we believe in that influence our teaching, norms that can nurture a playful environment, connections to speaking and listening, and ways of organizing our physical spaces. In chapter 3 (page 45), we shared teacher tools for planning, representing mathematical ideas, and communicating. This chapter is about using instructional routines to show us how we can embed the ideas from chapters 2 and 3 in our classrooms as we incorporate mathematical explorations. The specific routines are Number of the Day, choral counting, and true or false. For each routine, we'll share vignettes, public records, and connections to argumentation. In appendix A (page 211), there are examples of the "Instructional Routine Planning Template" that you can adapt to plan the routines for your own classroom.

As we nurture a classroom community where students listen to each other and share ideas, routines have the power to leverage meaningful discussions. It is easy to create a superficial or generic experience in routines where we go through the motions but don't accomplish much mathematically. Instead, we want to encourage a curious exploration that can lead to conversations about patterns, observations, questions, conjectures, and justifications. With examples, questions, and the planning template to guide you, we hope that the instructional routines can be a great introduction to integrating mathematical argumentation.

This book is about more than instructional routines, but routines are a place for us to start. In later chapters, we'll use the routines to explore how each layer of argumentation unfolds in practice.

Using Instructional Routines

Many teachers we work with find instructional routines to be valuable learning experiences for students and themselves because they provide a predictable structure. For students, this predictable structure provides space for engagement and participation as they know how the routine works. For teachers, a predictable structure allows time and attention to be spent planning the content and working on their practice, such as eliciting student ideas and considering how to represent these ideas and how to pose purposeful questions. As we discussed in the chapter introduction, there are various classroom routines that lend themselves to mathematical argumentation. Authors Stylianou and Blanton (2018) describe *routines* as a "low-stakes activity" that provides "a familiar place for important habits of participation to develop and take root in our classrooms" (p. 54). They are excellent opportunities to build classroom norms—students see that being part of the mathematical community means being curious explorers who ask questions and share ideas. Students also see that everyone has important ideas to contribute; we can learn from each other as we share those ideas and listen to others. The frequency with which you include instructional routines in your mathematics classroom will vary; perhaps you have a curriculum that incorporates instructional routines into every lesson or maybe you'll be creating them to enhance your curriculum materials. Either way, we can use instructional routines to build powerful mathematical experiences for our students.

As we nurture a playful environment, instructional routines help us build a space where curiosity and questions are modeled by the teacher and encouraged by students. For example, we introduce a mathematical concept and provide time for students to explore the idea. Students are encouraged to share ideas knowing that all ideas are valued. Instructional routines also connect deeply to communicating, such as students speaking and listening and, with practice, participating in collaborative conversations and using established norms for discussions. We also hope that during the instructional routines, teachers can practice representing mathematical ideas and try the teacher tools and questions that we shared in chapter 3. More broadly, the instructional routines provide teachers and students with the opportunities shown in table 4.1, building a foundation for the layers of argumentation and curious mathematical exploration.

Table 4.1: Teacher and Student Opportunities

Teacher Opportunities	Student Opportunities
• Make student thinking visible with representations. • Elicit student thinking. • Encourage explanation and reasoning. • Grow a community of young mathematicians with a strong mathematical identity. • Support students as they develop listening skills. • Highlight the value of each student's ideas. • Engage the students' minds in a topic that will be discussed during the lesson.	• Share ideas with classmates. • Look for patterns. • Explore observations. • Reason and make sense of patterns, structures, and operations. • Explore ideas from multiple perspectives. • Make connections between ideas. • Access the mathematical ideas for the day's lesson. • Listen to ideas from classmates. • Participate in collaborative conversations.

TEACHER VOICES

INSTRUCTIONAL ROUTINES

"Instructional routines are a fantastic container that gives space and structure for students to play, explore, and engage in each other's thinking and for teachers to be responsive to what they're hearing. When I started routines, I was a bit intimidated because I wondered if I would do them right or be able to support my students. But diving in and trying instructional routines made me realize that the students love them, and they dive in with you! They start to think about mathematics the way that you dreamed they would—as a place where ideas are encouraged, where understanding and sense-making matter most, and where they can truly be present and excited by the challenges. We tried instructional routines specifically to celebrate each other's ideas and thinking. We're going to look at it in a different way. We will see different things, and when we share those differences, we see richness and perspective emerge. I don't think I'll ever stop doing instructional routines in my classroom because I've seen the power of creating learning together. I've seen the power that routines can have to help shape my classroom culture and the way we approach math and each other's thinking." (Anonymous teacher, grades K–2)

Just as there are many opportunities for teachers and students, there are also important roles. Table 4.2 (page 68) lists some characteristics for the teacher role, the student role, and a routine role.

Table 4.2: Community Roles for Teacher, Student, and Routine

Teacher Role	• Model curiosity by sharing noticings and wonderings with students. • Think deeply about the mathematical opportunities within a routine and plan ahead to take advantage of the opportunities. • Ask thoughtful questions about patterns, student reasoning, and mathematical ideas. • Observe students' work with a sense of wonder. • Ask reflective questions after the lesson. • Model making connections between patterns and wondering about conjectures. • Think out loud and share ideas.
Student Role	• Make observations. • Be curious. • Ask thoughtful questions. • Listen to classmates. • Notice patterns in classmates' ideas. • Make connections. • Wonder.
Routine Role	• Provide open-ended opportunities. • Allow for entry points and perspectives. • Connect to deep mathematical ideas.

PAUSE AND PONDER

INSTRUCTIONAL ROUTINES

What instructional routines have you used or seen other teachers using?

_____
_____
_____
_____
_____
_____
_____
_____
_____
_____
_____
_____
_____
_____

While you may recognize the routines discussed in this chapter, remember that our purpose is to re-envision the routines to allow for more argumentation. Throughout part 2, we will build on the instructional routines and share examples of other tasks that can be used in each layer of argumentation (noticing and wondering, conjecturing, justifying, and extending). The instructional routines provide us with a common place to start, and then we'll dive deeper. First, let's review the routines to get a sense of what they look like. Then, we'll offer examples as we describe them so you can start to reimagine their potential.

Exploring Number of the Day Instructional Routine

The Number of the Day instructional routine invites students to share ways of thinking about a particular number. The teacher identifies one number, the Number of the Day, and poses an open-ended question, such as, "What do you know about the number _____?" Students share ways they think about that number while the teacher records those ideas on a public record as we saw in chapter 3. Like with other instructional routines, the routine itself is simple, yet there is so much power waiting to be uncovered. In figure 4.1, we have an example of the Number of the Day routine with the number 10.

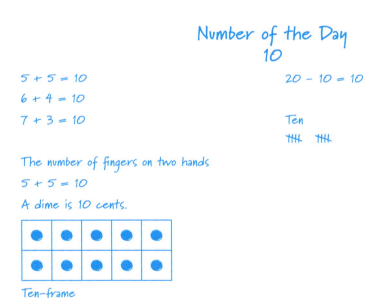

Figure 4.1: Example with 10 as the Number of the Day.

nurturing math curiosity

YOUR TURN

64

Imagine the Number of the Day routine enacted in a first-grade classroom toward the end of the school year and students are exploring the number 64. What are some responses you would anticipate as students explore the number 64? Which ideas are related and why?

_____
_____
_____
_____
_____
_____
_____
_____
_____
_____
_____
_____
_____
_____

In our experience working with primary students, we often observe them sharing representations, connections to the classroom and the real world, expressions, and equations. For the number 64, we've seen students share ideas related to the following.

- Physical or drawn manipulative representations
  + Sticks and dots representing base ten blocks; for example, 6 tens sticks and 4 ones units to show 64
  + Ten-frames showing six complete ten-frames and a ten-frame with four spaces filled
  + Tally marks showing twelve groups of 5 and four single tally marks
- Addition and subtraction expressions and equations
  + Adding two digits and one digit, such as 60 + 4
  + Adding two digits and two digits, such as 24 + 40
  + Equations with multiple addends that show place value, such as 10 + 10 + 10 + 10 + 10 + 10 + 4 = 64
  + Subtraction expressions such as 64 − 0 and 65 − 1 with numbers close to the quantity students are trying to achieve
  + Subtraction expressions like 74 − 10 as students use their knowledge of place value

+ Exploring large quantities; for example, identifying a number that, when subtracted from 100, will result in the given number, such as 100 − ? = 64

Throughout the Number of the Day discussion, many hands often excitedly emerge and wave as ideas are shared. Students see equations and use their understanding of numbers to generate more ideas. For example, after seeing the equation 20 + 20 + 20 + 4 = 64, another student might offer up 40 + 20 + 4 = 64. Student ideas are endless!

We're excited to show you how using something as simple as Number of the Day aids in deep discussion and mathematical curiosity and argumentation. All four layers connect to the Number of the Day instructional routine, where students share their understandings about a particular number. The students *notice and wonder* when they observe patterns and the relationship between different ways to represent a quantity. They also have opportunities to wonder how patterns could extend to other numbers, similar situations, and expressions. Students *conjecture* when they extend patterns and relationships and consider generalizations based on their observations. They also make sense of properties of operations. Students *justify* when they explain their reasoning about the patterns and observations and explain their conjectures with peers, convincing them that their conjecture is true. Finally, students *extend* when they share ideas, modify based on feedback, and extend to related content. By sharing their ideas, they are communicating using precise language, hearing feedback from their peers, and modifying their ideas based on the discussion.

CLASSROOM VIGNETTE: WAYS TO MAKE 64 IN FIRST GRADE

Let's drop into Rachael's first-grade classroom as she and her students engage in the Number of the Day routine in February. Rachael introduced her students to this routine in the fall, and they used it frequently. She began the lesson by introducing the Number of the Day, 64. As students came up with ways to make 64, they showed a thumb at their chest to signal they had a response. When they developed additional responses, they signaled by showing more fingers. Having a signal to indicate progress helped Rachael know that everyone had enough time to form an idea before she began calling on students to share their thinking.

She used this signal rather than raising hands because it's a private signal and doesn't make public who has a response and who doesn't yet. She didn't want students who take more time to feel that they are behind. As you read this vignette, consider the ways Rachael elicits student thinking and how she makes an in-the-moment decision to support students to build on a mistake.

Also, notice the public record in figure 4.2 (page 72). We shared ideas about public records in chapter 3 (page 51), and this is an example of how a teacher uses color and placement to make connections between ideas visible.

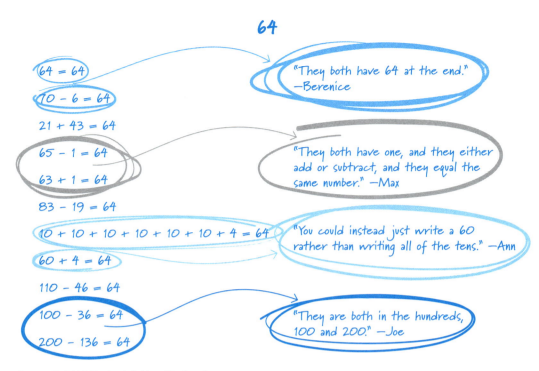

Source: © 2023 Rachael Gildea. Used with permission.

Figure 4.2: Public record for 64, grade 1.

Visit *go.SolutionTree.com/mathematics* for a free, full-color version of this figure.

Rachael launched the discussion with an open-ended question to elicit student ideas.

Rachael: Who wants to share an equation that you came up with for the number 64?

Ann: 6 tens . . .

Rachael: So, you're saying 6 tens, so 10 + 10 + . . .

Ann: Plus 4 and then it equals 64.

Rachael: So, 1 ten, 2 tens, 3 tens, 4 tens, 5 tens, 6 tens, plus a 4 at the end equals 64? I like how you said that.

Rachael clarified that she understood Ann's idea and made the idea explicit to other students by representing her contribution on the chart. While writing down the mathematical equations, Rachael also quoted the students' thinking and color coded it on the public record. In this case, she wrote Ann's idea in red and circled the corresponding equation in the same color.

Berenice: 83 minus 19 equals 64.

Rachael: 83 minus 19 equals 64. What else?

Rachael could have asked a follow-up question to dig deeper into Berenice's thinking. For example, "How do you know 83 − 19 = 64?" She also could have brought other students into the discussion by posing a question, such as, "Who has a strategy we could use to understand why 83 − 19 = 64?" There are many decisions that teachers make in the moment.

It's possible that Rachael wanted to get as many ideas written on the chart as possible rather than take a detour that could set the learning goal off track.

Brayden: 100, I think, minus 36 equals 64.

Max: 200 minus 164 equals 64.

Rachael: 200 minus what?

Max: 164.

Rachael: Equals 64?

Max: No, 200 minus 164 equals 64.

Students: 164.

Rachael: Why don't you double check that? 200 minus 100-something equals 64. Maybe let's find out what that is? Does anyone have any ideas? These are very high numbers. Try to see some similarities between other problems.

Rachael invited students to think about Max's idea in relation to Brayden's idea. A question she could have asked to make this more explicit could be, "I wonder how Brayden's equation, 100 – 36 = 64, can help us think more about Max's idea." This positions the ideas of both students as worthy of investigation and may provide a scaffold to the relationship between the numbers.

Scarlet: Well, he's just saying if you take 164, if you take half of it, it's 64.

Rachael: Half of it? What do you mean by half of it?

Scarlet: The ones, you take the ones away.

Rachael: The 100 away?

Scarlet: Yeah, the 100 away, and then there's a 4 right there, and a 6 right there, and then a 4. It would be 64.

Rachael: So, think of an equation where that would work. I see what you're saying. Think of an equation where if you started with a number, and then you took 100 away, there's 64 left; what number would you have to start with? You have a number, and you take exactly 100 away from it, then there's only 64 left. What number would you have to start with? Turn and talk to a neighbor.

Rachael invited students to think-pair-share. This gave students an opportunity to make sense of Scarlet's idea through partner discussion. It also gave Rachael an opportunity to listen to student conversations and select ideas that would further group understanding.

Emma: 164.

Rachael: So, what's an equation we can write? How do you know it's 164?

After eliciting more student ideas, Rachael encouraged her class to notice mathematical ideas that emerged during the discussion.

Rachael: We have all these equations that equal the number 64. They are similar to each other. What does the word similar mean?

Ann: Like if you were a twin, you are similar to your twin, like José and Jesús.

Rachael: All right, José and Jesús, come on up. So, these boys, they're twins. They're similar in a lot of ways. Does similar mean they're the same exact thing?

Students: No.

Rachael: What's one thing that is similar about these boys?

Brayden: They're both wearing shorts.

Max: They are both funny.

Rachael: Yes, they both have a good sense of humor.

Emma: They're both my friends.

Rachael: They're both your friends. They have that in common, so they're similar. They have a lot of qualities that are the same, but they also have differences, too. What's one thing that's different between these two boys?

Sarah: Their brains are different.

Jessica: José's hair is a little longer than Jesús's.

Rachael: Totally. José is missing a front tooth. Jesús wears glasses. They're similar in a lot of ways, but they're different in some ways, too. So, boys, go sit down. OK, we know the word similar now, right?

Students: Yeah.

Rachael identified the word *similar* in her planning as one that might be helpful when students look for relationships and connections across equations. She paused to discuss the meaning of the word, giving students access to the question and building their vocabulary.

Rachael: Looking at these equations, what equations are similar? Find two that are similar. They don't have to be the same, but they have to be similar.

Jack: They are all similar because 64, 64, 64, 64, 64, 64, 64, 64, 64, and 64.

Max: 63 plus 1 and 65 minus 1 equal 64.

Rachael: So, Max says this one, 63 plus 1 is 64, and 65 minus 1 is 64. How are they similar?

Max: Because they both have 1. They are both plus 1 or minus 1, and they both make the same number.

As we think about the discussion that unfolded in Rachael's classroom, it's important to consider how discussions like these develop over time. Rachael and her students engaged in the Number of the Day routine many times prior to the example in the vignette. When introducing a new classroom routine, it's important to aid students in understanding how to participate. We find beginning with small numbers that students have access to is helpful. This makes space for the routine itself to be the new learning with numbers that students are comfortable with. If only a few ideas emerge, let's celebrate those ideas! It may take time for conversations to sound like the one in the vignette. Students will only grow if we give them these experiences and practice the routine. The beauty of these routines is that they are accessible and follow the lead of students' thinking.

Exploring Choral Counting Instructional Routine

Choral counting brings together number patterns, a sense of community, and playful exploration. For the choral counting instructional routine, the teacher strategically picks a starting number and determines what the class will count by. Then, students count in unison as the teacher records the sequence. Once the sequence is recorded to intentionally bring out the mathematical structure, students notice patterns and talk about their observations. According to Megan Franke, Elham Kazemi, and Angela C. Turrou (2018), "Choral counting gets to the heart of what we desire for our mathematical communities. This activity creates space for all students to notice, to wonder, and to pursue interesting ideas" (p. 79).

For example, figure 4.3 comes from a choral count Lynn did with a second-grade class. This was the fourth time students participated in a choral count. They counted aloud by ten starting at 1. Lynn recorded the count vertically, recording ten numbers in each column. She hoped this recording would help students notice the relationship between columns and use that relationship to predict numbers that would appear in the fourth column. She recorded the numbers in black marker as they were chorally chanted by students during the count. Lynn paused periodically and asked students to share what they noticed. As students shared their noticings, she added their ideas to the chart and color coded them to make them visible. Lynn and the students explored structure within the number system, place value, and the relationship between numbers. These noticings led to observations and early conjectures about the structure of the number system.

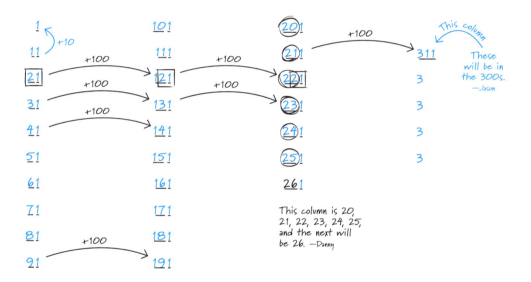

It's counting forward. —Jason

1, 2, 3, 4 . . . —Sam

It starts over again for each column. —Natasha and Bryant

They all have 1 in the ones place. —William

I think there always will be a 1 in the ones place. —Karen

The tens count up like 1s: 1, 2, 3 . . . —Jade

Figure 4.3: Choral counting public record.

Visit go.SolutionTree.com/mathematics for a free, full-color version of this figure.

nurturing math curiosity

YOUR TURN

COUNT BY TEN STARTING AT 8

Begin counting by ten, starting at 8.

- Write down the sequence of numbers up to 198.

- What do you notice about the numbers?

- Will that always be true if you continue to count in this way?

- Is there another way to write your sequence so that other patterns emerge?

- What do you think students would conjecture about this sequence?

CLASSROOM VIGNETTE: FIRST GRADERS INVESTIGATE SARAH'S CONJECTURE

Let's drop into Rachael's first-grade classroom where she and her students have been choral counting since the beginning of the school year. This lesson took place in May. As you read, consider the ways Rachael's first graders explore, test, and modify a conjecture.

Rachael began the lesson by revisiting a choral count she did with the class last week. During the choral count, the students started at 8 and counted by ten (see figure 4.4, page 78), and they shared many ideas about how the sequence of numbers was growing and what the digits represented. In a previous lesson, the class had explored counting by ten starting at 3. The public record in the classroom showed students some of the ideas and observations their classmates shared. As they reviewed the choral count, students remembered that the numbers always got bigger as they continued counting because they were adding ten each time. Rachael reminded the students about one particular observation, which guided that day's lesson.

> *Rachael: Sarah said something really interesting when we did this choral count. She made a conjecture. A conjecture is like saying something that Sarah thinks is true. Today, we're going to check if it's always true. Let me read her conjecture. It says, "No matter how far you go, there will always be an 8 at the end." There will be an 8 in the ones place. What do you think about that? Turn and talk to a neighbor.*

nurturing math curiosity

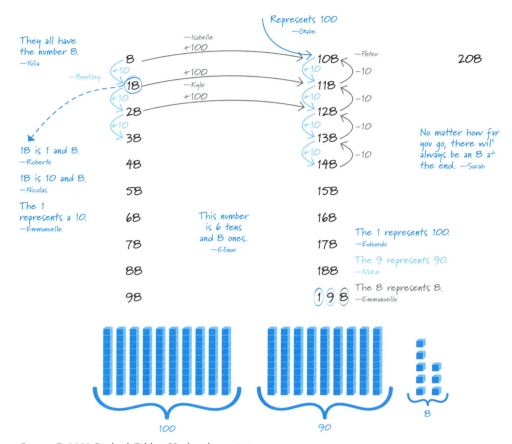

Source: © 2023 Rachael Gildea. Used with permission.
Figure 4.4: Choral counting public record from grade 1.

Rachael recognized Sarah's contribution as something to further investigate. She positioned Sarah as competent and invited other students to think about her conjecture.

One pair of students and Rachael had the following discussion during a turn and talk.

Rachael: What do you think about that conjecture?

Jane: I think it's true that no matter how far you go, there is an 8.

Rachael: How do you know?

Peter: It goes like 10 each time, so if you keep counting and counting and counting, it never stops, we'd keep going.

Jane: No matter how many numbers you do, there's always going to be an 8.

Rachael: How do you know that?

Jane: Because when you count, the last numbers are always going to be there. If we started at 5, it would always be like 5, 15, then like 25 and stuff, so it's always going to be at the end.

Peter: If we add 10s to each number, the numbers keep getting bigger and bigger all over.

Connecting the Classroom Environment and Teacher Toolbox Through Routines

By utilizing turn and talks, students have an opportunity to explore the question posed, and the teacher can listen to students' thinking. In this case, Rachael listened to student ideas and noticed they had made sense of Sarah's conjecture. She decided after eliciting a few ideas that it would be a good time to introduce the task based on this choral count.

As the whole group got back together, students continued to share their observations about the ones place—the ones place stays the same no matter how high the sequence goes. Yulia shared, "There's an 8 here and an 8 here and an 8 here until it stops." Isabelle said, "The 8 will never change." The students also think this will happen with other numbers; for example, if you start with 5 and count by ten, then all ones places will be a 5 as the sequence continues. To further explore this idea, Rachael gave students a recording sheet (see figure 4.5) and said, "Use this space to show me your thinking. If you run out of room, you may use the back. Now, at the very bottom, it says 'make your own conjecture.'" Students had time to work individually and received the freedom to use tools they thought would be helpful, like base ten blocks.

Name _____ **#** _____ **Date** _____

8, 18, 28, 38, 48, 58, 68, 78 . . .	**Conjecture:** "No matter how far you go, there will always be an 8 at the end."

Will this happen no matter what number you start with?

Show your thinking!

Make your own conjecture (use the conjecture above to help you).

Source: © 2023 Rachael Gildea. Used with permission.

Figure 4.5: Grade 1 recording sheet for exploration.

Visit **go.SolutionTree.com/mathematics** for a free reproducible version of this figure.

When Rachael brought the whole group back together, she said, "I saw a lot of really interesting thinking, and I noticed that this was kind of hard, too. I was asking a lot of you today. It was really exciting seeing what you were all thinking. Maybe we can make this conjecture into something that can be true for any number. Addison said something super interesting. Can you read your conjecture to everyone?"

Addison said, "No matter how far you go, the number you start with will always stay the same." Students added to the conversation with the following.

Ben: No matter what you start with, if you start with 4, it will always be 4 at the end, or it will be just 4 or like 24, for any number.

Cristina: Yeah.

Brian: If you add any number, it will start with that number at the end.

Philip: It will always be the same number that you start with all over again. Because if you keep adding the 10, it will be 8 at the end.

As the class discussed a modified conjecture that worked for other numbers, one student helped make the conjecture more precise by adding "the number at the ones place" doesn't change.

Roberto: No matter how far you count by tens, there will always be the same number in the ones place.

Rachael: Can someone come up and read this new idea out loud to the class that we have made together?

Nick: No matter how far you count by tens, there will always be the same number in the ones place.

Rachael asked a pair of students to share their reasoning, which involved using base ten blocks to model the situation.

Amanda: The tens place changed, but the ones place never changed.

Rachael: Why does the ones place never change?

Amanda: Because when you add 10, the 8 doesn't change. It cannot . . . not.

Elinor: 15, 28, 35, 67, that doesn't make sense.

Rachael: It doesn't make sense because you're not counting by ten. Can you show me using these ones cubes and ten sticks? Show me what it looks like. What do you start with?

Amanda: We started with 8 [grabs cubes].

Rachael: OK.

Amanda: 1, 2, 3, 4, 5, 6, 7, 8. We started with 8, and we added 10 [adds a ten stick].

Rachael: So, what is that right there? So, then what do we do next?

Elinor: Add another 10 [adds a ten stick]. That's 28.

Rachael: And then what's next?

Elinor: 38 [adds a ten stick].

Rachael: And then what's next?

Elinor: 48 [continuing to add ten sticks], 58, 68, 78, 88, 98, 108.

Rachael: So, could you keep doing this forever? If we had unlimited ten sticks, could you do that forever?

Girls: Yes.

Rachael: What number changes?

Girls: The 8 never changes.

Rachael: So, you're saying that the ones place always stays the same?

Girls: Yes.

Rachael selected these students to share their thinking with the group because they had used a tool that concretely showed why this conjecture held true. This provided all students with a visual representation of how and why the numbers were changing within the choral count and why that pattern would continue.

In the public record, Rachael used colors to make connections between annotations, arrows, and students' statements (as did Lynn in the second-grade example). These colors made connections and told the story of how the conversation unfolded. Rachael also used base ten blocks as a visual representation that connected to the numbers, supporting students that were working in a concrete phase. When you considered the sequence of counting by ten, starting at 8, how did different ways of writing it affect what patterns emerged? One of the most interesting things we have seen with this routine is how the sequence is written impacts what patterns get discussed! Different ways of recording might elicit different observations from the students.

PATTERNS IN A CHORAL COUNT

Let's think about this choral count:

5	10	15	20
25	30	35	40
45	50	55	60

- What patterns do you notice within the count?

- Why is that pattern happening?

- Why did we write the sequence in this way? How else could we have written it?

- What language did you use to describe why that pattern is happening?

- Write a conjecture from one of your noticings. Make it as precise as possible.

- How can you convince someone that this will always work?

With the choral counting instructional routine, there are many connections to mathematical argumentation. In Rachael's first-grade class, we see how a choral count resulted in Sarah *noticing, wondering*, and using the structure of the base ten system to make a *conjecture*. She and her classmates explored her conjecture, using representations to develop *justifications*, and finally, co-constructed a generalization that they modified throughout the process, extending ideas. With choral counting, students begin making observations about a number pattern, noticing patterns like detectives, and wondering about the patterns they see. They may wonder how the pattern will continue and why the patterns are present. Students have opportunities to make predictions and conjecture about how the structure of this choral count connects to numbers more generally. Students also have opportunities to explain their reasoning, justifying their predictions with others, and modifying predictions based on feedback.

We've unpacked the learning experience from the student's lens; let's also think about this from the teacher's lens. As we learn to listen and see our role as we can learn with and from kids, we increase our mathematics knowledge (Philipp et al., 2007) as well as our knowledge of student thinking. So much of argumentation is possible from our ability to notice (van Es & Sherin, 2006) and interpret what happens in a classroom, creating opportunities to leverage our students' brilliance as Rachael did with Sarah! How we listen can transform how children talk and what they learn (Empson & Jacobs, 2008).

Exploring True or False Instructional Routine

True or false and open number sentences invite students to think about the meaning of the equal sign and relationships between values. Teachers give students an equation or a set of equations and ask if it is true or false. For example, $5 = 1 + 4$. True or false? How do you know?

Students decide if the equation is true or false and explain their reasoning. Student justification provides teachers and peers with insight into their thinking and an opportunity to make sense of mathematical ideas. As more equations are added to the string, students can look for patterns across examples, notice and wonder about their observations, and make conjectures about the structure and properties that they are making sense of.

No matter what answers the students give, teachers can learn a lot about their thinking and their understanding of the equal sign. Every response can build the conversation!

Building an understanding of the equal sign is a beginning step in using true or false and open number sentences. Think about the equation $2 + 3 = 5$. Students may see this as 2 plus 3 makes 5 or 2 plus 3 is the same as 5. Students generally agree this is a true statement and typically see equations written in this way. We can present the same students with $5 = 2 + 3$ and hear them say things such as the following.

- "You can't write it like that."
- "It's backward."
- "5 doesn't equal 2 + 3."

In this case, students are still coming to understand the equal sign and the meaning it carries. As students understand the meaning of the equal sign, we might hear them say things like, "That's true. It's like saying 5 is the same as 5" or "Both sides are 5."

As students come to understand the meaning of the equal sign, teachers can use true or false and open number sentences to get at particular mathematical ideas. Think about the equation $6 + 2 = 2 + 6$. In this example, students may begin to reason about the commutative property of addition, realizing that numbers can be added in any order and the sum will remain the same. A similar equation, $6 - 2 = 2 - 6$ can be used for students to consider whether the commutative property holds true for both addition and subtraction. While numbers can be added in any order, this isn't true of subtraction.

nurturing math curiosity

YOUR TURN
EXPLORE TWO EXAMPLES

Are the following equations true or false? How can you justify your thinking?

4 + 9 = 4 + 10

36 + 17 = 17 + 35 + 1

- What representations are helpful as you think about these equations?

- How might the first equation connect to the second?

- What do these equations have in common?

- What conjecture might come out of these?

- What are some responses you would anticipate from your students? What could you learn about their understanding?

Connecting the Classroom Environment and Teacher Toolbox Through Routines

In addition to true or false statements, such as the earlier example, teachers can also present open number sentences. For example, 4 + 3 = ___ + 2. What number would make this statement true? How do you know?

In this example, students identify the missing quantity and justify their response. When given the open number sentence as shown, we may hear responses such as, "5 because 4 plus 3 is 7, so I know the other side needs to equal 7, and I know 5 and 2 is 7." The student understands the meaning of the equal sign and knows that each side must have the same value to be true. We may also hear responses such as, "7 because 4 plus 3 equals 7 plus 2." In this case, the student may think about the equal sign as a placeholder before the answer, adding 4 + 3 and ignoring the + 2. Another common response to this example is 9. In this case, a student may see the addition sign and add all the values, again, not having yet developed an understanding of the equal sign.

True or false and open number sentences provide students with opportunities to make their thinking visible and reason about the relationship of numbers and operations. For example, presenting an equation, 2 + 5 = 5 + 2, and following up with questions such as, "Is that true or false? How do you know?" creates space to think about the relationships within the equation and articulate that thinking. Students may *notice and wonder* about the equation and make observations about how it could extend to other situations. These observations may lead to *conjectures* about properties of operations. The question, "How do you know?" puts student thinking at the center and provides students the opportunity to use precise language as they *justify* their reasoning. At the same time, space is created for other students to listen, interpret, and *extend* their thinking. This may include agreement, disagreement, or adding to the original ideas. Through interaction around the student's thinking, statements can be revised and modified.

Planning true or false and open number sentences begins with teachers recognizing their students' understanding of the equal sign. Do your students think of the equal sign as a symbol that means the answer comes next? Do they understand it shows a relationship between quantities on either side? Do they see it as meaning "the same as"? Eliciting student ideas about the equal sign is an important step. You might pose the question, "What do you know about the equal sign?" and invite students to share their thinking. If you notice some students don't have a solid understanding of the equal sign, building the foundation could be an important place to start. Depending on your curriculum materials and students' past experiences, you may have the opportunity to introduce them to this concept and explore.

Researchers Thomas P. Carpenter, Megan Loef Franke, and Linda Levi (2003), in their book *Thinking Mathematically: Integrating Arithmetic and Algebra in Elementary School*, identify a set of benchmarks students may encounter as they begin to make sense of the equal sign:

1. Getting children to be specific about what they think the equal sign means is a first step in changing their conceptions.
2. Children accept as true some number sentence that is not the form *a + b = c*.
3. Children recognize that the equal sign represents a relation between two equal numbers. They compare the two sides by carrying out calculations.
4. Children are able to compare the mathematical expressions without actually carrying out the calculations. (p. 19)

Consider equations that provide opportunities to help students to construct their understanding of the equal sign.

> **CLASSROOM VIGNETTE:** FIRST GRADERS MAKE SENSE OF THE EQUAL SIGN

Let's drop into a first-grade classroom in September when Rachael and her students engaged in a true or false activity for the first time. She posed the equation 5 + 2 = 2 + 5 (see figure 4.6) and invited her students to consider whether the statement was true or false and provide reasoning to justify their thinking. Rachael gave students individual think time as well as a recording sheet to represent their thoughts.

$$5 + 2 = 2 + 5$$
$$\uparrow$$
$$\text{is the same as}$$

Lily	→	𝍫𝍫 𝍫𝍫 ⅠⅠⅠⅠ 14
Alec	→	5 + 2 ≠ 2
EJ	→	5 + 2 = 7 2 + 5 = 7
Paige	→	𝍫𝍫 ⅠⅠ = ⅠⅠ 𝍫𝍫

Figure 4.6: Grade 1 true or false.

As you read this vignette, consider the routine itself and the opportunities for argumentation within it. Also, notice the ways Rachael's first-grade students make sense of the equal sign, a foundational understanding in using true or false equations.

First, Rachael called on Lily, who shared that it was false because 5 + 2 = 2 + 5 is 14. The teacher asked, "How did you get 14?" Lily explained that she counted on her fingers to get 14, showing on the paper with tally marks, adding all numbers in the equation.

Next, Alec stated, "5 + 2 does not equal 2." Perhaps Alec overlooked the + 5 of the second expression.

EJ noticed that it's not just 2; it's 2 and 5. EJ explained that "5 and 2 is 7, and 2 and 5 is 7." Rachael then revoiced, "I know that 5 and 2 equals 7, and we also know that 2 and 5 also equals 7. Any connections? Who else saw that? EJ thinks it is true."

> Paige: Well, it's like a switch but it's the same number but it's like switched [moves hand back and forth].
>
> Rachael: Paige just said that it's the same numbers except they're switched. Who else sees that? So, Paige, show me what you did.
>
> Paige: I drew like 1, 2, 3, 4, 5, . . .
>
> Rachael: Paige says they're 5 and 2 more; 7 is the same as 5 and 2 more. Let's count together as a class and see if it's the same. Ready?
>
> Class: 1, 2, 3, 4, 5, 6, 7. [Each individual mark is visible in the tally marks drawn.]
>
> Rayna: I'm thinking that the equal sign is the same as.

Within this exchange, Rachael elicited and recorded student thinking as students co-constructed an understanding of the equal sign through the true or false instructional routine.

Connecting the Classroom Environment and Teacher Toolbox Through Routines

Common misconceptions surfaced within the discussion as Rachael called on students with correct and incorrect responses. Lily, Alec, and EJ each had different interpretations of the task, each a common way for students to approach similar tasks as they develop an understanding of the equal sign. Sequencing the strategies of EJ and Paige allowed students to consider the idea presented in those strategies from both an abstract and more concrete representation of their thinking. In addition to identifying that the numbers in both are the same, as we saw in EJ's strategy, Paige made the quantities visible.

Rachael's first graders were working to understand the meaning of the equal sign. True or false equations can also be used to get at a particular mathematical idea or relationship. For example, if students understand the meaning of the equal sign, the equation presented to Rachael's class, $5 + 2 = 2 + 5$, could be posed to get at the meaning of the commutative property.

As an extension, we have seen a powerful way to illuminate similarities in a set of equations. Once students have determined whether equations are true or false, they then modify the false statements to make them true.

YOUR TURN
HOW MIGHT STUDENTS RESPOND?

Consider the following true or false equations and how students may respond to each. What does their response tell you about their understanding?

$3 + 2 = 5$

_____
_____
_____
_____
_____
_____
_____
_____
_____

$5 = 3 + 2$

_____
_____
_____
_____
_____
_____
_____
_____
_____

nurturing math curiosity

5 = 5

5 = 5 + 1

3 + _____ = 5

2 + 3 = 5 + _____

We recommend starting with quantities that are familiar to students. This way, students can construct new learning around the meaning of the equal sign in the context of numbers they are comfortable with. In Rachael's routine, her goal was for students to think about the equal sign and what it means to add numbers. She also wanted to introduce students to the commutative property of addition, with the idea that you can add numbers in any order and still get the same sum. Consider figure 4.7 and the mathematical ideas these equations potentially lend themselves to.

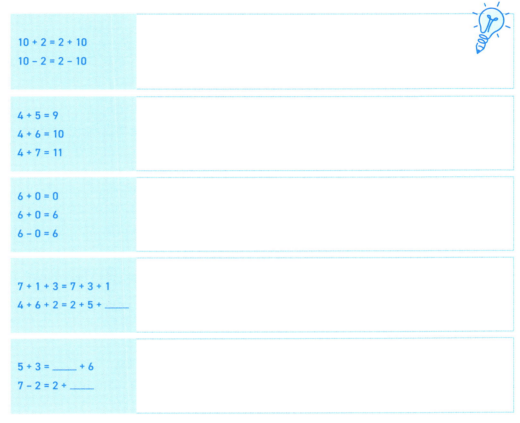

Figure 4.7: What mathematical ideas can you draw from these equations?

TEACHER VOICES
TRUE OR FALSE?

"I feel that my students will enjoy the true or false questions and have fun explaining their thinking. With true or false questions, students can come up with noticings and explanations. Through these noticings, they can come up with a conjecture they can test to create a generalization." (Christina, grade 2 teacher)

Making Connections to Classroom Community and Teacher Toolbox

As you add these routines or re-envision them in your classroom, the following are some ideas to think about.

- Consider ways you will support all students' participation.
  + Will you pose the task and ask students to signal when they have an idea?
  + Will you give students an opportunity to share their idea with a partner prior to launching a whole-group discussion?
- Think about how you will record student contributions.
  + Will you record ideas in the order they were shared?
  + Will you record related ideas?
  + Will you record all ideas in the same color and then use different colors to show relationships?
- Consider what questions you could ask the students as you move from recording student-generated ideas to looking for patterns. We find general questions open doors for student participation and lead to ideas that can be further investigated.
- Think about where the record will be written and how you will display student contributions. Make sure you have a large space to capture student ideas.
  + Will you record ideas on chart paper, allowing students to return to and build from their ideas?
  + Will you record on a whiteboard where ideas will be removed at the end of the discussion?
- Consider how you will close the experience.
  + How will you connect student ideas to the mathematical ideas that emerged?
  + How will you encourage student reflection on the big idea of the goal?

Questions for Further Reflection

The following questions will help you synthesize your learning by reflecting on chapter 4.

- What did you notice about the classroom vignettes?
- What did you notice about what the teacher did to support students to develop and use precise language?
- While you are teaching, attend to the ways that students notice patterns. What conjectures might they come up with related to those number patterns?
- What topics are you teaching that would relate to these instructional routines?
- What other instructional routines do you use that might lend themselves to argumentation?

Chapter 4 Summary

Classroom instructional routines can create space and opportunity for students to engage in the process of argumentation. They are a hidden gem because they have so much potential while being unassuming and deceptively simple. When students have opportunities to engage in open-ended mathematical routines that elicit thinking and generate ideas, they can notice patterns and structures. As we've seen in Rachael's classroom, young students have important ideas to contribute, and they can see things from different perspectives. Using predictable classroom routines allows students and teachers to focus on the content and ideas shared, engage in sense-making, and introduce the layers of mathematical argumentation in natural ways. Look at the ways that routines connect to the layers of argumentation in table 4.3, which we'll focus on in part 2 of this book.

Table 4.3: Connections Between Routines and Layers of Argumentation

Layer of Argumentation	Opportunities Embedded in Instructional Routines
Noticing and Wondering	• Explore mathematical ideas. • Observe patterns and relationships. • Wonder how patterns could extend to other numbers, similar situations, and expressions.
Conjecturing	• Extend patterns and relationships. • Consider generalizations based on their observations. • Make sense of properties of operations and put their ideas into conjectures.
Justifying	• Explain their reasoning about the patterns and observations. • Explain their conjecture with peers and convince them that their conjecture is true.
Extending	• Share ideas and listen to other students' ideas. • Modify ideas based on feedback. • Extend ideas based on the current content and patterns discovered.

The "Chapter 4 Application Guide" (page 92) can help you connect the ideas in chapter 4 to your classroom. In chapter 5, we start growing the layers of argumentation by exploring the first layer: notice and wonder. We will also revisit the Number of the Day instructional routine as we investigate the first layer.

Chapter 4 Application Guide

Use the following application guide to connect these ideas to your classroom.

Chapter 4 Topics	Connect to Your Classroom
Instructional Routines	• If routines are already incorporated into your curriculum, look for connections between this chapter and your curriculum materials. • Look at the structure of your lessons and your daily schedule. Begin thinking about how you could make space for routines two to four times a week. • Look at the routines described in this chapter. Pick one and explain what it has to offer your upcoming mathematical content.

PART 2:
Growing the Layers of Argumentation

CHAPTER 5

Exploring the First Layer: Notice, Wonder, and Beyond

Young children live in a state of wonder, ever attuned to small details and curious questions. In the introduction (page 1), we learned from Huinker (2020) that "children enter this world as emergent mathematicians, naturally curious, and trying to make sense of their mathematical environment" (p. 17). They naturally explore, notice patterns, categorize what they see, and bring a curiosity and a sense of awe to many things they do. For example, while building a ramp, kindergartner Jackie noticed a ball went fast when placed at the top and, after several observations, wondered what would happen if the ramp was steeper. Building ideas from their observations is what students do as they are learning. We can nurture these experiences in mathematics class, too, but what does it look like to notice and wonder about numbers and patterns? How can we build on what students naturally bring to our classroom to help develop important skills they will use throughout their lives?

When we notice, we attend to details. We can communicate our observations and ask questions as we make connections and build new ideas. In a mathematics classroom, students may notice shape categories or the way numbers build in a pattern. They also may notice how numbers or objects are the same or different, or they may notice different things than adults. We all can grow in our ability to notice and make sense of the world. As teachers, we have a chance to notice and wonder in two ways: (1) we can notice and wonder along with students, and (2) we can notice and wonder about what students are thinking. These layers of argumentation are an invitation for our students *and* ourselves to grow wonder and curiosity.

As we nurture the mathematician in each of our students, remember that all students' ideas are worth sharing because everyone can notice and wonder. Educator Rick Wormeli (2014) writes about middle school students, "Our goal should be a classroom culture that cultivates curiosity and personal investment, one in which students feel safe to engage in the activity or topic without fear of embarrassment or rejection" (p. 27). This goal applies to K–2 classrooms, too. We can also focus students' attention on the small, curious details that connect to our lesson so that our lessons build on their ideas, and they have a sense of ownership. Williams (2022) writes:

> If I routinely ask: *What do you notice?* I will receive a range of responses which we can talk about and children will learn that all contributions are equally valued and all add towards our mathematical understandings. It positions children as authoritative and capable, respecting their interests and them as emerging mathematicians. (p. 124)

Whatever we bring to our lesson, we don't have to stop at just noticing and wondering. We can build powerful ideas, but only if we let the wonder grow beyond the initial share. We'll show what this looks like by unpacking a first-grade classroom vignette. Then, we'll learn more about this layer of argumentation and understand task characteristics that lend themselves to noticing and wondering, questions to nudge students to notice and wonder, and connections back to the consecutive sums task that you explored in chapter 1 (page 18) as a learner. This structure will repeat for all four chapters on layers (chapters 5 through 8).

As we explore noticing and wondering together, let's look at a classroom vignette to see how students curiously attend to the details shared during the Number of the Day routine (we described this and other routines in chapter 4, page 65). We will continue to follow this first-grade example in other chapters so we can see how the layers of argumentation grow, build on, and relate to one another. As you read, let your mind notice and wonder about the students' thinking, what the teacher does and says to facilitate the lesson (the teacher moves), and the number 100 (see "Your Turn: 100").

YOUR TURN
100

What do you know about 100? Think of five to seven ideas, expressions, or connections and write them down. Then, use different colors to draw lines or circles to show how your ideas relate to each other (if they do relate). Remember, no observation is too small, all ideas are worth sharing, and every idea gives us a place to start.

Exploring the First Layer: Notice, Wonder, and Beyond

> **CLASSROOM VIGNETTE: NUMBER OF THE DAY AND NOTICE AND WONDER**

In this first-grade classroom, students were engaged in the Number of the Day routine, generating ways to represent 100 and what they know about 100. The teacher, Josephine, called on Mason, who was holding a thumb to his chest as a silent hand signal, indicating he has an idea to share.

Mason: You can buy 100 things at the store.

Lili: It's a big number.

Samuel: There are numbers bigger, for example 2,030.

Maria: 100 is ten groups of 10.

Jayden: 100 has three numbers [digits].

Emily (holding her hands to form a square): 100 is the big square in the [base ten] blocks.

Trey: 100 plus 10 equals 110.

Josephine recorded each contribution on chart paper as it was shared. With the addition of the equation, students' brains shifted gears toward more equations. Next, the teacher called on Rafael.

Rafael: 100 plus 0 equals 100.

Josephine: Is there an equation that is related to Rafael's idea, 100 plus 0 equals 100?

Jocelyn: 0 plus 100 equals 100, you can switch it.

Grady: 99 plus 1 is the same as 100.

Molly: 98 plus 2 is 100.

Students continued to share ideas, and Josephine continued to record. She strategically placed the equations in order, and students continued adding equations as a pattern emerged. After a student offered 90 + 10 = 100, Josephine asked, "Is there another equation that uses decade numbers, like 90 + 10 = 100?" With this new prompt, which stemmed from a student idea, students generated another set of equations, with the teacher organizing them so that addends went up by ten in one column and down by ten in the next. This was an intentional choice made in the planning stage that allowed her to respond in real time to the ideas of her students in an organized way.

Once the chart included a variety of ideas (see figure 5.1, page 100), with students indicating they still had more thoughts to share, Josephine invited them to turn and talk. "I notice there are more ways to show 100, as I see many of you wanting to share ideas. Take a minute and tell a partner how else you might show 100." This teacher move gives all students a chance to share their ideas, to feel heard, and to wrap up the generating ideas portion of the instructional activity.

Pointing to the resulting chart, Josephine said, "You came up with a lot of ways to show 100 today. Let's pause and look at the ideas that you shared. What do you notice? What do you wonder?" Some students began to hold a thumb up in front of their chest. Others joined in. Some added a finger up along with their thumb to signal that they had multiple ideas to share with the group.

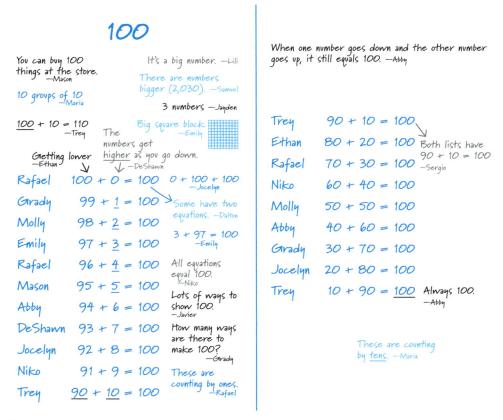

Figure 5.1: First-grade public record about the number 100.

Visit **go.SolutionTree.com/mathematics** for a free, full-color version of this figure.

Josephine posted two sentence frames on the whiteboard to promote noticing and wondering (see figure 5.2). Once she saw that most students had an idea to share, she opened the discussion.

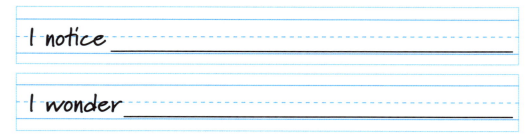

Figure 5.2: Notice and wonder sentence frames.

Josephine: Javier, I notice you have an idea. What do you notice, or what do you wonder? You can use one of the sentence frames to share your idea."

Javier: Lots of ways to make 100.

The teacher revoiced Javier's response, "You noticed there are lots of ways to make 100." She recorded Javier's idea on chart paper and added his name to his contribution. In her revoicing, she added the word *noticed*, signaling to students they can use the common language as they offer ideas. She continued calling on students to share ideas.

Grady: I wonder how many ways there are to make 100. We have even more ideas!

Related to that idea, Dalton noticed that some rows have two equations. DeShawn noticed that the numbers go 1, 2, 3, 4 as you look down the equations, saying, "The numbers get higher as you go down." He made a motion like an elevator with his hand going down. That prompted Ethan to notice that the other number (addend) is getting lower as you go down the equations. Niko noticed that all the equations equal 100. The students were excited to explore the equations, sharing connections between both sets of equations.

Abby pointed to the red equations and noticed, "When one number goes down and the other number goes up, it still equals 100." Having towers of ten connecting cubes available and ready, Josephine took out the towers to represent the red equations. With the help of a student to hold the cubes, the teacher showed one tower of ten and nine towers of ten to represent the two addends of the first equation (see figure 5.3). To show the next equation, she passed one of the nine towers to the other pile. This concrete visual connected the abstract equations to the quantities they represent and how the equations were related.

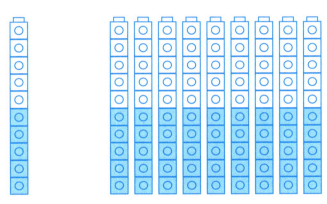

Figure 5.3: Using towers of ten to represent the two addends.

In this vignette, the teacher gave students an opportunity to explore and share ideas. She built on what students do naturally: they notice and wonder about things they see, make connections to what they already know, and connect ideas as they generate new knowledge. The questions were open-ended, and everyone had something they could contribute. In our classrooms, we ideally want to keep this curiosity alive rather than diminish it with time and curriculum constraints. We know that students learn through exploring, connecting, and sense-making, so how do the layers of argumentation allow us to build on that to keep the curiosity alive? Let's keep exploring!

Understanding Notice and Wonder

Notice and wonder is the first layer that we can grow as we nurture an environment of curiosity and exploration in our classroom that will support mathematical argumentation and deep conceptual understanding. In fact, we can't build other layers as well without the foundational notice and wonder layer. In this layer, students slow down and intentionally observe patterns, collect information about the patterns, make connections between examples, ask curious questions, and share ideas (Rumsey, Guarino, & Sperling, 2023). In the vignette, we saw the teacher recording ideas as the students generated them and giving all students a place to share. No observation was insignificant; Emily's idea that there is a base ten block that represents 100 was no more or less valuable than the equations other students shared. Once the teacher wrote down some equations, students noticed a pattern and generated related equations by adjusting the addends. The teacher gave students space to share ideas, and every idea was valued.

The notice and wonder layer wasn't finished just because the students' great ideas were recorded. Stopping at that point would diminish some of the momentum and potential for mathematical argumentation and exploration. The next step is to go beyond notice and wonder. The teacher's next prompt invited the students to look for patterns among the ideas. "Let's pause and look at the ideas you shared. What do you notice? What do you wonder?"

Next, the students were noticing and wondering about the ideas, making connections, and exercising their curiosity. One student noticed that there are "lots of ways to make 100," and another student wondered, "How many ways are there to make 100?" The idea that some numbers in the equations were getting higher, some were getting lower, and some were staying the same was exciting to the students. These ideas were also recorded as a public record that would become a permanent part of the classroom. Learning doesn't end at the end of the mathematics block; the public record can be added to as more ideas emerge on other days, too.

The main goal of noticing and wondering is to create space for curiosity and exploration so that students can generate ideas to be built on in other layers. The classroom norms and environment are crucial to nurture a space where students can share freely and explore without judgment. Teachers and students in the community of learners have a role to play in each layer. For example, teachers carefully select tasks that lend themselves to noticing and wondering.

The environment cultivated by the teacher needs to position all students as mathematical knowers. At the notice and wonder layer, every idea is worth sharing, and every student has something to contribute. Yet, some ideas will naturally lend themselves more to future layers of mathematical argumentation and propel the discussion further. But how do we know which ideas to leverage and probe further? As we look at the chart in figure 5.1 (page 100) that resulted from the vignette, we see some noticings and wonderings that could lead nicely to mathematical argumentation. While it's important to value all student contributions, it's helpful to consider which contributions will lead to conversations of important mathematical ideas and argumentation so that we know where to go next.

As you look back at figure 5.1, ask yourself the following questions.

- What ideas stand out? Which pair nicely together?
- What ideas would you want to probe further? What questions would you pose?
- What ideas lend themselves to important mathematical understandings?
- How do the ideas connect to and extend the goal of the lesson? Are there generalizable parts of the lesson goals that connect to the observations?

Exploring the First Layer: Notice, Wonder, and Beyond

In thinking about generalizable observations that lend themselves to important mathematical understandings, we noticed DeShawn, Ethan, and Niko's ideas went well together and could lead students to discuss addition and the idea of compensation. Abby's contribution built on these ideas when she noticed, "When one number goes down and the other number goes up, it still equals 100." She was attending to the relationship between addends, now from the lens of groups of ten. The teacher can leverage these two ideas to guide student thinking about adding one more or ten more to a quantity—an important understanding for young students. The concrete visual helps to make that concept more accessible for all students and establishes a foundation for other layers.

Further investigation of this noticing might also seed the idea of decomposing and recomposing within the strategy of compensation. For example, when adding 39 + 46, one might consider taking 1 from 46 to have 45 and adding the 1 to 39 to make 40, thus changing the problem to 40 + 45, which are friendlier numbers to work with. When students share important ideas like these, it's up to us as teachers to recognize when these ideas emerge and then do something with them. That's an important role—one that takes practice.

There will likely be so many student ideas that we won't be able to probe all of them. Pushing some ideas further with questioning generates observations to use in future activities related to other layers. In our experience, we have found it helpful to anticipate student thinking within our planning process. We can value all ideas while also knowing that we will leverage some ideas further, especially those that have the potential to lead to generalizations or patterns. The initial ideas shared ("100 is ten groups of 10," "It's a big number," "100 has three numbers [digits]," and "100 is the big square block") were great places to start, but they are not as connected to other observations, so they likely will not be leveraged or questioned further at this point.

If ideas emerge that aren't used right away, we encourage teachers to create a bulletin board or wall called a conjecture wall, where curiosity can continue to flourish beyond the recording that is happening in the specific lesson. Ideas that aren't leveraged in one lesson can be kept alive on a conjecture wall, and students can continue the conversation. When noticing and wondering becomes a valued activity that is part of the fabric of our classroom, it can change who we are and how we see the world. When we and our students see the world, mathematics, and our fellow learners through the lens of curiosity and wonder, it propels learning and understanding. Noticing and wondering make us doers and sense-makers of mathematics rather than passive receivers of knowledge. Indeed, we can notice and wonder about all areas of learning!

Connecting Notice and Wonder to Consecutive Sums

In chapter 1 (page 18), we explored the consecutive sums task, and you wrote about patterns, pictures, and charts and then made observations. Look back at what you noticed and wondered about as a learner. How is what you noticed similar to what K–2 students noticed in the vignettes that we read since exploring that problem? What did you wonder about? How did looking at the examples of other teachers' work in figure 1.3 (page 22) spark more ideas for you? Look at your responses in the first row of figure 1.4 (page 25), where we asked you questions about your experience with noticing and wondering.

We provided an opportunity to slow down and explore in a way that we don't often make time for in our busy days. Just like in the classroom vignette, no observation was insignificant; there were a lot of related ideas with consecutive sums that emerged when we put lots of clues together. This task gave you a chance to experience the sense-making detective work of playing with numbers and to see what discoveries you could make, like we do for our students. As we look at what makes a task work well for noticing and wondering, continue thinking about the consecutive sums task and what made it engaging for you.

YOUR TURN
REVISING 100

We explored the number 100 and a vignette from a grade 1 classroom.

- What do you think might emerge in a kindergarten classroom when they are given the number 10 to explore?

- How could the ideas about the number 10 connect to the ideas Josephine and the first graders in the vignette generated about the number 100?

Exploring the First Layer: Notice, Wonder, and Beyond

Using Tasks for Noticing and Wondering

We used the example of the Number of the Day routine for the vignette, but many other routines and tasks lend themselves well to noticing and wondering. In this section, let's unpack the vignette a little more before thinking about what makes the routine work as a launching point for noticing and wondering. There are some characteristics to consider as we look for tasks.

The grade 1 routine about 100 could have been split into two days, where one day was about generating ideas and observing patterns and the next day was about conjecturing and justifying. In fact, this would be a great way to do this routine for the first time so that you can have a chance to see what students come up with and consider how you could reorganize ideas and what conjectures might emerge. We made notes of this in the "Instructional Routine Planning Template" in appendix A (page 227). Related to the Number of the Day routine, teachers can also show an intentional list of expressions or equations that relate to the Number of the Day to highlight ideas instead of generating a list of observations, as we showed in the first part of the vignette. For example, in figure 5.4, the teacher could display expressions to highlight the idea that numbers can be decomposed in different ways or show that by increasing one addend and decreasing the other, the sum (7) stays the same.

$$1 + 6 \qquad 3 + 4 \qquad 5 + 2$$
$$2 + 5 \qquad 4 + 3 \qquad 6 + 1$$

Figure 5.4: Decomposing 7 in different ways.

To highlight these decomposition ideas, we could also start with two-color counters as a representation, shown in figure 5.5.

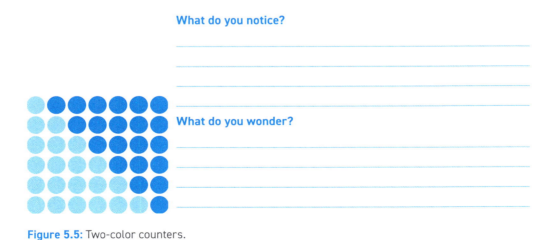

Figure 5.5: Two-color counters.

Letting students notice and wonder first, and then building the lesson from student-developed ideas, is a powerful way to include their voices, even if you already had an idea of where you wanted to go and you use their words to get there.

TWO-COLOR COUNTERS

The following questions are related to the two-color counter image in figure 5.5 (page 105).

- What do you predict the next row will look like? What other row could be added to the image?

- How could you represent each row with an expression and what advantage do we have in using that representation? Do any other patterns or questions emerge?

- What might students notice and wonder? While all ideas are valuable, which might be worth pursuing further in the activity?

Exploring the First Layer: Notice, Wonder, and Beyond

The goal of showing you these examples is to help you see different tasks that could lend themselves to noticing and wondering in a way that goes beyond a basic share-out. These tasks also provide open-ended opportunities and multiple entry points to noticing and wondering. It can be helpful if there are possible generalizations connected to mathematical concepts and learning goals of the lesson as we think beyond this layer. Like the earlier examples, the task may have a picture, figure, or set of expressions to be explored. The following characteristics are helpful in noticing and wondering tasks, and we will revisit these in chapter 9 (page 177) when we look at how to modify curriculum materials to include the four layers of argumentation.

- Everyone can enter the task and share something.
- The task sparks curiosity and there are many possible observations.
- There are connections to relevant mathematical concepts.
- There are opportunities to extend the examples to general cases.
- The descriptions of patterns can lead to generalizations.
- There are connections to mathematical representations that show the structure of mathematical ideas (for example, see figure 5.5).

As students share ideas, you might ask questions to probe deeper or nudge connections. For example, after an idea is shared, you might ask, "Does anyone have an idea that is related to what [student] shared?" We've seen in classrooms where teachers regularly ask questions like the following that students begin to think in similar ways, generating and sharing connected ideas as the students did in the opening vignette (page 99) by seeing and using structure. We believe the teacher's nudging leads to students having more connected observations. Whatever task you use, it can be helpful to have the following questions ready to nudge students toward noticing and wondering.

- What do you notice? What do you wonder?
- What patterns do you see? Will that pattern continue?
- What do the equations have in common?
- How do the equations relate to other observations?
- Who has a related observation?
- Where do you see connections?

Let's look at a common addition task related to the addition table. You may have seen something like figure 5.6 (page 109) in your curriculum materials or maybe your students have been given a blank table like this to fill out. After completing the table and checking with their group members, imagine that students are asked to look for patterns in the table to engage in the notice and wonder layer. Then, show them a table with all the sums of 10 colored in to further highlight the organization of the addition sums, recording their ideas on the public record. As you look at this task and the routines we've been sharing, consider how they fit with the characteristics of tasks we've been discussing.

PAUSE AND PONDER
CHARACTERISTICS OF TASKS

- How does the Number of the Day routine address the characteristics in the bulleted list on page 107?

- How do the choral counting and true or false instructional routines from chapter 4 (pages 74 and 83) fit these characteristics?

We envision students noticing number pairs that make 10 and perhaps number pairs that compose other sums within the table. They might consider why this is happening. Students might also notice that some sums show up in the table more than others; for example, there are eleven times that a sum of 10 appears in the table but only four times that a sum of 3 appears. We'll return to this task in chapter 8 (page 161).

Exploring the First Layer: Notice, Wonder, and Beyond

+	0	1	2	3	4	5	6	7	8	9	10
0	0	1	2	3	4	5	6	7	8	9	10
1	1	2	3	4	5	6	7	8	9	10	11
2	2	3	4	5	6	7	8	9	10	11	12
3	3	4	5	6	7	8	9	10	11	12	13
4	4	5	6	7	8	9	10	11	12	13	14
5	5	6	7	8	9	10	11	12	13	14	15
6	6	7	8	9	10	11	12	13	14	15	16
7	7	8	9	10	11	12	13	14	15	16	17
8	8	9	10	11	12	13	14	15	16	17	18
9	9	10	11	12	13	14	15	16	17	18	19
10	10	11	12	13	14	15	16	17	18	19	20

Figure 5.6: Making tens in the addition table.

PAUSE AND PONDER
REPRESENTATIONS

- How do the representations in figures 5.5 (page 105) and 5.6 show related concepts? What are the benefits and limitations of each?

- How is the addition table in figure 5.6 connected to Ava's conjecture (page 9)? Where do you see Ava's conjecture in the addition table?

_____
_____
_____
_____
_____
_____
_____
_____
_____

Noticing and Wondering and the Number of the Day Routine

It's helpful for students to learn what it's like to notice, wonder, share, and listen through the structure of a routine (chapter 4, page 65). In appendix A (page 211), we provide guidance on noticing and wondering with the Number of the Day instructional routine. Chapters 6 through 8 (pages 117 through 174) discuss how to build the other three layers following the Number of the Day routine. What you practice with Number of the Day can be extended to other routines and tasks (see examples in appendix A).

When someone observes noticing and wondering happen in a classroom, they may not be attuned to all the details and planning that went into making the activity powerful. Let's build on the ideas about routines in chapter 4 now that we've unpacked the notice and wonder layer. In addition, let's remember the ideas about nurturing a classroom community and growing our teacher toolbox from part 1 (page 7) as we implement Number of the Day. The first step is to think about the learning goal. What is it you hope students will think about and understand through the learning experience? What experience will support the learning you're working toward? Thinking about connections to the learning goal, selecting strategic numbers, anticipating students' responses, recording student thinking, working with representations, asking questions, and providing language supports during the planning phase will lead to a smoother, more strategic enactment. But it's a lot to think about! We have a Number of the Day example in the "Instructional Routine Planning Template" in appendix A (page 222) that has a lot of information from part 1. To make much of our thinking visible, we have annotated our "Instructional Routine Planning Template" for the grade 1 vignette in appendix A (page 227) as if we are sitting next to you looking at the template. We are sharing our thoughts and reminding you about connections to previous parts of the book. See figure 5.7 for an example.

Exploring the First Layer: Notice, Wonder, and Beyond

Number of the Day Example With Annotations

This version of the "Instructional Routine Planning Template" includes annotations as if we were there with you pointing things out.

Task:
What do you know about 100?

Content Connections:
Where could argumentation emerge?

- Adding and subtracting within 100
- Composing and decomposing numbers
- *Compensating addends*

Materials:
- Chart paper
- Markers
- Base ten blocks
- *Two large clear zipper bags*
- *Connecting cubes*

Anticipate Possible Student Responses
Before trying the instructional routine with students, brainstorm ideas that students might come up with. Consider how to organize the ideas in a way that could support patterns to emerge, like using writing expressions in an order that shows how addends change (see green and red in full-color version).

Anticipating helps us to be responsive and intentional. Ch. 3 (Williams, 2022)

Give credit to students by including their name next to their idea.

Ten groups of 10
Three numbers
100 is big

Group A
100 + 0 = 100
99 + 1 = 100
98 + 2 = 100
97 + 3 = 100
96 + 4 = 100
95 + 5 = 100

These equations have the same structure; the addends shift by 1.

These equations have addends that shift by 10.

Group B
50 + 50 = 100
40 + 60 = 100
30 + 70 = 100
20 + 80 = 100
10 + 90 = 100
40 + 50 + 10 = 100

Even though it's repetitive, the = 100 helps make a pattern obvious.

Group C
100 − 0 = 100
100 − 1 + 1 = 100
100 − 2 + 2 = 100
101 − 1 = 100
102 − 2 = 100
103 − 3 = 100
104 − 4 = 100

Subtraction equations might emerge!

Possible place value connections

It has a 1 in the hundreds place, zeros in the tens and ones.

It can be made of tens and ones.

The public record may not look exactly like this! See example record in figure 5.1 (page 100).

Students Explore and Generate Ideas
As a class, invite students to generate ideas related to the number 100. Organize related ideas and equations together with the same color. We have organized them by Group A, B, and C to show which colors would be grouped together.

What do you know about the number _____? Let's write down all of the things we know.

- Is there another way to think about 100 that's related to what _____ shared?
- Can you say more about _____?
- What equations can you come up with that have a sum of 100?
- Can you think of an equation with decade numbers and with a sum of 100?

Figure 5.7: Page 1 of the annotated Number of the Day "Instructional Routine Planning Template" found in appendix A.

Visit *go.SolutionTree.com/mathematics* for a free, full-color version of this figure.

If you are ready to start intentionally practicing notice and wonder, you can start with one of the Number of the Day routines shared in chapter 4. A full example of the one we have focused on in this chapter (What do you know about 100?) is located in appendix A (page 222). You can use the "Instructional Routine Planning Template" in appendix A or modify our example for your own students. Then, you can explore a different routine or a different kind of task. We have several examples in appendix A (page 211). You don't need to get argumentation to happen on the first try, just explore the routine and give students a chance to talk. Give students adequate time to think, and when you notice that most or all students have an idea to contribute, begin calling on them to share ideas. Once you and your students have had a chance to practice this layer, you can introduce them to conjecturing in chapter 6.

TEACHER VOICES
NOTICE AND WONDER

"I have noticed that my first graders this year are using the sentence starter 'I notice.' This is so exciting for me, because they are not only finding patterns during a math lesson, but they are also finding patterns in English language arts and science lessons! I feel my class knows to listen to each other when their peers are speaking. They love discovering patterns and sharing their thinking with their peers." (Rachael, grade 1 teacher)

"Exciting to see my kindergartners using the language frames, I notice, I wonder. I notice that I need to support precision in language. Often, students say, 'I saw *it*' or 'If you move *it*, it's the same.' I want to support them in articulating what *it* is, by asking, 'Can you tell me more?' or 'Can you explain what you mean?'" (Bethany, grade K teacher)

Questions for Further Reflection

The following questions will help you synthesize your learning by reflecting on chapter 5.

- What are your students noticing and wondering about? Which ideas have you thought about and which ideas are new?

- Sometimes we tell students about patterns before they have a chance to explore, notice, and wonder for themselves. Is there an upcoming lesson where you could shift some of the noticing and wondering to the students?

- Consider making a conjecture wall for students to add noticings and wonderings that you don't have time to discuss. What do they notice and wonder? You will observe that student noticings become more detailed as the school year progresses.

- In what ways are you noticing and wondering more now as a teacher?

Chapter 5 Summary

Noticing and wondering open the doors to argumentation. We've shared instructional tools (tasks and routines) and teacher moves that we've found useful in observing noticing, wondering, and beyond. Building on students' curiosity and sense of wonder, this layer encourages students to look for and make use of patterns and structure. The "Chapter 5 Application Guide" (page 114) can help you connect the ideas in chapter 5 to your classroom. In chapter 6, we'll explore the second layer: conjecturing.

Chapter 5 Application Guide

Use the following application guide to connect these ideas to your classroom.

Chapter 5 Topics	Connect to Your Classroom
Notice and Wonder	• Model noticing and wondering for your students by sharing your curiosity out loud. • Explore the mathematics of an upcoming lesson yourself by spending 10 minutes noticing and wondering about the task or topic. Record your ideas here.
Questions	• Incorporate one of the suggested questions into an upcoming lesson. Write it here:
Language Supports	• Create language frames and post them in your classroom: 　+ I notice _____ 　+ I wonder _____
Characteristics of Tasks	• Look at tasks in the upcoming lessons to see if they meet some of the characteristics listed for noticing and wondering.
Number of the Day Routine	• Use either the Number of the Day (100) "Instructional Routine Planning Template" in appendix A (page 222) or use another number to begin incorporating routines into an upcoming lesson.

Nurturing Math Curiosity © 2024 Solution Tree Press • SolutionTree.com
Visit **go.SolutionTree.com/mathematics** to download this free reproducible.

CHAPTER 6

Exploring the Second Layer: Conjecturing

Young students come up with great ideas about how the world works, taking their observations and wonderings and describing how patterns might continue. Revisiting the introductory story from chapter 5 (page 97), let's see how Jackie continued to think about the ramp.

While exploring, she noticed that the ball went fast down the ramp and wondered what would happen if the ramp was steeper. She began to notice patterns with more iterations and tried to generalize the ideas she was witnessing. She conjectured that the steeper the ramp, the faster the ball went. She also conjectured that a bumpy, larger ball will go slower than a smoother, smaller ball. Elementary education professor Amy Noelle Parks (2015) writes that:

> The free-wheeling context of play creates many opportunities for children to offer conjectures and to have their conjectures critiqued by others.... Voicing these theories and listening to the reasoning of peers in response gives children practice in making and evaluating evidence and arguments. (p. 86)

We can nurture experiences like exploring the ramp with numbers and patterns in grades K–2, building on the notice and wonder layer we discussed in chapter 5. Let's see what that looks like.

When we conjecture, we take what we notice and wonder and make predictions about how patterns continue and what might be true beyond the examples we have in front of us.

In our context, a *conjecture* is a generalized statement we believe to be true about a mathematical idea. We can also conjecture in other subjects—young students often do this naturally and are not bound by subject area divides. Sharing a conjecture is a starting point for a conversation—a launching-off point rather than an absolute truth. It's based on what we know right now and can be modified as we explore further. Similarly, researchers Thomas P. Carpenter, Megan Franke, and Linda Levi (2003) write:

> The goal in engaging students in making conjectures is more than simply getting students to talk about mathematics and make mathematical ideas explicit. We want students to make conjectures not just for the sake of making conjectures, but because the ideas that they make conjectures about are important mathematical ideas that provide them power to learn new mathematics, to solve problems, and to understand mathematics they are learning and using. (p. 53)

We agree with researchers Traci Higgins, Susan Jo Russell, and Deborah Schifter (2022) that:

> Conjecturing is a critical mathematical practice for young students. It is the bridge between noticing regularity and justifying why that regularity holds. Conjectures arise as students consider examples of mathematical regularities, are refined as students work on articulating their idea with precision, and continue to be reconsidered as students move toward justification. (p. 196)

In a mathematics classroom, students may conjecture about how shapes are related to each other or what is true about categories of numbers. As students explore a number pattern, they may conjecture about how the pattern continues no matter how high the numbers go. While everyone is making sense of the world and the patterns we see, students may conjecture about different things than us, and that is something to celebrate and learn from. Every conjecture will provide an opportunity to generalize and understand the noticings and wonderings in a deeper way, even if they might not turn out to be true. Even when conjectures aren't true, deep learning can emerge from the experience of exploring the ideas.

Some students may move toward conjecturing without prompting after building a rich foundation of observations in the notice and wonder layer. They naturally want to build an understanding of what they see. While some students may start to conjecture without prompting, others may need some purposeful questions to nudge them in that direction. In this chapter, we address these different ways of conjecturing so that you can build and integrate this layer into your classroom. Remember that students aren't aware of the layers in the same way as we discuss them in this book. The layers will likely flow for the students. We are distinguishing the layers for you so that you can explicitly attend to the important features and build them in your classroom in parts. Eventually they will flow in your lessons as well.

In this chapter, you'll learn what conjecturing is, what it looks like, and how to nudge students to make and share their conjectures. Your students have big ideas about the world and how it works, and they may already be conjecturing, so we'll talk about how to identify it as well. We'll also unpack the idea of conjecturing and what that looks like for students and explore the types of conjectures that students typically make.

Exploring the Second Layer: Conjecturing

DECOMPOSING NUMBERS

Conjecturing, like noticing and wondering, can emerge from many different mathematical topics and activities. Imagine your students have been decomposing numbers and the following expressions are organized on public records hanging in the room (see figure 6.1, page 120). Explore these lists of decomposed numbers to see what you notice and wonder and how those observations prompt you to think of conjectures—things that you believe to be true.

- What do you notice and wonder about the charts?

- What patterns do you see?

- How do you think the patterns will continue?

- What do you believe to always be true about decomposing numbers?

- Based on what you've noticed, what predictions do you have for decomposing larger numbers?

3	4	5	6	7
0 + 3	0 + 4	0 + 5	0 + 6	0 + 7
1 + 2	1 + 3	1 + 4	1 + 5	1 + 6
2 + 1	2 + 2	2 + 3	2 + 4	2 + 5
3 + 0	3 + 1	3 + 2	3 + 3	3 + 4
	4 + 0	4 + 1	4 + 2	4 + 3
		5 + 0	5 + 1	5 + 2
			6 + 0	6 + 1
				7 + 0

Figure 6.1: Charts related to decomposing numbers, organized into strategic lists.

In the opening vignette of this book (page 9), we shared a kindergartner's conjecture about decomposing numbers. Look back at Ava's conjecture and see how it connects to this set of decompositions. How is her conjecture similar to or different from yours?

Exploring the Second Layer: Conjecturing

CLASSROOM VIGNETTE: NUMBER OF THE DAY AND CONJECTURING

In chapter 5, we dropped into a first-grade classroom that was generating ways to show 100 as they worked on the instructional routine Number of the Day. Students got excited and shared ideas, and the teacher recorded the students' thinking in a strategic way using color and placement. Students engaged in the first layer of argumentation: notice and wonder. Where we paused the vignette in chapter 5 (page 101) corresponds to where the lesson ended for the day with the students. The next day, the students revisited the public record to refresh themselves on what they had noticed and wondered about the previous day. We can look back at the public record to refresh ourselves in figure 6.2.

Figure 6.2: Grade 1 public record for Number of the Day—100.

Visit *go.SolutionTree.com/mathematics* for a free, full-color version of this figure.

Josephine nudged students to make conjectures, which are general statements about what they believe to be true, by connecting back to the students' ideas from the previous day's public record.

> *Josephine: You've come up with many ways to show 100 and shared many noticings and wonderings. Sometimes, mathematicians gather all their equations or shapes and look for patterns across all the examples, and that's what we're doing. You are doing the work of mathematicians right now. You're noticing really good things. We're wondering to ourselves, Is this idea always going to be true? Is there something you think might always be true based on what we have written so far?*

The idea of a conjecture was still new to these students at this point, so the teacher focused the students' attention on a promising statement from the previous lesson. "Let's revisit Abby's statement that 'when one number goes down, and the other number goes up, it still equals 100.'" As she pointed to the equations shown on the chart, Josephine asked Abby to restate her idea and point to what she was thinking on the public record. Josephine then said, "Abby noticed that when one number goes down, and the other number goes up, it still equals 100. What does Abby mean? Is that observation always true? When will it be true?"

Josephine prompted the students to turn and talk with a neighbor as they considered the observation and whether it was true. As students talked with a partner, Josephine monitored the conversations, listening for ideas about general patterns and observations to bring back to the whole group. She overheard Ethan connecting to his original statement as he talked with his partner, so she asked him to share when they regrouped. Ethan said, "The numbers are getting lower as you go down: 99, 98, 97, 96."

> *Josephine: I can see that Abby's observation fits with the green equations that Ethan is pointing to. Does it also work with the red ones?*
>
> *Nakia: The ones in green go up or down by 1 and the ones in red go up or down by 10. The hops are different sizes. All on the left side equal 100. On the right side, it's the same thing but you just get bigger numbers.*
>
> *Josephine: Let's look at the right equations. If we start with the expression 50 + 50, what does Abby mean about numbers going up and down? What number goes up and what number goes down? How much do they go up and down by?*

Josephine is working to engage all students in making sense of Abby's idea and connecting both sets of equations, using Abby's initial language, while also encouraging the students to add precision to the conjecture.

> *Daniela: Maybe she meant that 60 is 10 more than 50 and 40 is 10 less than 50?*
>
> *Josephine: Who can revoice what Daniela said?*
>
> *Student: The number goes down by 10, and the other number goes up by 10.*

Josephine's talk move of asking a student to revoice Daniela's observation drew attention to an idea Josephine wanted all students to access before moving to the conjecturing phase. Since students were still learning about conjecturing, she took this opportunity to highlight this example of a conjecture. "A conjecture is an idea that we think might always be true; let's write it so we can explore it more." The detail of "by 10" was added to add clarity to Abby's conjecture (figure 6.3).

With the example highlighted and written on the public record, students began thinking of other ideas that might also be true. Dalton seemed drawn to the idea that there were two equations written for some of the rows: for example, 97 + 3 = 100 and 3 + 97 = 100. Pointing to those equations, he said, "You can write them two ways. You can flip the numbers." Josephine asked, "Who can restate this conjecture?" She added the conjecture to the conjecture chart, at the bottom of figure 6.3.

While not a conjecture, Sergio noticed that both sets of equations included 90 + 10 = 100. To honor this idea, Josephine added it to the noticing chart paper, since it's not a conjecture but a worthy and connected observation.

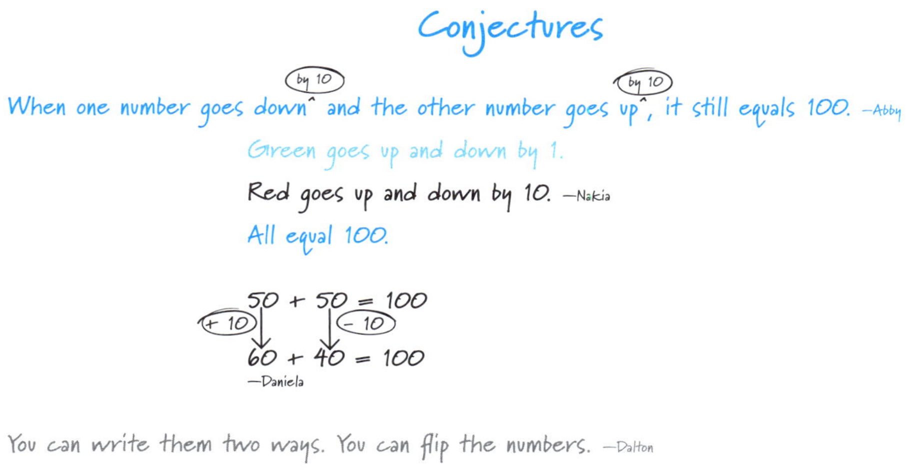

Exploring the Second Layer: Conjecturing

Conjectures

When one number goes down (by 10) and the other number goes up (by 10), it still equals 100. —Abby

Green goes up and down by 1.

Red goes up and down by 10. —Nakia

All equal 100.

$$50 + 50 = 100$$
$$\downarrow {+10} \quad \downarrow {-10}$$
$$60 + 40 = 100$$
—Daniela

You can write them two ways. You can flip the numbers. —Dalton

Figure 6.3: Conjectures chart for grade 1 shows cumulative student ideas throughout the lesson.

Visit **go.SolutionTree.com/mathematics** *for a free, full-color version of this figure.*

As the students developed conjectures, Josephine had to decide which conjectures to leverage for the next part of the lesson. Starting the lesson, Abby's conjecture was the direction she tentatively planned to go, so she decided to focus on that conjecture and save the other for another exploration. There are lots of directions that teachers can go, and there is no right or wrong way. It depends on the content students are currently working on and how the conjecture can enhance and amplify that learning.

Focusing on the commutative property idea that Dalton proposed makes sense in another lesson. In fact, the class can revisit that idea anytime if it is placed on a conjecture wall. Another way this could unfold would be to have students work in groups and pick a set of equations to think about and then state a conjecture. This would make sense once they have had more experience conjecturing and it becomes a typical thing they do. In this lesson, students continued to explore Abby's conjecture, so Josephine said, "These are both great conjectures. Let's explore Abby's conjecture today and continue to talk about Dalton's conjecture another day because this is an important idea that is going to continue to come up as we are exploring math equations."

At this point, we'll pause the vignette to unpack what we just witnessed related to conjectures. We'll see what happens next in this classroom in chapter 7.

Understanding Conjecturing

Building from the notice and wonder layer, we can nurture an environment that allows students to be mathematical knowers and creators. Students can build ideas and make connections, and they can do that in mathematics class with patterns and numbers. By taking the patterns that they observed in the previous layer and the questions they were curious about, students can extend from the examples in front of them, generalize their ideas, and make predictions about what they believe to be true. Researchers Susan Jo Russell, Deborah Schifter, Virginia Bastable, Traci Higgins, and Reva Kasman (2017) write about the importance of conjecturing, saying:

> When elementary students have the opportunity to create mathematics that is brand-new to them, participating in the act of innovation can empower them. As students start to make their own conjecture and arguments, the goal of mathematics ceases to be about providing correct answers to someone else's questions. Instead, mathematics becomes focused on the creative process and the search for understanding. (p. 26)

In the grade 1 vignette, we saw Abby and Dalton sharing conjectures about what they thought might always be true. Even though these are initial assumptions and not as mathematically precise, they are general statements about the patterns and are great places to begin. We recognize them as conjectures because they are general statements that go beyond specific numbers. Sergio's statement was very specific about an example (90 + 10 = 100) that both sets of equations had in common. The teacher made the decision to acknowledge it as a noticing rather than as a conjecture. This is an example of valuing and recording students' ideas in a space where all ideas are welcome.

Connecting Conjecturing to Consecutive Sums

In chapter 1, we explored the consecutive sums task (page 18), and you observed how the patterns continue and what might always be true after trying many examples. Look back to remind yourself of the statement you wrote that you think will always be true. With the students in this chapter's vignette, there is power when they can create new mathematics and show creativity. In a similar way, we want you to explore something that you might not have seen for a while in a new way as you developed a conjecture in the consecutive sums task. Look back at your conjecture (see page 19). How would you describe it? Here are some conjectures we have heard from other educators.

- "If you add two consecutive numbers, the sum will always be odd."
- "With four addends, the sum is always even."
- "Not all whole numbers can be written as the sum of consecutive positive numbers."
- "With three addends, the sum is a multiple of 3."

Was your conjecture about an arithmetic property that is always true? Was your conjecture about types of numbers, a procedure and why it works, when to use a procedure, or how operations act and behave? As we continue this chapter, we'll describe some different types of conjectures we have seen with K–2 students.

Let's look at another example as we continue exploring the idea of conjecturing. In a kindergarten lesson built from the true or false routine, students were looking at a set of true equations they generated as a class (see figure 6.4). These were listed in a long column in the classroom. As they worked as number detectives, they came up with three class conjectures, ideas that they thought might always be true. By conjecturing about the equations, students were developing a deeper understanding of teen numbers and place value while practicing the language of the discipline. While an adult may look at the kindergarten conjectures in figure 6.5 and think they are obvious, they may not be obvious to students who are early in their exploration of these topics.

Exploring the Second Layer: Conjecturing

10 + 1 = 11	10 + 4 = 14	10 + 7 = 17
10 + 2 = 12	10 + 5 = 15	10 + 8 = 18
10 + 3 = 13	10 + 6 = 16	10 + 9 = 19

Figure 6.4: True equations organized to elicit a pattern.

Conjectures

Teen numbers always have a 1. —Noah

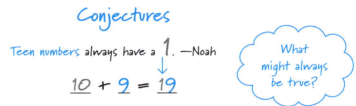

10 + 9 = 19

What might always be true?

Teen numbers don't have a 2 in front. —Luis

When you count, numbers get bigger. —Elsie

Figure 6.5: Kindergarten conjectures.

The main goal of conjecturing is to open a space for building knowledge together based on the noticings and wonderings of the previous layer.

TEACHER VOICES
CONJECTURES

"Conjectures are statements that students believe to be true, and they can be revised (get more specific) with time and with new information." (Rachael, grade 1 teacher)

"Conjectures need to be general and able to be tested. I think conjectures are the starting point of creating a generalization or theory. A key feature is that they are not fixed and able to be changed based on what the student knows." (Christina, grade 2 teacher)

The classroom norms and environment are crucial in nurturing a space where students can share freely and explore without judgment. Williams (2022) writes:

> If the culture of the setting is one where learners feel safe, where they are strongly encouraged to ask their questions and offer their conjectures, in mathematics as in any area of learning, they often reveal understandings beyond those we might expect. (p. 124)

Students may be eager to share their ideas with a sense of pride at having discovered a new statement they believe is true. We can share in their excitement and encourage them to clarify their ideas, while also encouraging classmates to engage curiously. We also know that not all conjectures will be true, but all are worthy of being explored. Learning can happen from exploring statements, whether they are true or not.

As discussion facilitators, we can be aware of which conjectures to leverage and probe further. Some contributions will lead to conversations of important mathematical ideas and argumentation. Look back at figure 6.2 (page 121) from the vignette and ask yourself the following questions.

- What conjectures lend themselves to important mathematical understandings?
- How does the conjecture connect to and extend the goal of the lesson?
- Does the conjecture generalize patterns that were observed in the previous layer?
- What questions would you pose to clarify the conjecture?

As we move toward conjecturing, we may need to provide more time for the classroom community to explore a conjecture. First-grade teacher Rachael turned a conjecture into a task the next day when she put Sarah's conjecture on a recording sheet for students to write about (figure 6.6). The conjecture came from a choral count; its purpose was to investigate an idea that emerged the previous day so that the class could discuss it and decide if it was true.

Name _____ **#** _____ **Date** _____

| 8, 18, 28, 38, 48, 58, 68, 78 . . . | **Conjecture:** "No matter how far you go, there will always be an 8 at the end." |

Will this happen no matter what number you start with?

Show your thinking!

Make your own conjecture (use the conjecture above to help you).

Source: © 2023 Rachael Gildea. Used with permission.
Figure 6.6: Grade 1 recording sheet for exploration.

Exploring the Second Layer: Conjecturing

YOUR TURN
CONNECTING TO TASKS

Figures 6.7 and 6.8 (page 128) are two examples of images that could give students a chance to notice and wonder. It doesn't need to be a whole task; perhaps you have images like this in your curriculum materials that students could notice and wonder around.

- After you've noticed and wondered about an image from your curriculum, how do you think the observations you've made will extend beyond the numbers shown? What do you believe to always be true about the situation in the image? What conjectures might emerge after students notice and wonder about the image?

- How might the students state the conjectures? There might be some conjectures that you think are too obvious but remember that there are no insignificant ideas. We can build on the students' ideas!

In figure 6.7, students may make many different observations, which could each lead to different possible conjectures. Students may notice that if you add one to a number, you get the next counting number. This could lead to the conjecture that when you add one to a number, the sum is one larger than the addend you started with. They may also notice that each pair of towers has a cube without a partner, which could lead to conjectures about even and odd numbers and the relationship of the addends.

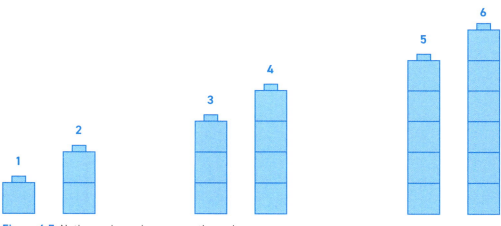

Figure 6.7: Notice and wonder—connecting cubes.

When observing the number lines in figure 6.8, students might notice that one arrow is showing adding 4 and one is showing subtracting 4. They might notice that if you add 4 and then subtract 4, you end up where you started. Students might conjecture that addition and subtraction are inverse operations.

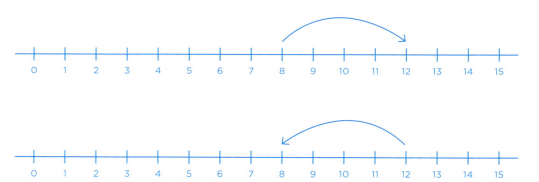

Source: Illustrative Mathematics, n.d.a. This work is licensed under a Creative Commons Attribution 4.0 International License (https://creativecommons.org/licenses/by/4.0).

Figure 6.8: Jumps on the number line.

Exploring the Second Layer: Conjecturing

PAUSE AND PONDER
CONNECTING CUBES AND NUMBER LINES

- How does figure 6.7 relate to the consecutive sums task and samples of the teacher work shown in figure 1.3 (page 22)?

- Is figure 6.7 a helpful representation for any of your observations?

- How could number lines, like those in figure 6.8, be helpful in supporting students as they explore a choral count?

Looking at More Examples of K–2 Conjectures

As we envision what conjectures might look like in our classroom, let's explore some examples we have heard from K–2 students, organized by categories based on the work of researchers (Carpenter et al., 2003; Higgins, Russell, & Schifter, 2022; Rumsey, 2012; Rumsey & Langrall, 2016). Like the tasks in figures 6.7 and 6.8, different tasks, situations, images, and equations will lead to different opportunities for students to conjecture, and it's helpful to know the different types of conjectures they may come up with. An awareness of the different kinds of conjectures can help us to identify students' brilliance and not miss a conjecture because it's different from others. Depending on the types of conjectures, different justifications may be more likely used by students. We'll talk about that in chapter 7, in which we discuss the justifying layer (page 139).

CONJECTURES ABOUT ARITHMETIC PROPERTIES

Conjectures about arithmetic properties are focused on "basic properties of numbers and operations on them. These conjectures represent important ideas about arithmetic that make the learning of arithmetic easier and that are critical for learning algebra" (Carpenter et al., 2003, p. 62). The context of arithmetic properties provides a rich context for making conjectures and can also support students as they develop early algebraic concepts (Blanton, 2008; Carpenter et al., 2003). The following are some examples of K–2 student conjectures about arithmetic properties in their own words.

- If you add 0 to a number, it doesn't change the amount.
- You can switch the order of two numbers that you are adding together, and the sum stays the same.
- We can add three numbers together in any order and get the same sum.

CONJECTURES ABOUT TYPES OF NUMBERS

Conjectures about types of numbers are focused on characteristics of groups of numbers—for example, even and odd numbers or multiples of ten. They help us to understand what it means to be in the group of numbers. The following are some examples of K–2 student conjectures about types of numbers in their own words.

- Whenever you add two odd numbers, you will get an even number.
- A multiple of 10 will always have a 0 in the ones place.
- All doubles equal even numbers.
- Teen numbers always have a 1.

CONJECTURES ABOUT PROCEDURES

Conjectures about procedures are "rules for carrying out specific computational procedures" and the general outcomes of the calculations (Carpenter et al., 2003, p. 62).

They help us understand what happens when we do a procedure. The following are some examples of K–2 student conjectures about procedures in their own words.

- If you start with 8 and count by tens, you will always have an 8 in the ones place.

- If you add 10, the ones place doesn't change but the tens place goes up by one.

- If you have a teen number and you subtract 10, what's left is the last number in the teen number (grade K).

CONJECTURES ABOUT WHEN TO USE PROCEDURES

Conjectures about when to use procedures are focused on the efficiency of a procedure. The conjecture is not about how to use it or the outcome, but rather when it makes sense to use it. Multiple procedures are compared to decide which is best for a certain situation. Some examples of K–2 student conjectures in their own words about when to use procedures include the following.

- With subtraction, if the subtrahend is bigger than the ones place of the minuend, decomposing is helpful.

- When using a counting strategy to subtract, it's easier to count up when the numbers are far apart (18 – 2) and count down when the numbers are close together (18 – 16).

CONJECTURES ABOUT THE BEHAVIOR OF OPERATIONS

Conjectures about the behavior of operations are focused on the general outcomes of calculations. The following are some examples of K–2 student conjectures about the behavior of operations in their own words.

- If you add two numbers, you get a bigger number.

- If you add 1 to a number, the sum is bigger than what you started with.

- Every time you keep counting, the numbers keep getting bigger.

- Addition and subtraction are opposites.

- When you are adding two numbers and one number goes up and the other number goes down by the same amount, it equals the same sum.

Now that we've shared some examples of conjectures we've heard with K–2 students and shown the different categories of conjectures, let's talk about two things that are not conjectures. First, definitions are not conjectures, but they are useful tools to talk in mathematically precise ways. Carpenter and colleagues (2003) write that unlike conjectures, "definitions cannot be justified. They are true by definition" (p. 62). Second, the calculated answers to a specific equation can be explained but are not generalizable as a conjecture. Patterns across several equations could be generalized into a conjecture, but not a single answer. For example, "The answer to 4 plus 5 is 9" is a statement but, taken along with other related equations, could lead to a conjecture.

PAUSE AND PONDER
CONJECTURES

- What kinds of conjectures have you heard from your students or which are they most likely to come up with?

- What types of conjectures do you think your students might come up with for the Number of the Day instructional routine?

Using Tasks for Conjecturing

We followed the example of a Number of the Day routine for the vignette, but let's look at some characteristics of tasks and routines that would lend themselves to conjecturing. When students conjecture, they are making sense of bigger ideas beyond the examples in front of them. In the choral counting instructional routine, students can make conjectures about how the pattern extends and why. They look beyond the numbers listed to generalize the patterns that they see. In the true or false instructional routine, by looking across equations for patterns, students also generalize the number properties and structure of the operations that are represented. As students are noticing and wondering, we can encourage conjecturing within the tasks. We can look for opportunities to ask how patterns extend, when certain strategies make the most sense, and what students believe to be true. Consider the following characteristics of tasks that we find helpful to search for in opportunities to conjecture.

Exploring the Second Layer: Conjecturing

- The task sparks curiosity, and there are multiple patterns or properties to explore.
- There are connections to relevant mathematical concepts or procedures.
- There are multiple related examples (for example, to the same arithmetic property or to a specific pattern).
- The examples provide a window into a generalizable property or pattern. There are opportunities to extend the examples to general cases.
- The descriptions of patterns can lead to generalizations.
- There are connections to mathematical representations that show the structure of mathematical ideas.

In grade 2, you may see tasks in your curriculum materials where students are given representations and asked to find one-half (see figure 6.9). This may seem like a procedural task, but there are deep connections to mathematical argumentation embedded in making observations.

Task

Which pictures represent one-half?
___

How do you know?
___

What do you notice and wonder about the pictures?
___

What might always be true?
___

i. ⊘   ii. ◩   iii. ▭   iv. ⊕

Figure 6.9: Looking for one-half.

Let's look at how this task connects specifically to conjecturing. This task is relevant to mathematics concepts in its grade level, and the examples provide a window into a pattern. As students talk about the patterns they notice, it can lead to generalizations about what one-half is. The images also build connections to the structure of one-half (with the area model) and could lead to students noticing one-half in other real-world situations. Through this task, students are building an idea of what counts as one-half, with some examples and nonexamples. As the image of the square incorrectly shaded shows us in figure 6.9, it's not just about drawing a single line through the shape to make two parts—they must be equal parts. Precise language is important as students explain why a picture shows one-half. A student may conjecture that if you cut a shape into two parts, one of the parts is one-half.

To make it more precise, peers may push the student to also add that the two parts must be exactly the same size. Students might also conjecture that any shape can be cut into two equal pieces, and some can be cut in more than one way.

Continuing With the Number of the Day Instructional Routine

Let's think about how to extend the Number of the Day routine in your classroom, building on what you did in chapter 5 (page 110) and applying the new ideas from this chapter. Sometimes, students begin to conjecture without prompting, and we can listen for clues in the students' language that a conjecture is emerging. The language of generalizing can include words such as *whenever*, *always*, *sometimes*, and *for any number*. Just because those words are used doesn't guarantee a conjecture is being formed, but it's a clue to listen to the statement's language to see if there is something to build from.

Sometimes, conjectures don't emerge on their own, but we can encourage them through purposeful questioning that focuses students' attention on the patterns or properties and how they extend. The goal is to generate some statements that extend beyond the cases shown, so if we hear observations about the specific examples, we could ask, "Are there other numbers that idea will work for?" or "Will that always be true as the pattern continues?" If there is a general observation related to the direction of the argumentation lesson, we could also ask, "Is that statement always true?" or "Which types of numbers is that true for?" In the "Instructional Routine Planning Template" in appendix A (page 211), we have sample questions listed. Our questions can nudge students to take a step forward and look beyond the specific examples listed. This is an opportunity to develop ideas about what they believe is always true. It's not that all questions in the "Instructional Routine Planning Template" need to be asked in that order, but they are listed to provide examples of question types that could prompt more global thinking. The following questions nudge at conjecturing.

- Is that observation always true? When will it be true?
- What do you believe to always be true about _____?
- How will the pattern continue?
- Is that true always, sometimes, or never? How do you know?
- Can you draw a visual representation to show what you mean? What does each part of your representation show and how does it connect to the conjecture?
- How can you use a tool to show what you mean?

Sometimes, students want to add to the conversation but aren't sure how. Language frames (chapter 3, page 59) encourage a common language and a way to enter the discussion. With this layer, we can model the language frames or write them out for students. Some language frames for this layer include the following.

- My conjecture is _____.
- It will always be true that _____.
- An idea I have is that _____.

Exploring the Second Layer: Conjecturing

PAUSE AND PONDER
STUDENTS' NUMBER OF THE DAY THINKING

- When you were working on the Number of the Day routine in chapter 5 with your own students, did you hear words like the ones on page 134 emerging in the conversations?

- Did students start to conjecture without your prompting?

TEACHER VOICES
CONJECTURING

"Finding patterns in numbers and making conjectures drives student thinking into making generalizations for math. I am excited to lead the students in making a conjecture. They will be able to use their knowledge and the correct language to make a conjecture about 10 more and 10 fewer, perhaps by noticing place value and the patterns they see." (Rachael, grade 1 teacher)

"Students were actually making generalizations without me even knowing! I now want to further their thinking and ask them to apply these conjectures to any number. I want students to practice how to turn and talk, and make sure they are working together to come up with conclusions or ideas. I want them to be using the academic language we are focusing on." (Rachael, grade 1 teacher)

"If I do the sequence with the zeros, I think my students will notice that the number does not change when zero is added. I would like to then turn this statement into a conjecture and try to get students to use more academic language to be more specific. I would like them to reference the word *amount*, as well as the word *sum*. I think it would be beneficial for students to have more specific language when talking about the commutative property." (Rachael, grade 1 teacher)

"My students were able to articulate and build generalizations within the course of a lesson. They had practice with a concept and then even the students who typically struggled to make a connection were able to do so (except for one). But one girl who consistently struggles said, 'If I have a unicorn plus zero, I'd still have a unicorn.' She was able to then take this thinking and apply it to her number work." (Bethany, grade K teacher)

Questions for Further Reflection

The following questions will help you synthesize your learning by reflecting on chapter 6.

- Look through grade-level standards and consider properties and big ideas. What kind of lessons would lend themselves to conjecturing?
- What surprised you within the vignette in this chapter?
- How do you see conjecturing as an opportunity for students to develop deep understandings and see their own ideas and the ideas of others as valuable?
- What do you want to remember as you support your students to make conjectures?

Chapter 6 Summary

As Higgins, Russell, and Schifter (2022) write:

> Conjecturing is a critical mathematical practice for young students. It is the bridge between noticing regularity and justifying why that regularity holds. Conjectures arise as students consider examples of mathematical regularities, are refined as students work on articulating their idea with precision, and continue to be reconsidered as students move toward justification. (p. 196)

We've described the conjecturing layer of argumentation and shared what conjecturing looks and sounds like in primary classrooms. Giving students opportunities to notice and wonder and adding follow-up questions—such as "Is that observation always true?"—to our repertoire can shift noticings and wonderings into conjectures. The "Chapter 6 Application Guide" can help you connect the ideas in chapter 6 to your classroom. In chapter 7, we'll explore the third layer of argumentation: justification.

Chapter 6 Application Guide

Use the following application guide to connect these ideas to your classroom.

Chapter 6 Topics	Connect to Your Classroom
Conjecturing	• Model conjecturing for your students by sharing your ideas out loud.
Types of Conjectures	• Look at the types of conjectures described in this chapter and compare them to some of the upcoming work in your curriculum to determine which types of conjectures might connect with your lessons.
Questions	• Incorporate one of the suggested questions into an upcoming lesson. Write it here:

Language Supports	• Create a language frame and post it in your classroom:
	  + My conjecture is _____
	  + It will always be true that _____
	  + An idea I have is that _____

Characteristics of Tasks	• Look at tasks in the upcoming lessons to see if they meet some of the characteristics listed for conjecturing.
Number of the Day Routine	• Continue with the Number of the Day routine that you started in chapter 5 (page 110), focusing on the conjecturing ideas from this chapter.

CHAPTER 7

Exploring the Third Layer: Justifying

Young students like to understand the world, often asking *why* as they make sense of what they are seeing. They are learning to communicate and listening to explanations of answers to their questions, whether they be about why there are certain rules or how something works. For example, let's return to the example of Jackie and the ramp. As she explored with a ramp and conjectured that a bumpy, larger ball would go slower than a smoother, smaller ball, she wanted to understand why. She tried to convince someone first using examples, restating some of what she had observed with the balls. Then, she used some reasoning about the characteristics of the balls and how they related to the ramp. The large bumpy ball went slower because it rubbed along the edge of the ramp walls more. The small smooth ball didn't have anything in its way, so it slid more easily without rubbing on the ramp. We can nurture experiences like explaining and justifying ramp conjectures with numbers and patterns in grades K–2, building on the conjecturing layer we discussed in chapter 6.

When we *justify*, we communicate our ideas and convince someone that a conjecture or idea is true using examples, representations, and reasoning. There are many ways that students may try to convince someone a conjecture is true; by exploring the conjecture further, students are creating a deeper understanding of the mathematical ideas. Even though the students' justifications aren't going to be close to mathematical proofs, students are building a conceptual understanding and taking ownership of the mathematical ideas. Students may show multiple examples, using larger and larger, more abstract numbers as they build a convincing explanation that the conjecture is true. They may use a representation for a specific example first and then use the same representation in a general way to show that the conjecture works for any number. Students may explain by connecting or extending a previously known statement, building from information on an anchor chart or public record. Their justifications may not be complex at first, and that's OK. We recognize and value justifications in the early grades as a stepping-stone to more sophisticated justifications in later years.

In this chapter, you'll learn more about what justifying is, why it's important, what it looks like, and how to nudge students to make justifications. Your students have big ideas about the world and why things work—they already convince people that their ideas are true! There are different types of justifications used by students; we'll unpack those so that you can be aware of them in your own classroom.

YOUR TURN
JUSTIFYING ADDENDS CONJECTURE

In previous chapters, we've explored the conjecture that, when adding two quantities, if you take 1 or 10 from one addend and add it to the other addend, the sum will stay the same.

- Try some examples to better understand what the conjecture is stating.

- Draw a picture to represent this conjecture.

- Are you convinced that this will always be true no matter what quantities you start with for the two addends? How can you convince someone that the conjecture is true for all numbers?

CLASSROOM VIGNETTE: NUMBER OF THE DAY AND JUSTIFYING

In chapter 6 (page 121), the students articulated two conjectures, and Josephine focused on Abby's conjecture as the lesson progressed, keeping Dalton's conjecture for another time. They explored Abby's conjecture that "when one number goes down by 10 and the other number goes up by 10, it still equals 100." Josephine asked, "How can we convince someone that when one number goes down by 10 and the other number goes up by 10 that it'll still equal 100?" Students shared several ideas, including the following.

- "If someone doesn't know it's real, you can show them the examples."
- "You can show them in other ways. You can use fingers."
- "You can show them with piles. When one pile goes up and the other pile goes down, it still equals the same."

At table groups, students had a chance to pick one of the suggestions shared in the whole group or explore a different way to convince someone that Abby's conjecture was true. Some students wrote out the equations in red from the public record to show examples. Abby wrote two equations that were next to each other on the chart: 20 + 80 = 100 and 30 + 70 = 100; she also wrote the sentence, "It still equals 100." You can see an example representation of her work in figure 7.1.

20 + 80 = 100
30 + 70 = 100
It still equals 100

Figure 7.1: Equations and justification for the conjecture.

Several groups used towers to show that the conjecture was true, creating an equation using the towers and then moving a tower from one pile to the other, as in figure 7.2. DeShawn put the towers of ten into two containers to move them back and forth.

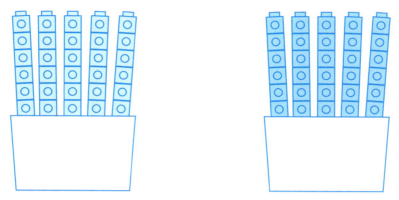

Figure 7.2: Groups of towers to represent the conjecture.

To make a record, some tried to draw each tower in detail, while others drew lines to represent the tower of ten. Jocelyn drew one tower of ten as part of her equation, which you can see in figure 7.3.

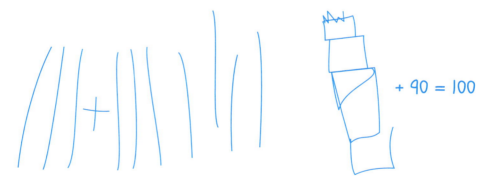

Figure 7.3: Tower representation and equations.

Using the context of the towers, another student said the conjecture was true: "Because they're all the same height, we still have the same amount." Molly drew a picture similar to what is shown in figure 7.4, with the numbers counting by tens and towers in two piles. She drew an arrow to show one tower moving to the other pile. In the classrooms we worked in, students had open access to tools and were encouraged to use them. Using tools can help students understand, represent (Jacobs & Kusiak, 2006), and explain important mathematical ideas and relationships.

Exploring the Third Layer: Justifying

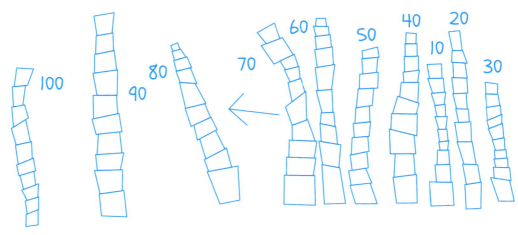

Figure 7.4: Representation with numbers, towers, and arrows.

We can see from the examples that students communicated and justified in different ways that were meaningful to them to show that Abby's conjecture was true.

Understanding Justifying

Our third layer builds on the (1) noticing and wondering and (2) conjecturing layers to justify whether the conjecture is true or false. We wrote earlier in this chapter that when we justify, we convince someone that a conjecture or idea is true using examples, representations, and reasoning. In the vignette, we saw students using previous examples to convince or justify that this conjecture was true, while other students were drawn to concrete representations and pictures. Allowing students to justify in a way that makes sense to them is important, and letting them share with peers helps them to see other ways of justifying the same conjecture. Schifter and Russell (2020) write:

> The goal of having students articulate and justify claims about how the operations behave is not merely one more piece of content for teachers to squeeze into an already full agenda. Through these discussions, students develop richer understandings of the meaning of the operations and their relationships, which in turn support greater flexibility with computational procedure. (p. 26)

Let's revisit the consecutive sums task and then dive into some of the ways students justify so we can identify them in our classrooms.

Connecting Justifying to Consecutive Sums

Looking back at the consecutive sums task in previous chapters can help you make connections between your work as an explorer and the types of experiences you want to embed for your students. Revisit the ways you would convince someone that your conjecture is always true. Is your go-to way of justifying using examples, a representation, reasoning, counterexamples, or story problems? What makes your go-to way convincing to you? What ways do you think are most convincing to students?

One of the conjectures we explore with the consecutive sums task is that "the sum of two consecutive positive whole numbers is always an odd number." Which of the three justifications in figure 7.5 is most convincing to you? Why do you find it convincing?

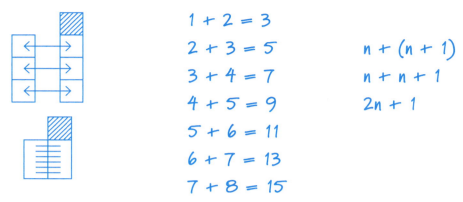

Figure 7.5: Three justifications for the odd sum conjecture.

As we continue this chapter, we'll describe some different types of justifications we have seen with K–2 students. You can continue thinking about what kind of justifications you could use and why they are convincing to you.

Learning Ways That Students Justify

There are many ways that young students justify, and they typically fall into the following categories, based on research (Carpenter et al., 2003; Kazemi & Hintz, 2014; Lannin, Ellis, & Elliott, 2011; Rumsey, 2012; Russell, Schifter, & Bastable, 2011; Russell, Schifter, Bastable, Higgins, & Kasman, 2017).

- Appeal to authority
- Examples (including numerical examples and story problems)
- Representation of a generic example
- Reasoning
- Counterexample

We'll look at each of these along with short examples so that you can imagine what it sounds like with young students.

APPEAL TO AUTHORITY

Let's start with appeal to authority (Carpenter et al., 2003). When asked why something is true, students might say that their teacher or parent told them. They may also appeal to the perceived authority of a classmate as in the kindergarten vignette described in chapter 2 (page 32). Diego had a conjecture, but his classmate, Jason, told him that it wasn't true. He appealed to Jason's authority that his conjecture was not true when he retold the conjecture to a teacher. Ideally, we want students to reason and decide for themselves if something is true and go beyond appealing to authority.

Exploring the Third Layer: Justifying

EXAMPLES

Examples are a common way that students justify a conjecture is true, and there is a range of ways that examples are used. Students may start with a single example or multiple examples as they convince themselves or others that a conjecture is true. We've seen students start out with small, familiar numbers and then try examples with larger numbers. Larger numbers might be more convincing to students because they are less concrete to them. They can easily see single-digit numbers on their fingers or with concrete items, but a number like 100 is more abstract. Related to examples, students may even come up with a story problem to justify. While all these examples are places to start and may be quite convincing to students of all ages, it's essential to nudge them to go beyond. Even if we use large numbers or many different examples, that doesn't mean that the conjecture is always true because numbers are infinite. So, we can acknowledge students' thinking and sharing in the justification with an example; as students get older, they will continue to think about different ways to convince someone that a conjecture is true.

In Patrick's kindergarten classroom, when looking at equations that had a 0 as one of the addends (see figure 7.6), students were justifying the conjecture that "when you add 0 to a number, you get that number as the answer."

1 + 0 = 1	0 + 1 = 1
2 + 0 = 2	0 + 2 = 2
3 + 0 = 3	0 + 3 = 3
4 + 0 = 4	0 + 4 = 4
5 + 0 = 5	0 + 5 = 5
6 + 0 = 6	0 + 6 = 6
7 + 0 = 7	0 + 7 = 7
8 + 0 = 8	0 + 8 = 8
9 + 0 = 9	0 + 9 = 9
10 + 0 = 10	0 + 10 = 10

Figure 7.6: Kindergarten equations with zero as an addend.

For some students, examples were convincing, and someone suggested adding to the bottom of the chart (11 + 0 = 11) to justify that the conjecture is always true. Graham used a story problem example to justify, saying, "If you have 200 blue cars and 0 red cars, then you would still have 200 blue cars." He imagined holding a bag of blue cars in one hand and an empty bag for red cars in the other. He brought his hands together to combine them. Natalie then decontextualized the numbers from the story problem to add on to the conversation with her example of 200,000 + 0 = 200,000.

Moving from small numbers in story problems to large, abstract numbers is a common progression within a classroom as students use examples to justify. As students move toward larger and larger numbers, it becomes more abstract and generalized because they can't visualize the quantities that they are using.

REPRESENTATION OF A GENERIC EXAMPLE

Visual and concrete representations are important as students build mental models of mathematics, make sense of the concepts, and justify using generic representations (Russell et al., 2017). We know that "young children are capable of justifying claims of generality. Reasoning from representations to justify their conjectures is an effective route for establishing general claims in the elementary classroom" (Schifter & Russell, 2020, p. 21). In the kindergarten example related to figure 7.7, a student was building a generic example using representations when he imagined holding two bags of cars, one with 0 and one with 200.

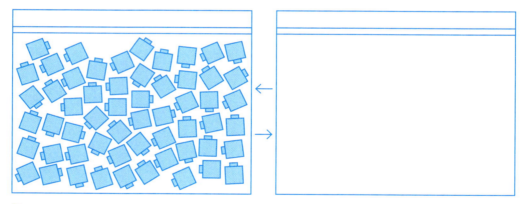

Figure 7.7: Using bags to demonstrate a generic example shared by a kindergarten student.

This is approaching a generic example because it doesn't matter if it is 200 or another amount; the motion still indicates that the total will be that number. Patrick, the kindergarten teacher, continued to push this idea further by bringing out two plastic bags, one with "some amount we don't know" and one that was empty. A generic representation, either concrete or pictorial, pushes students to think about generalizing the conjectures beyond examples and provides an entry into generalized justifications (Russell, Schifter, & Bastable, 2011). By intentionally integrating representations through the first two layers, we are helping make this kind of justification accessible for students.

In the first-grade vignette (Number of the Day) that we have been following since the beginning of the chapter (page 141), the students similarly were using a representation to show the examples, moving toward more generic examples. The tower of ten is a concrete, visual representation that's connected to the equations the first-grade students were exploring. The teacher intentionally introduced the concrete representation in the two previous layers to establish a solid understanding of the concepts, patterns, and equations. The exaggerated repetition of the examples made clear the action and movement of the patterns between the equations. The students could see the block move from one pile to the other (see figure 7.8).

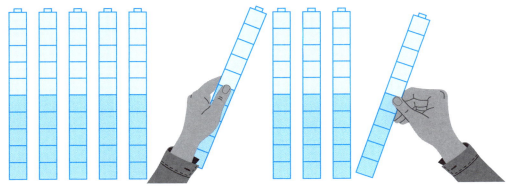

Figure 7.8: Using a specific example to move toward a generic example.

While the students were using the towers to show two decade-number addends that equal 100, the towers could also each represent 1. If each tower represented 1, then the sum would be 10. This is a more generic example where we can flexibly see the quantities and motions without focusing on the specific numbers.

In *But Why Does It Work? Mathematical Argument in the Elementary Classroom*, Russell and colleagues (2017) write that generic representations should have specific criteria. Let's see how the criteria relate to what we described in the previous paragraph.

1. The action and meaning of the operation are clearly represented.

2. The representation is not just about specific quantities but can be used to show what happens with "any number" or set of numbers that students are working with.

3. The representation shows why the conjecture must be true; the structure of the representation shows how the conclusion of the claim follows from its premise.

TEACHER VOICES
REPRESENTATIONS

"I feel like using representations is a way for students to communicate their thinking initially (using models). After providing their representation, it becomes easier to articulate their thinking, bridging the gap between finding a conclusion and talking about why their conclusion is true." (Rachael, grade 1 teacher)

"Representation plays a huge part in argumentation. It allows students to explain their ideas and their thinking in different ways. Many students may feel more comfortable explaining their ideas through various representations rather than just writing out their thoughts." (Christina, grade 2 teacher)

"Representation is a huge factor in argumentation. It sets up a visual for students to refer to and elaborate on. Talking is abstract; students benefit from having a visual to refer to, so they can center on an idea, but also be able to follow along with another student's thinking." (Rachael, grade 1 teacher)

REASONING

As students build their justifications from examples to generic representations, they may begin reasoning using only words. With the kindergarten conjecture of "When you add 0 to a number, you get that number as the answer," a student justified by saying, "It's the same number because you don't have any more or any less." He wasn't connecting with an example, story problem, or representation; he was using words and reasoning to convince someone. Similarly, a student from the first-grade vignette justified the conjecture by saying, "Because they're all the same height, we still have the same amount." In grades K–2, we can't expect proofs that mathematicians would come up with, but it is important to get them talking, thinking, and reasoning about the mathematics in their own words. We can always push for more precision by asking questions ourselves and encouraging peers to ask clarifying questions.

COUNTEREXAMPLE

Related to examples, one way to justify that a conjecture is not true is with a counterexample. This works when the conjecture is not true, and a single example can disprove it. Given the false conjecture of an even number plus an odd number equals an even sum, a simple counterexample like 4 + 3 = 7 is enough to show that the conjecture does not hold true.

Exploring the Third Layer: Justifying

ADDING AND SUBTRACTING THE SAME AMOUNT

Another conjecture that came out of the Number of the Day routine is that if you start with 100 and add an amount, then subtract that same amount, you end up with 100 again.

How can you convince someone that the conjecture is always true using the following?

- Examples

- Pictures or representation of a generic example

- Reasoning

nurturing math curiosity

MORE EXAMPLES OF K-2 JUSTIFICATIONS

Let's look at conjectures we've already explored in this book and the different ways students might justify. We organized them in figure 7.9.

Conjectures	Types of Justification			
	Examples (small and big)	Story problem	Representation of a generic example	Reasoning
Whenever you add two odd numbers, you will get an even number.	3 + 5 = 8 3 + 3 = 6 43 + 5 = 48 43 + 3 = 46	If 3 people and 5 people make a large group, it will be an even number. Everyone will have a partner. Eight is an even number.		If you have two odd numbers, they would each have one without a partner. When you put them both together, the two leftovers become partners.
If you add 0 to a number, it doesn't change the amount.	5 + 0 = 5 3 + 0 = 3 100 + 0 = 100 999 + 0 = 999	If I have 5 pencils and add 0 more, I still have 5 pencils in my box.		When you add 0 to a number, you are not changing it, so the sum stays the same.
You can change the order of the addends and the sum will be the same (commutative property of addition).	2 + 3 = 5 3 + 2 = 5 97 + 3 = 100 3 + 97 = 100	If I have 2 pencils in one hand and 3 in the other, that is the same amount as if I switched hands.		If you switch it, it's still the same amount, just in a different order.

Figure 7.9: Types of justifications for conjectures we have explored.

Using Tasks for Justifying

We used the example of the Number of the Day routine for the vignette, but there are other types of tasks that promote justifying. When students justify, they are making sense of the idea at a different level than believing it themselves; they are explaining and convincing someone else that the conjecture is true. Students develop a deeper understanding of the mathematical content when they consider why something is true, and they make connections to other big mathematical ideas. When students come up with generalizations, we can seek opportunities for them to go beyond the conjecture and justify why it is true. We need to be intentional about the questions and prompts that we use to encourage students to justify. We may sometimes use other similar words, like *explain*, but we must be thoughtful about what we really expect students to discuss when we ask the prompts. For example, we may ask students to explain, but they don't necessarily need to justify in order to explain how they thought about their solution or conjecture. A prompt like, "*Justify* why the conjecture is true," requires that a student convince another person.

When students make conjectures, we can add prompts like, "Justify why that is true" or "Why is that true?" We can also provide a conjecture to the class discussion, being intentional about how we state the prompt, and ask students to justify the given conjecture. For example, in chapter 4 (page 77), we shared the vignette where Rachael provided a conjecture from the previous day for students to investigate. We discussed that prompt as a group and ended up with, "Will this happen no matter what number you start with? Show your thinking." While the original intent was for students to justify, when we (the authors and the teacher) debriefed about the lesson afterward, we realized that it wasn't explicit enough for the students. We need to be specific about what we ask students to do. If we want them to justify or convince someone, then we need to prompt for that. Instead, we could have used one of the following justification prompts.

- Do you agree with this conjecture? Why do you agree or disagree?
- Use pictures or words to convince someone that this is always true.
- Justify why this conjecture is true.
- Why is this true? How do we know it is true?
- Explore this conjecture. Convince someone that this is true.

Notice the difference between the justification prompts and the following prompts, which do not necessarily get at justification.

- What did you do to find your answer? Explain your steps.
- Explain your thinking.

As we imagine integrating the justifying layer into tasks, the following characteristics might be helpful to keep in mind.

- There are connections to the relevant mathematical concepts and previous conjectures.
- There are conjectures that students can explore.

- Students can explore why the conjecture is true using pictures or words.
- If there are examples, there are opportunities to extend the examples to general cases.
- If there are representations, they show the structure of mathematical ideas and can help students see why it works. For example, see the first example in figure 7.5 (page 144).

Let's look at a grade 1 Illustrative Mathematics (n.d.b) task from its curriculum and see if it fits with characteristics of tasks that lend themselves to justifying (and the previous two layers). In this subtraction card game, students have a double ten-frame and two sets of cards: number cards 0–10 and number cards 11–20. Students pick one card from each pile and subtract the smaller number from the teen number. For example, if a student picks 17 and 3, they would represent 17 on the double ten-frame and act out subtracting 3 (see figure 7.10).

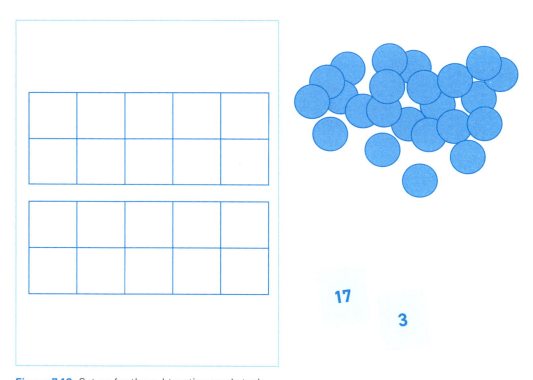

Figure 7.10: Set up for the subtraction cards task.

While students engage in the task, teachers can monitor how they subtract. For example, some students will take away part of the quantity to get to ten and then take away the remaining part of the quantity and count what is left. Other students may take the smaller number directly from the full ten-frame and add the remaining amounts (Illustrative Mathematics, n.d.b). For the end of the lesson, it suggests the teachers ask students to "pick your favorite round. Show how you found the value of the difference using drawings, words, or numbers."

Exploring the Third Layer: Justifying

SUBTRACTION CARD TASK

- Where do you see the characteristics of tasks that support justification in the subtraction card task?

- Based on our suggestions of what teachers can monitor for, what are the goals of the lesson?

- How might the representation support the students' developing idea of the structure of subtraction?

- What might students notice and wonder?

- What might students conjecture? How might the conjectures relate to the goals of the lesson?

- How might students begin to justify their conjectures, or convince someone that their generalizations are true?

Exploring the Third Layer: Justifying

PAUSE AND PONDER
JUSTIFICATION

- What tasks in your instructional materials encourage justification?

- What tasks or learning activities have you used in the past that lend themselves to justification?

Continuing With the Number of the Day Routine

Let's think about how we can continue building the Number of the Day routine through this layer of argumentation. Your students have had a chance to (1) notice and wonder and (2) conjecture. Now, you can begin to nudge them toward justifying and convincing others that their idea is true. They may already begin to add justifications, or they may need some prompting (see appendix A, page 211). The following are questions to nudge at justifying.

- Why do you believe that to be true?
- Can you draw a picture to show why that works?
- Can you use tools to show why that works?
- How can you convince someone the conjecture is always true? Never true?
- Why is that true? Why is it not true?

By connecting back to the representations used in the justification layer, we position students to use models to represent the generalization's structure, which can support their language. In the first year of the project, second-grade teacher Christina wrote that "representations are super important, and their use allows students to make huge conceptual understandings and bridges. I also think that it helps students understand how to explain their ideas to others in a different way besides using words." Representations create a bridge between the concrete image and the abstract words to describe the situation. As you look back at your Number of the Day work in the previous two layers, were there some representations that might be especially helpful to refer to as you ask students to justify?

As students justify and convince others that their conjecture is true, listen for other ways to justify that we mentioned earlier in the chapter in figure 7.9 (page 150). It can be helpful to intentionally connect different representations throughout the layers, especially as students are doing the justifying.

TEACHER VOICES
TEACHER REFLECTION

"Students need the opportunity to develop language through class discussions, examples given orally by other students, or from themselves. There is a hierarchy of explaining and justifying thinking, starting with listening, then moving to oral communication, and ending with written communication." (Rachael, grade 1 teacher)

"Conjectures and generalizations can be abstract, so it's helpful to have that concrete representation to root [students'] understanding. Also, making their thinking visible by charting—need to chart more and have clear, specific visuals that stay up and that we refer to." (Bethany, grade K teacher)

"When a student constructs an argument about a mathematical concept, they are justifying their thinking; they are proving something that they believe to be true. There *is nothing more exciting for a teacher than having a student think about something they are 100 percent sure about, then having another student think the exact opposite; instead of fighting, the students can articulate their thinking either through words or pictures. When they can take turns speaking and come to a solution together, that shows true collaboration, and isn't that the goal? These students are on their way to being solid communicators!" (Rachael, grade 1 teacher)*

Questions for Further Reflection

The following questions will help you synthesize your learning by reflecting on chapter 7.

- Sometimes it's easier for teachers to explain why something is true instead of asking students to justify. Is there an upcoming lesson where you could shift some of the justifying to the students?

- When you ask students to write, explain, show, convince or justify, pause, and think about, (1) what are you hoping to learn from them and (2) how might they respond? Are those two parts aligned? How can you adjust the question using the preceding ideas to revise your question?

- How do you imagine justification will strengthen student language?

- As students justify, what are ways you might support their use of language?

- How might representations support students to explain and understand one another's thinking?

- What tasks do you use that encourage students to justify?

Chapter 7 Summary

Justification is an important life skill and one that can be developed by young students through argumentation. As we saw within this chapter, students can justify their thinking using examples, counterexamples, representations, and reasoning. As teachers, we can select tasks and routines that incite justification and use thoughtful prompts, questions, and supports as students develop communication skills. The "Chapter 7 Application Guide" (page 158) can help you connect the ideas in chapter 7 to your classroom. In chapter 8, we will explore the extending layer.

Chapter 7 Application Guide

Use the following application guide to connect these ideas to your classroom.

Chapter 7 Topics	Connect to Your Classroom
Justifying	• Model justifying for your students by sharing your ideas out loud, asking for their input.
Ways of Justifying	• Look at the ways of justifying described in this chapter and consider which you might hear and see in your classroom.
Questions	• Incorporate one of the suggested questions into an upcoming lesson. Write it here:

Language Supports	• Create a language frame and post it in your classroom:
	  + It is true because _____
	  + I agree because _____
	  + I disagree because _____

Characteristics of Tasks	• Look at tasks in the upcoming lessons to see if they meet some of the characteristics listed for justifying.
Number of the Day Routine	• Continue with the Number of the Day routine that you started in chapter 5 (page 110), focusing on the justifying ideas from this chapter.

Nurturing Math Curiosity © 2024 Solution Tree Press • SolutionTree.com
Visit **go.SolutionTree.com/mathematics** to download this free reproducible.

CHAPTER 8

Exploring the Fourth Layer: Extending

As young students make sense of the world, they connect ideas and extend their thinking to similar contexts. For example, going back to Jackie exploring the ramp, she explained why some balls go faster than others, making a connection to sledding on a hill a few months later. The hill was faster when it had snow covering it, but as she slid more, the leaves underneath began to show through. Now, the sled was not as fast. It's not just the steepness or the object that goes down the ramp that affects the speed; it's also the ramp or hill itself. She modified her conjecture to acknowledge that the characteristics of the ramp or the hill affect the speed, too, and she extended her idea to another situation. There are so many things to consider, and there are so many ways to make a ramp or hill faster and slower.

We also can nurture connections and opportunities to modify and extend ideas with numbers and patterns in grades K–2, building on the previous layers. Not only can we modify conjectures and justifications, but we can also extend ideas and notice and wonder again, beginning the layers again in a cyclical, creative way. This is how we learn and build knowledge—by making connections, clarifying what we mean, extending on ideas, and continuing to notice and wonder. In this chapter, we unpack extending and follow our Number of the Day vignette into the final layer. Then, we look at tasks that lend themselves to extending.

YOUR TURN
PREVIOUS CONJECTURES

In chapter 7, we looked at a subtraction card task (see figure 7.10, page 152), and we talked about what students might (1) notice and wonder and (2) conjecture, and how they could (3) justify their ideas. Let's revisit that task; think about how we could extend ideas as we cycle back to noticing and wondering with new learning and perspective from the three layers. What if students notice that when you subtract, there are times when you take from both ten-frames and times when you only take from one? This gets at the idea of when to decompose and can lead to a conjecture about when to use a procedure.

- Where is your mind wanting to continue with this idea? What are you curious about?

- What other topics might connect with this idea, in both addition and subtraction?

- How might this idea naturally extend to other types or sizes of numbers or other operations?

Exploring the Fourth Layer: Extending

> **CLASSROOM VIGNETTE:** NUMBER OF THE DAY AND EXTENDING

As we explore extending together, let's look at the classroom vignette and see how the Number of the Day routine is progressing. In chapter 7 (page 141), the first graders justified Abby's conjecture that when one number goes down by 10, and the other number goes up by 10, it'll always equal 100. They used examples, reasoning, representations, and drawings. Now that students had a clearer understanding of the conjecture and were convinced that it was true, they began to extend the conjecture and explore related ideas.

There were two specific details in the conjecture: how the numbers increase (by 10) and what the constant sum is (100). Josephine nudged the students to think about what else might be true.

Josephine: Does it only work if we go up and down by 10?

Student: No, it also works if we go up and down by 1 [pointing to the set of equations that starts with 100 + 0 = 100; figure 5.1, page 100].

To prompt the students, Josephine asked if you could go up by 10 and down by 1. Most students said no, but some were unsure. DeShawn said, "They have to step by the same thing." As he said this, he motioned with his hands so that one made steps up and one made steps down in the air. Then, he exaggerated the motions so that one was big and one was little to say, "It can't go like this."

Josephine: OK, so it needs to go up and down by the same amount, either 1 or 10?

DeShawn: Anything as long as it's the same.

Josephine: And if we have a sum of 100, it'll stay 100. What if we had a different sum?

DeShawn: It could be a different number instead of 100.

Josephine: Like what kind of number?

DeShawn: Any number.

Josephine: What if we have two numbers added together and have a sum of 10? Imagine one addend goes up by 1 and the other addend goes down by 1. Would the sum still be 10? Let's explore this conjecture with cubes. [See figure 8.1.]

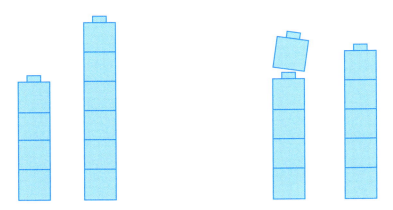

Figure 8.1: Representation of the conjecture with cubes.

Students worked in groups of two or three to explore this extended idea to Abby's conjecture. Students made two piles of cubes and repeatedly moved one cube from one pile to the other, as in figure 8.1, noticing that the sum was still 10 cubes. One group noticed that you could move two cubes at a time from one pile to the other and it would still be a sum of 10. Gathering the groups back together, Josephine asked, "Are there other things you think might be true now that we've explored this conjecture?" Based on the experience with the cubes, some students began to move toward a more generalized conjecture: When one number goes down *by an amount* and the other number goes up *by the same amount*, the total stays the same. This is a more general version of Abby's original conjecture, and the representations helped students to see a general situation from specific examples. To push for precision and make the conjecture less wordy, Josephine reminded the students that the numbers they were adding together were addends and the total was the sum. This led to the following, more precise, conjecture that built from the original: "When one addend goes down by an amount, and the other addend goes up by the same amount, the sum stays the same" (see figure 8.2).

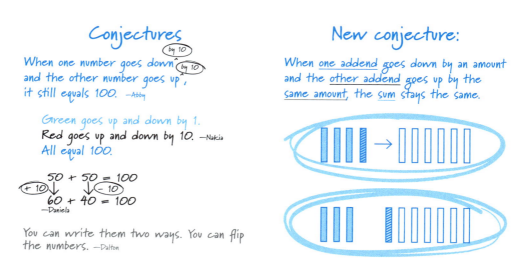

Figure 8.2: Extending a conjecture and adding precise language.

Visit *go.SolutionTree.com/mathematics* for a free, full-color version of this figure.

Understanding Extending

Extending is the fourth and final layer, but it's not the end of the exploration. Just as we lose some of the power when we stop noticing and wondering too soon, there is much power that occurs in argumentation when we extend our ideas. Remember in chapter 1 (page 15) that Su (2020) writes that we can "think of exploration as a continuous cycle, passing from one phase to the other and back again" (p. 57). That's what this layer invites us to do as we modify and extend to make strong connections and understand in a deep way. A second grader helped us think of it this way when she drew what she called a conjecture circle for the conjecture wall. She labeled it "Plan, Make, Test, Repeat" (see figure 8.3). We aren't ever done because we can keep extending and connecting as we add new knowledge; that's where the *repeat* comes in.

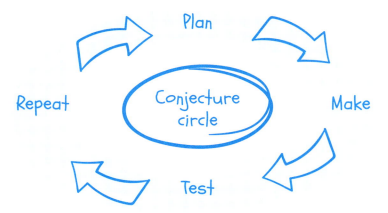

Figure 8.3: Conjecture circle.

The perspective that we can modify our ideas is valuable to nurture a classroom community where we learn from our mistakes and keep trying when things are challenging. Thoughts don't have to be fully formed to be shared and valued. We can revisit conjectures to make them more precise and we can modify and adjust as we explore. In the first-grade vignette, we saw students exploring the details of the conjecture, adjusting how the numbers increase (by 10) and what the constant sum is (100) using the representations. Together as a class, they were playfully extending to see what else might be true and modifying their conjectures to make them more precise after learning more through the justification process.

We've witnessed modifying and extending repeatedly in lessons where a spirit of exploration is fostered. Remember, in Diego's kindergarten conjecture (page 32) that he was curious about Jason's conjecture and extended it to include larger numbers. In another first-grade lesson where we explored subtraction decomposition (Rumsey, Guarino, & Sperling, 2023), students conjectured about when to use the decomposing strategy, focused on the efficiency of the procedure. While the initial conjecture was a good place to start, it was not precise and needed to be modified for clarity. We realized that introducing precise language like *subtrahend* (a number subtracted from a minuend) made the conjectures less wordy and more understood by students. Since *big* and *bigger* are subjective words, adding more detail made that part of the conjecture clearer. Modifying the conjecture was an important part of the exploration and aided students to develop a deeper understanding of the procedure. Notice the following modifications to the conjectures made by a first-grade class as they shifted to more precise language.

1. "If the second number is big, decompose. If the second number is small, you don't need to decompose."

2. "If the *subtrahend* is big, decompose. If the *subtrahend* is small, you don't need to decompose."

3. "If the subtrahend is *bigger than the ones place of the minuend*, decomposing is helpful. If the subtrahend is *smaller than the ones place of the minuend*, decomposing is unnecessary."

PAUSE AND PONDER
CONJECTURES

Notice how the language in the list of three conjectures on page 165 becomes more precise. What changes were made between conjecture 1 and conjecture 3?

How are the changes more precise?

How might they support students' understanding of the ideas and their ability to communicate clearly?

Students may also modify as they attempt to make a false conjecture true after exploring and realizing that it is not true as stated. Valuable learning happens as students decide how they can modify a false conjecture to make it true. For example, if a student has an initial (false) conjecture that "when you add two odd numbers, you get an odd sum," a classmate might provide a counterexample like 3 + 1 = 4 to help them see that the conjecture isn't true. As they modify the conjecture, students can decide what they would need to change to make it true. Do they want to modify one of the addends or the sum? A modified conjecture could be the following.

- "When you add two odd numbers, you get an even sum."
- "When you add an odd number and an even number, you get an odd sum."

We extend ideas when we make connections and apply our learning to new cases or types of numbers. We want to nurture classroom communities where everyone's contributions are valuable, and we can learn and make connections between ideas. When exploring the conjecture that "when you add 0 to a number, you get that number as the answer" (page 145), students in Patrick's kindergarten classroom were eager to find more ideas that would also be true. Patrick nudged the extended exploration by asking, "If that's true, what else might be true?"

Adeline: Zero can be the first number or the second number of the equation.

Poppy: There is the same amount altogether even if you flip them.

Patrick: Is there another idea to add to this new idea?

Graham: Because you turn the numbers, but it will still be the number because we didn't add anything. If I had 0 red cars and I had ten million thousand and eight hundred fifty-three blue cars and we do this, there would still be the same amount.

The student used a switching motion with his hands so that his arms were holding two amounts and then they crossed. Patrick repeated the motion so that everyone could see.

Patrick: So, you're making this motion [while holding two bags of square tiles to represent the cars] like this, or I could have them like this [switches the bags across to show the exaggerated movement from one side to the other]. And it's still the same amount? So, you think this is going to work if one of the numbers is 0, that we can add 0 here or here and it's still going to be the same?

Graham: It doesn't have to be 0.

Michael: Yes, it does have to have 0 to flip-flop.

Some students extended their equations to the commutative property of addition saying that zero could be in either addend position. This idea got students to think about the commutative property more broadly, although not everyone thought it worked for all numbers. For example, Michael thought that you could flip the addends only if one of them was 0. With this kindergarten lesson, students continued to extend their ideas, with one student wondering, "What if the answer is 0? Consider: 0 plus 0 equals 0."

Another student, Wendell, focused on a different detail of the equations, wondering, "Instead of 0 + 5, it could be 1 + 5; then it's not going to be the same answer."

Patrick: We could make up another conjecture.

Wendell: Then, it would be 1 more instead of the same.

Patrick: If we add 1 to any number, it's not going to be the same. We could add that to the conjecture chart.

Natalie: If you add 200,000 to a number, it's going to be way bigger than that number.

Patrick: Is that always going to be true?

Natalie: Yes, because . . . [uses a large example to show that it's bigger] if we add 200,000 and we add 8, it will be 200,008; that's bigger.

The students were eager to share new noticings and wonderings, building from the original conjecture and justifying these new ideas. The extending layer is the part of argumentation where exploration continues and new mathematical knowledge is built from existing knowledge.

Connecting Extending to Consecutive Sums

One aspect that we like about the consecutive sums task is that it can go in so many different directions, and there are many connections to be made between mathematics content areas. Revisit figure 1.4 (page 25) to see what other ideas drew you in and what connections you made. We learn when we make connections and extend our thinking. For example, what have you learned as we continue to revisit this task and where would you want to go next? Were there some parts of the sample work that didn't seem related when you saw them at first but now they do? We want to create rich experiences with K–2 students so that they can continue to think about a task and make connections between previous and new information.

TEACHER VOICES
EXTENDING IDEAS

"Argumentation both spirals and builds. It is an ongoing process as students continue to come back and add on to previous conversations and discussions." (Josephine, grade 1 teacher)

Using Tasks for Extending

Playful curiosity fosters an environment where ideas can be extended and explored beyond the initial task by both students and teachers learning together. Teachers can model curiosity and extending by saying the following.

- "I wonder what would happen if . . ." (For example, we used a different number.)
- "I wonder what would change about our idea if . . ." (For example, we used even numbers instead of odd.)

One goal is to help students restart the cycle and get back to noticing and wondering. Here are some characteristics of tasks for extending that may be helpful to keep in mind.

- The task invites students to be curious and connect different ideas.
- There are connections to relevant mathematical concepts and previous conjectures.
- There are opportunities to extend the conjectures with other content (types or sizes of numbers or other operations).
- If there are representations, they show the structure of mathematical ideas and have the potential to help students see why it works.

Let's look at a task to see where it connects to these characteristics. In chapter 5 (page 109), we looked at an addition table that you may have seen in your curriculum materials (figure 8.4). We wondered if students might notice the pairs that make 10 and then extend to notice other sums in the table and the pairs of addends that make those. For example, they may notice where 9 shows up as a sum and count how many times it is there. They may also notice that there are more sums of 10 in the table than sums of 9 and wonder if the amount of sums increases as the table continues.

+	0	1	2	3	4	5	6	7	8	9	10
0	0	1	2	3	4	5	6	7	8	9	10
1	1	2	3	4	5	6	7	8	9	10	11
2	2	3	4	5	6	7	8	9	10	11	12
3	3	4	5	6	7	8	9	10	11	12	13
4	4	5	6	7	8	9	10	11	12	13	14
5	5	6	7	8	9	10	11	12	13	14	15
6	6	7	8	9	10	11	12	13	14	15	16
7	7	8	9	10	11	12	13	14	15	16	17
8	8	9	10	11	12	13	14	15	16	17	18
9	9	10	11	12	13	14	15	16	17	18	19
10	10	11	12	13	14	15	16	17	18	19	20

Figure 8.4: Making tens in the addition table.

How do you think students might extend their thinking to other sums or other observations? The following questions can help prompt extending on this task.

- "Can someone restate _____'s conjecture?"
- "Does anyone have a similar idea or something you'd like to add?"
- "Does anyone have a different idea?"
- "Are there words in the conjecture that anyone has a question about?"
- "How can we rewrite our conjectures to make them more precise?"
- "Are there other things you think might be true now that we've explored this conjecture?"
- "What else might be true?"

YOUR TURN
ADDITION TABLE

Figure 8.5 (page 172) is an addition table, this time with expressions in the place where the sums were. This is a first-grade notice and wonder warm-up from the Illustrative Mathematics (n.d.c) curriculum. Students notice and wonder about the addition table and there are opportunities to dive deeper through the four layers of argumentation.

- What deep mathematical content does this table connect with and how does it fit into each layer of argumentation?

- How is this table similar to and different from the table in figure 8.4 (page 169)?

Exploring the Fourth Layer: Extending

- What are the advantages to each table?

Let's think about all four layers with this task, especially considering how to extend the learning with the extending layer.

- What do you notice and wonder?

- What conjecture might be true based on your observations?

- How could you justify that the conjecture is true?

- Are there other things you think might be true now that we've explored this conjecture? What else might be true?

	0	1	2	3	4	5	6	7	8	9	10
0	0 + 0	0 + 1	0 + 2	0 + 3	0 + 4	0 + 5	0 + 6	0 + 7	0 + 8	0 + 9	0 + 10
1	1 + 0	1 + 1	1 + 2	1 + 3	1 + 4	1 + 5	1 + 6	1 + 7	1 + 8	1 + 9	
2	2 + 0	2 + 1	2 + 2	2 + 3	2 + 4	2 + 5	2 + 6	2 + 7	2 + 8		
3	3 + 0	3 + 1	3 + 2	3 + 3	3 + 4	3 + 5	3 + 6	3 + 7			
4	4 + 0	4 + 1	4 + 2	4 + 3	4 + 4	4 + 5	4 + 6				
5	5 + 0	5 + 1	5 + 2	5 + 3	5 + 4	5 + 5					
6	6 + 0	6 + 1	6 + 2	6 + 3	6 + 4						
7	7 + 0	7 + 1	7 + 2	7 + 3							
8	8 + 0	8 + 1	8 + 2								
9	9 + 0	9 + 1									
10	10 + 0										

Source: Illustrative Mathematics, n.d.c. This work is licensed under a Creative Commons Attribution 4.0 International License (https://creativecommons.org/licenses/by/4.0).

Figure 8.5: First-grade notice and wonder warm-up.

Questions for Further Reflection

The following questions will help you synthesize your learning by reflecting on chapter 8.

- What upcoming mathematics content could be extended and explored?
- What are you curious about and what might your students be curious about?
- What big ideas at your grade level might you encourage students to further explore?
- Think about your grade-level content; what ideas can you revisit as students build additional knowledge?
- What spaces (like a conjecture wall) can you create for students to later revisit and extend ideas?

Chapter 8 Summary

Considering how conjectures can be extended by thinking about different operations and different numbers is an important part of the mathematical work that students are doing. This is an opportunity to encourage students to curiously explore and extend their thinking, revisiting the noticing and wondering layer that we started with. In this way, the learning is never finished; we can always continue to extend our ideas and learn more. The "Chapter 8 Application Guide" (page 174) can help you connect the ideas in chapter 8 to your classroom. In chapter 9, we'll find opportunities for argumentation.

Chapter 8 Application Guide

Use the following application guide to connect these ideas to your classroom.

Chapter 8 Topics	Connect to Your Classroom
Extending	• Model modifying and extending for your students by sharing ideas and further wonderings with the class.
Questions	• Incorporate one of the suggested questions into an upcoming lesson. Write it here:

Language Supports	• Create a language frame and post it in your classroom:
	  + Another idea I have is _____
	  + I think it's also true that _____

Characteristics of Tasks	• Look at tasks in the upcoming lessons to see if they meet some of the characteristics listed for extending.
Number of the Day Routine	• Continue with the Number of the Day routine that you started in chapter 5 (page 110), focusing on the extending ideas from this chapter.

Nurturing Math Curiosity © 2024 Solution Tree Press • SolutionTree.com
Visit **go.SolutionTree.com/mathematics** to download this free reproducible.

PART 3:
Growing More Mathematical Ideas

CHAPTER 9

Finding Opportunities for Argumentation

We discussed preparing our classroom environment, learning teacher tools, and re-envisioning instructional routines in part 1 (page 7). We explored the four layers of argumentation and how instructional routines can be used to leverage the ideas in part 2 (page 95). In part 3, we will explore how viewing lessons from an argumentation lens opens up lots of opportunities! In this chapter, we examine some instructional resources, consider the elements that make resources argumentation ready, and explore teacher moves and strategies to enhance the learning experiences we design for our students.

Discovering Opportunities

Now that you have a vision of argumentation with young students, you'll be surprised at the connections and opportunities within your own mathematics tasks, games, and instructional materials. Let's start by looking at an activity from the Illustrative Mathematics (n.d.d) curriculum: the 9 Plus Game, as depicted in figure 9.1 (page 178). It's a simple game that might not suggest mathematical argumentation at first glance. For this activity, each pair of students has a set of number cards 0 to 10, a double ten-frame with nine counters displayed on a ten-frame, and extra counters. Students draw a number card, add that many counters to the nine counters on the double ten-frame, find the sum, and record an equation. Students play five rounds of the game and then are directed to "talk with your partner about the patterns you notice as you play the game" (Illustrative Mathematics, n.d.d).

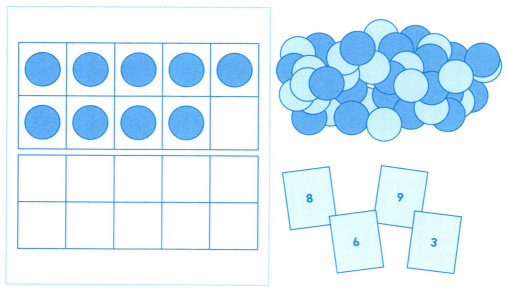

Figure 9.1: Game materials.

Let's take a look at the purpose of the activity as described within the teacher's guide of the curriculum (Illustrative Mathematics, n.d.d; see figure 9.2:

> The purpose of this activity is for students to find sums when one addend is nine. Students represent sums on the 10-frame to encourage them to use the structure of a ten. During the launch, the teacher demonstrates playing a round of the game. It is important to let students discover patterns as they play the game. For example, when finding the sum of 9 + 5, some students may represent each addend on a separate 10-frame and count to find the sum. Other students may use the associate property and move one counter from the five, and add it to the nine to make a ten.
>
> Students may generalize that when they take one from an addend to make 10, the sum has one less than that addend. When students build this understanding, they may no longer need to show their thinking on the 10-frame and can just write an equation. By repeatedly making the ten by taking one from an addend, students may see and use the structure of ten to add on.

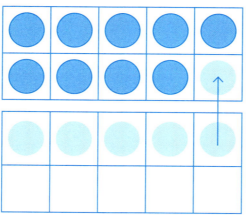

Source: Illustrative Mathematics, n.d.d. This work is licensed under a Creative Commons Attribution 4.0 International License (https://creativecommons.org/licenses/by/4.0).

Figure 9.2: 9 Plus Game purpose.

Finding Opportunities for Argumentation

PAUSE AND PONDER

OPPORTUNITY FOR ARGUMENTATION?

What are your thoughts about the 9 Plus Game?

Is there an opportunity for argumentation within this game? Why or why not?

Let's review some of the opportunities we see for argumentation within the game. First is the use of representation to support sense-making. Within each round of the game, students use a double ten-frame with nine displayed and add counters to match the number card. The visual and physical representations allow students to see one of the counters being added to the nine to complete a ten-frame and then additional counters being added to the second ten-frame to create a teen number. For example, when adding 9 + 3 with the representation, students may show 9 + 1 + 2 by adding 1 to the top ten-frame and then adding 2 more below. Mathematically, they are using properties to break 3 into 1 + 2, add 9 + 1 to get 10, and then 10 + 2 to get 12.

The second opportunity is the recording of corresponding equations. Teachers ask students to record an equation for each round, ending with five equations after the game. Figure 9.3 (page 180) includes equations from one student pair. Because the game calls for five rounds of play, students have multiple equations to analyze and see patterns and structure.

$$9 + 3 = 12 \qquad 9 + 8 = 17 \qquad 9 + 9 = 18$$
$$9 + 5 = 14 \qquad 9 + 2 = 11$$

Figure 9.3: Student equations.

Finally, teachers encourage students to talk with a partner about the patterns they notice when adding with 9 through the final prompt, "Talk with your partner about the patterns you notice as you play the game." This prompt launches the first layer of argumentation: noticing and wondering.

Teachers can expand the game to provide even more opportunities. For example, after students discuss their ideas, the teacher could invite students to share an equation with the whole class. As students share ideas, teachers can add notes to a public record in a way that supports students to see structure. Here's what that could look like (see figure 9.4).

$$9 + 0 = 9 \qquad 9 + 5 = 14 \qquad 9 + 8 = 17$$
$$9 + 1 = 10 \qquad 9 + 6 = 15$$

Figure 9.4: Classroom public record from the 9 Plus Game.

The teacher could follow up by asking, "What do you notice?" They could then add student contributions to the chart and nudge toward conjectures, supporting the sequential phases of argumentation. Students might notice that the second addends and the sums increase as you go down the equations. Some students might want to fill in the blanks with equations that fit between the equations listed. For example, a student might want to add $9 + 7 = 16$ after $9 + 6 = 15$. There are many things for students to notice and wonder about!

Let's step back and think about what makes a task argumentation ready.

- Opportunities for sense-making and reasoning
- Being open ended
- Connecting representations
- Understanding why or how something works
- Connections to big ideas, places to see patterns and make generalizations

Finding Opportunities for Argumentation

IDENTIFYING ARGUMENTATION-READY TASKS

Now that we've explored an activity together, it's your turn. Look at the task in figure 9.5 (page 182). Would you consider the task to be argumentation ready? Why or why not? If the task isn't argumentation ready, how might you modify it to make it argumentation ready?

_____
_____
_____
_____
_____
_____
_____
_____
_____
_____
_____
_____
_____
_____
_____
_____
_____
_____
_____
_____
_____
_____
_____

Card sorts might not look like argumentation-ready tasks at first glance, but we have found many to be rich opportunities. We noticed opportunities for argumentation within this activity as students made sense of odd and even numbers. After student pairs sort cards and talk to a partner, we imagine the teacher inviting students to share card pairs along with their reasoning—why they sorted the cards in a particular way or how they know it's odd or even—and recording their ideas on a public record. Then, the teacher might pose a question like, "What do you notice about odd numbers?" or "What do you believe to be true about odd numbers?" Students may conjecture about the composition of odd and even numbers or operating with them. We're curious about the ideas that might emerge!

1. Sort your cards into a group that shows an even number and a group that shows an odd number. Explain your thinking to your partner.

2. Find three cards that show the same number. Explain to your partner how each card shows whether the number is even or odd in a different way.

Even and Odd Card Sort

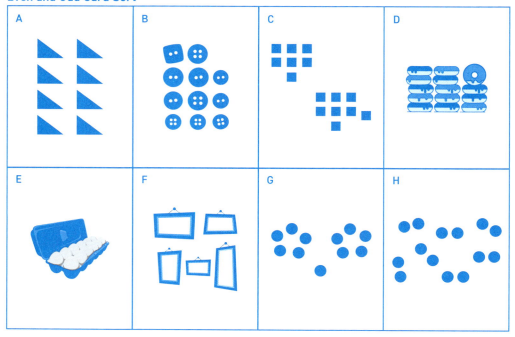

Even and Odd Card Sort

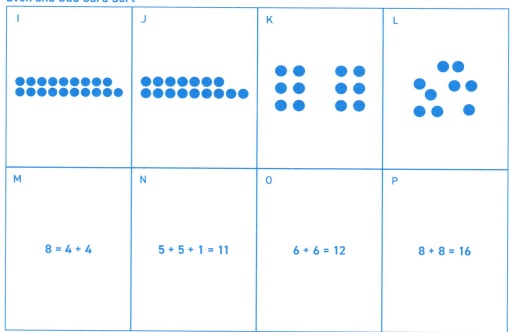

Source: Illustrative Mathematics, n.d.e. This work is licensed under a Creative Commons Attribution 4.0 International License (https://creativecommons.org/licenses/by/4.0).

Figure 9.5: Card sort—even or odd.

Finding Opportunities for Argumentation

CLASSROOM VIGNETTE: UNDERSTANDING TWO-DIGIT NUMBERS

Now, let's drop into Michelle's first-grade classroom to see how one lesson from grade-level instructional materials unfolded as we attend to what argumentation opportunities are present in the activity. We hope that you can see more opportunities in tasks than you might have when you started this book. Like figure 9.5, this lesson also includes a card sort and is part of the Illustrative Mathematics (n.d.f) curriculum.

Michelle's first-grade students were working on understanding place value, specifically that two-digit numbers are made up of tens and ones. She began by showing students an image of base ten cubes, an expression, and a written quantity of tens and ones (see figure 9.6. She then asked students which two representations showed the same two-digit number. Students had a partner discussion and decided that 40 + 1 and the image of 4 ten sticks and a 1 unit had the same value, 41.

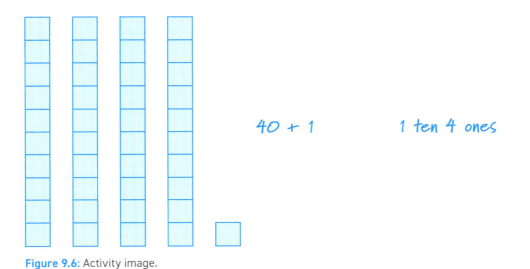

Figure 9.6: Activity image.

Next, Michelle introduced a card sort activity and students worked in pairs to explore the cards. Each card had a written numeral, an expression, a quantity of tens and ones (for example, 2 tens, 3 ones), or an image of ten sticks and ones units, similar to the image they had just discussed. As students worked, Michelle walked around the room, posing questions and listening in as students sorted cards and explained their ideas. She had them come to the carpet where pairs were invited to share how they sorted. As student pairs shared, Michelle placed the cards into a pocket chart (see figure 9.7, page 184). Once she placed all the cards in the chart, she invited students to notice and wonder, launching the first phase of argumentation. The lesson's design, and inclusion of specific numbers and representations, led to noticing and wondering regarding some core ideas.

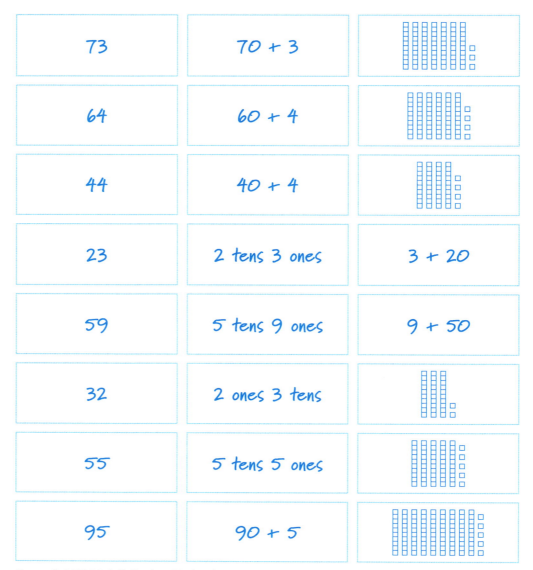

Source: © 2023 Michelle Sperling. Used with permission.
Figure 9.7: Cards placed into a pocket chart for a card sort activity.

Within the discussion, students were drawn to the numbers 23 and 32 and how the words were written in the second column of the cards. Bella noticed 23 is 2 tens and 3 ones and 32 is 2 ones and 3 tens. She shared, "It looks like 23 if you don't read the words." Other students noticed, "They match in a row." David wondered, "Why are the ones and tens switched in the word representations? It can confuse us."

The next day, following her students' lead, Michelle posted the cards for 23 and 32, which the students had focused on the prior day. Luca shared that with the numerals 32 and 23, organization does matter. Then, he referred to the representation with words—2 ones, 3 tens and 2 tens, 3 ones—that organization doesn't matter. Itzayana added that the words were in different orders. Iker asked, "In 23, why is the 2 first and then 3 last?" Following these observations, students came up with a conjecture: "In a two-digit number, the order matters because if you change the order, it will make a different number" (see figure 9.8).

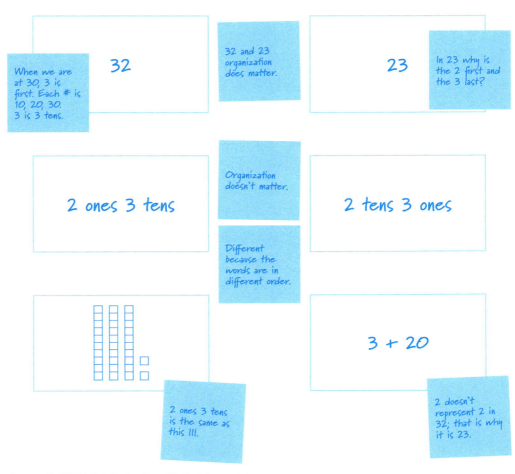

Source: © 2023 Michelle Sperling. Used with permission.
Figure 9.8: Class conjecture about the order of numbers.

Students then set off to justify their conjectures with many using base ten blocks to explore and make meaning. In addition to testing the numbers from the card sort activity, 23 and 32, students generated and tested other numbers—for example, 36 and 63 (as seen in figure 9.9, page 186) and 14 and 41.

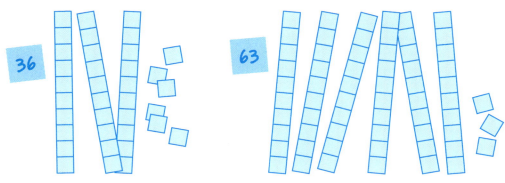

Figure 9.9: Student representation of 36 and 63.

Michelle used magnetic base ten blocks to represent 14 and 41 on the board, and students shared ways that they made sense of each quantity.

Aiden: 4 ones and a ten is still 14.

Luca: 1 goes first because there is 1 ten, 4 ones.

Maya: 1 needs to go first or it might make 41.

Francisco: 1 and 4 together.

Angel: In 41, 4 is first because there is 40.

Iker: There is 1 one; it's the second number.

As they extended their thinking, they revised their original conjecture (see figure 9.10): In a two-digit number, the order of the numbers matters because the first number is the tens place. The second number is the ones place.

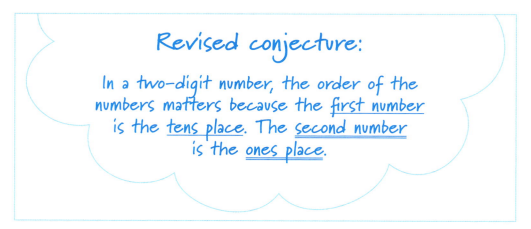

Figure 9.10: Revised conjecture.

Michelle and her first-grade students have gone through each of the four layers of argumentation as they've investigated the place values of two-digit numbers. Their work

Finding Opportunities for Argumentation

is built from a lesson within the Illustrative Mathematics (n.d.g) instructional materials. The specific lesson was argumentation ready as it offered students opportunities to see and use structure (of the base ten system). Students constructed meaning as they worked across multiple representations, including numbers, base ten blocks, and values of tens and ones. Additionally, they had opportunities to practice using language as they worked collaboratively to sort cards and discuss values. The goal of the lesson, as stated in the instructional materials, was to interpret different base ten representations of two-digit numbers (drawings, words, and addition expressions), which we argue was taken to a deeper level through argumentation.

Days later, students extended their thinking about double-digit numbers and made connections to their prior work. They created (and named) their own layer of argumentation: an add-on conjecture (see figure 9.11)!

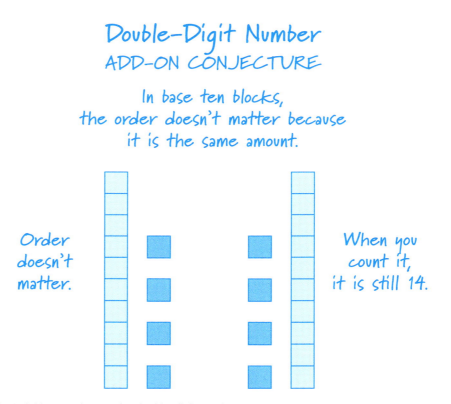

Figure 9:11: Add-on conjecture for double-digit numbers.

As we reflect on the experience in Michelle's classroom, we are excited by the opportunities she found in instructional materials and how she leveraged her knowledge and vision to create worthwhile learning experiences for her students.

PAUSE AND PONDER
ARGUMENTATION-READY TASKS

- Look at your instructional materials, mathematics tasks, and games your students have done or are about to do. Which would lend themselves to argumentation?

- How might you adapt these to make them argumentation ready?

TEACHER VOICES
INSTRUCTIONAL MATERIALS

"I feel like the textbook provides the meat of the lessons, but teachers must add in the support for the student conversations. This not only creates richer discussions, but the teacher can guide students in the direction they want the lesson to go. To reach a certain objective, the teacher can ask questions that will elicit specific conversations."
(Rachael, grade 1 teacher)

Questions for Further Reflection

The following questions will help you synthesize your learning by reflecting on chapter 9.

- What did you find interesting or surprising in the vignette?
- What activities or tasks do you use in your classroom that may be argumentation ready?
- What do you want to remember as you revisit your instructional materials?

Chapter 9 Summary

Now that you have a lens for argumentation and what it can look like in your classroom, you'll notice opportunities in tasks, games, and instructional materials. Sometimes the opportunities can be used exactly as they were designed; other times they can be modified or adapted. Intentional teacher moves, like we saw in the first-grade vignette, can extend resources we're already using and enrich the student learning experience. The "Chapter 9 Application Guide" (page 190) can help you connect the ideas in chapter 9 to your classroom. In chapter 10, we'll look at using children's literature to engage in argumentation.

Chapter 9 Application Guide

Use the following application guide to connect these ideas to your classroom.

Chapter 9 Topics	Connect to Your Classroom
Hidden Opportunities and Argumentation-Ready Tasks	• Look at your upcoming lessons and see where there are opportunities to include layers of mathematical argumentation. Make notes about how you might modify some tasks to enhance the opportunities.

CHAPTER 10

Using Children's Literature to Engage in Argumentation

Children's literature plays a central role in primary classrooms. As parents and teachers, we've spent countless hours reading to and with young students. Reading and rereading favorite books or parts of books, empathizing with characters, analyzing situations, and creating alternate storylines are all part of incorporating children's literature. The playful discussions within a community of readers are also a place to nurture argumentation. Students can interact with the text as they engage in the layers of argumentation.

In this chapter, we drop into a kindergarten classroom as students experience an interactive read-aloud and share ideas for using children's literature to spark argumentation. One student favorite is *This Is a Ball* by Beck Stanton and Matt Stanton (2015). This short story features images with statements that *misidentify* each image. In this chapter, we explore how to use books like *This Is a Ball* and others in the classroom, including making connections to mathematical argumentation and how to plan a read-aloud. We also look at other examples that you can incorporate into your lessons.

CLASSROOM VIGNETTE: *THIS IS A BALL* IN KINDERGARTEN

Let's drop into Bethany's kindergarten classroom as she reads the book aloud. Bethany began, "Today, we're going to read the story *This Is a Ball*." While reading aloud, she pointed to the image of a cube on the cover. Students responded immediately, calling out, "No! That's not a ball; it's a box." They had recently spent time learning about the attributes of shapes and couldn't wait to explain why the book's cover image was a box and not a ball as stated on the cover.

Throughout the interactive read-aloud, students enthusiastically shared their ideas. They had a keen interest in the text and wanted to share their thinking. For example, when read the text, "This is a bike," and shown an image of a car, student responses included, "The wheels are not training wheels" and "Bikes don't have windows." Student responses reasoned why the object was not what the text stated in some cases or how the image could have been interpreted in other cases. For example, when shown an image of buildings and hearing, "This is a beach," some students agreed that it could be the beach with the buildings in the background.

After the read-aloud, students participated in the first phase of argumentation: notice and wonder. Bethany asked, "What do you notice? What do you wonder?" The students' responses were charted on paper. As students shared their noticings and wonderings, we observed that Bethany created space for students to build on each other's thinking, and students took this opportunity. For example, after one student shared, "The elephant is not a dog," other students added to that explanation, sharing attributes that an elephant has, such as "a long nose, a loop tail, looks like an elephant." Another student shared that a dog has "no loop tail." The notice and wonder activity, which Bethany recorded on chart paper (figure 10.1), provided insight about how students were thinking, ways they were able to explain and justify their thoughts, and the language necessary to do so. This led us to wonder how this experience could be leveraged and built on.

I notice . . .

- The elephant is not a dog.
  - long nose
  - loop tail
- The scary green thing is not a princess. It's an alien.
- The box is not a ball. It has six corners and a ball doesn't have any corners.
- The blue bike is a car. Bikes don't have windows.
- The ice cream is not a cat. If you saw an ice cream with two sharp kitty ears, that would be an ice cream kitty. No ears. Kitty has four legs.

I wonder . . .

- If they wrote a different book where the princess is not an alien
- If the thing you said is a dog is really a dog
- How would a beach be like that? Has no windows
- Why are they trying to trick us?

Figure 10.1: Notice and wonder public record.

On a subsequent day, Bethany gave students a task that included an image of a cube along with the statement, "This is a ball. Do you agree? Why or why not?" See figure 10.2.

This is a ball. Do you agree?
Why or why not?

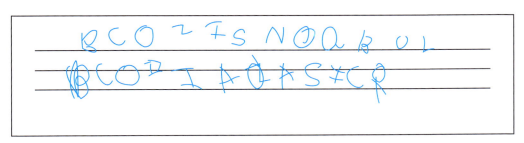

Figure 10.2: Recording sheet to go along with *This Is a Ball*.

This task led students to a variety of explanations.

Harry: It's not a ball.

Bethany: Why do you say it is not a ball?

Harry: Because it has six sides, there's no curves, and a ball is this [pointing to third image on his paper] but I put an X over here because that's not a ball, and I put a check mark because it is a ball.

Bethany: Why do you say this is not a ball?

Harry: Because it has six sides and no curve.

In this example, Harry has verbally articulated his thinking in a way that he's working toward communicating in writing. He's used his written representation as part of his verbal explanation as he points to the example (the ball he's circled) and nonexample (the cube he's placed an X over). Harry's also named an attribute of a ball—"curves"—and verbally suggested that this shape cannot be a ball "because it has six sides and no curves."

Lydia, like Harry, provides rationale for why the image is not a ball, attending to the attribute of sides (see figure 10.3, page 196). This student, as part of the verbal explanation, draws an image as she verbally explains. She also ends her explanation with a form of closure.

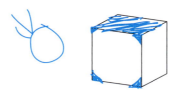

> This is a ball.
> Do you agree? Why or why not?

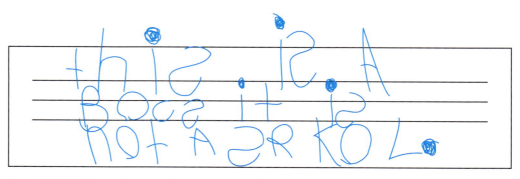

Figure 10.3: Rationale for why the box is not a ball.

Lydia: This is not a ball because it has six sides, and a ball would have no sides like this [points to circle], so it's a ball. A ball would be like this; you have to draw it like this [student draws a ball]. Do you see these edges [pointing]?

Bethany: Yes.

Lydia: That's how you know if it's a box or a ball.

Bethany: Can you tell me more about that? What do you mean that's how you can tell?

Lydia: So, I mean like somebody said this would be a ball. It would not because [a ball] wouldn't have four, like squares have four, like six, of like the sides. That's how you know it's not a ball.

You may notice a difference in the verbal and written explanations of Lydia. She writes, "This is a box. It is not a circle." Her verbal explanation shared additional insight into her thinking and provided us with a snapshot of the language she could pull from and the places where we could support her language development.

Logan wrote, "No, because they have seven sides. A circle has no [sides]." (See figure 10.4.) Logan has also drawn a diagram of a box that's labeled, "They have seven sides," and a circle that's labeled, "They look curve." She also has written on the side, "Look, this is a circle."

Using Children's Literature to Engage in Argumentation

This is a ball.
Do you agree? Why or why not?

Figure 10.4: Another student recording sheet.

This student's verbal explanation mirrored her written explanation. She, like her peers, referred to her written explanation when asked verbally to share her thinking.

Bethany: This is a ball. Do you agree?

Logan: No, because they have seven sides; a circle has no sides.

Bethany: Circles have no sides?

Logan: Yeah.

Bethany: What about this [pointing to diagram]? Tell me about this on your paper.

Logan: Look, this is a circle [leading paper and looking at circle]. They don't have curves. [Points to box] They have seven sides.

Finally, we share Ford's explanation (see figure 10.5, page 198). He also used his written explanation to support his verbal explanation. Ford added to it as he communicated to the teacher, drawing examples to support what he said. He elaborated on his explanation, giving examples of common objects to support his ideas, and he used classroom resources (a chart on the wall) as references. Ford also included multiple attributes.

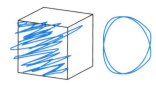

This is a ball. Do you agree? Why or why not?

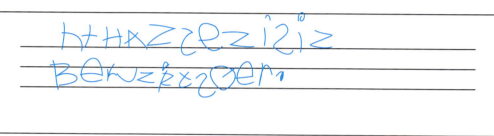

Figure 10.5: Student recording sheet.

Bethany: Tell me about your thinking. This is a ball. Do you agree? Why or why not?

Ford: No, because a ball has curves. This does not have this [draws a ball]. This has this kinda like this, kinda like, see [continues to add to his representation as he speaks in reference to it], kinda like an arrow like that. It has that instead of curves.

Bethany: So, tell me more about that. Are there other things besides curves that help you think about that?

Ford: Curves are kinda like an upside-down rainbow like this [adds to the bottom of the image, outlining the u-shape on the bottom of the circle] and this is like, they're kinda like a rainbow.

Bethany: Are there any other things that make you think that this is or is not a ball?

Ford: [Pointing to images on his paper] This bounces. This doesn't.

Bethany: Oh, one bounces, and one doesn't.

Ford: This one has 1, 2, 3, 4, 5, 6, 7 sides, and this one only has 1, 2, 3, 4.

Bethany: Oh, so you're thinking about the sides?

Ford: Yeah, so I'm gonna draw the circle right here and a box right here [draws on paper].

Bethany: Tell me about that.

Ford: So, this has lots of corners [the box], and this one doesn't have a lot of corners. This one does not have corners. This one has curves [the circle]. Curves are kind of like pizzas [points to chart on wall]. It has a curve on pizzas too.

Bethany: Oh, interesting, so that chart is kind of helping your thinking, too.

Ford: Yeah. Cuz a pizza, on its bread, it has a curve too.

Bethany: Interesting. You've told me about a lot of things. You've told me that it has curves. You've thought about sides and corners and rolling.

Ford: This one's more still than a bouncy ball. A bouncy ball bounces a lot, and this one doesn't bounce a lot, and it doesn't move a lot. It's really still. This one's not that still. It bounces. It bounces. It bounces.

While Bethany used the book to focus on mathematics content her students had been working on—understanding the attributes of shapes—similar activities could be developed around other mathematical content.

Making Connections to Mathematical Argumentation

Using children's literature can allow students to consider an author's ideas as they reason and make sense of stories. Young students can *notice and wonder*, *conjecture*, *justify*, and *extend* ideas—what we refer to as the layers of argumentation.

We can see examples of this in the explanations of Bethany's kindergarten students. Students had opinions about the claims the authors were making and agreed and disagreed using evidence and definitions. They had an opportunity to justify their perspective and convince someone that they were correct. The students also shared their ideas to get peer feedback.

We think about children's literature in a few different ways. Some children's literature lends itself well to argumentation, giving students opportunities to reason, explain their thinking, and engage in the layers of argumentation, without a specific mathematical focus. *This Is a Ball* is an example of this type of story. Students notice that the text misidentifies each image and offer explanations, sometimes explaining how they know the mismatch and other times justifying the correct text and how they know. There are also stories with an evident mathematical storyline, where students have opportunities to think about specific mathematical ideas and simultaneously develop argumentation skills.

Planning Read-Alouds

Selecting literature is the first step in planning. We included some of our favorites in this section along with a brief description of each text and ways it can promote argumentation. While this list is not extensive, our goal is to provide materials to help you get started and tools to build a lens for identifying additional resources.

READING MATHEMATICS-SPECIFIC CONTENT

The following lists some children's books that are specifically about mathematics concepts.

- ***One Hundred Hungry Ants* by Elinor J. Pinczes and Bonnie MacKain (1999):** In this story, one hundred hungry ants are en route to a picnic when one of them identifies ways to group themselves to get there more efficiently before all the food is gone. Students have opportunities to learn about arrays and different ways one value can be represented in rows and columns while also sharing and explaining noticings, patterns, and generalizations.

- ***The Doorbell Rang* by Pat Hutchins (1989):** In this popular children's book, siblings are about to share twelve cookies, until the doorbell rings. Each time the doorbell rings and new guests appear, the children have to decide how to share the cookies. The story can provide students with opportunities to develop understandings of equal groups, explain and justify their thinking, and notice patterns and structures within the number system as they share twelve in different ways.

- ***Ten Black Dots* by Donald Crews (1986):** In this short counting story, an increasing quantity of black dots are incorporated into each illustration. Students have an opportunity to count and see quantities from one to ten. They may notice that on each page, the quantity increases by one. Therefore, if additional pages are added to the book, they can conjecture and justify what quantity would be represented on each consecutive page.

- ***Equal Shmequal* by Virginia Kroll and Philomena O'Neill (2005):** In this story, animals consider ways to make equal teams to have a tug-of-war. Equality is considered from the lens of number and from the lens of size and weight. This story can provide students with an opportunity to construct and articulate their understanding of the equal sign.

READING GENERAL CONTENT (NOT MATHEMATICS SPECIFIC)

The following lists some general content books for children.

- ***This Is a Ball* by Beck Stanton and Matt Stanton (2015):** This short story features images with statements that identify each image; however, the statements *misidentify* each image. For example, when showing an image of a car, the corresponding text says, "This is a bike." Each page lends itself to argumentation as students reason why the object is not what is stated in the text, providing attributes and justifications of their thinking.

- ***Six-Dinner Sid* by Inga Moore (1991):** Sid the cat lives in six different houses, and he is fed dinner six different times. After getting sick and visiting the vet six different times, Sid gets discovered. Should Sid continue to be fed six dinners? The story provides an opportunity for students to engage in argumentation as they share their ideas, make a claim, and support that claim with reasoning.

- ***Any Kind of Dog* by Lynn Reiser (1994):** Richard wants a dog. His mother gives him many different creatures, but none of them are the dog he wants. How might Richard convince his mother that he should get a dog? The story provides an opportunity for students to consider if Richard's mom should give him a dog and provide reasoning to support their opinion.

Using Children's Literature to Engage in Argumentation

PAUSE AND PONDER
BOOKS IN YOUR CLASSROOM

- Which books that you read aloud to your students have opportunities for them to engage in argumentation?

- Which books have opportunities for students to form an opinion, justify their ideas, share, and extend?

GETTING STARTED WITH READ-ALOUDS

Once you select the literature, think about the purpose of using that particular book. Why this book? What do you hope students think about or learn by engaging with the text?

Another consideration is what the read-aloud will look and sound like. For example, how will this book be read aloud? Will the book be read through once in its entirety? Will there be pausing points as it is read aloud? Some books may lend themselves to one or the other. Also, consider how the richness of the text will be maintained. Will there be discussion throughout the reading or at the end?

After deciding how the text will be read aloud, consider how students will interact with the text. Will there be a whole-group discussion? Will students turn and talk with a partner at periodic points? What will be the role of questioning? What questions will be posed to elicit student thinking? How will you question to bring out mathematical goals (if relevant)? For example, with *The Doorbell Rang*, you might plan and pose questions, such as the following.

- "How would you share the cookies? Why? What did you think about?"
- "How do you know that's fair? What does it mean for each person to get an equal amount?"

What questions will press argumentation skills? For example, from the context of *This Is a Ball*, consider questions such as, "How do you know it's not a ball? How could you convince the author that it's not a ball?" After the book, you can think about a follow-up experience. Will there be a follow-up experience? If so, what is the purpose and goal? What will that look like and sound like?

In the example from Bethany's kindergarten reading of *This Is a Ball*, students engaged in noticing and wondering as a whole class and in an individual task. The purpose of noticing and wondering was to elicit student thinking and learn more about their reasoning, while also giving them an opportunity to develop listening and speaking skills as they used language to share and build on ideas of others. It was through this experience that the individual task was developed. Students had worked on attributes of shapes, and Bethany was curious how they would use that reasoning to construct an argument. Figure 10.6 can help you plan your read-alouds.

	Book Title: _____
Before Reading	Identify the purpose for reading the book.
During Reading	How will the story be read? ❏ In its entirety ❏ Pausing at points in the story What questions can I pose to: • Elicit student thinking • Bring out mathematical ideas (if applicable) • Press argumentation skills

After Reading	Consider the follow-up experience:
	• How will students engage with ideas from the text?
	• How will these ideas lead to use of argumentation skills?
	    + Language development
	    + Noticing and wondering
	    + Making and justifying claims
	    + Sharing and extending ideas

Figure 10.6: Planning considerations.

Questions for Further Reflection

The following questions will help you synthesize your learning by reflecting on chapter 10.

- What did you notice about the vignette? Did anything surprise you?

- In the follow-up activity connected to the read-aloud of *This Is a Ball* in Bethany's classroom, students responded to an image from the text, and the prompt, "This is a ball. Do you agree? Why or why not?" What prompts might you give your students that connect to specific content you're working on?

- You've considered books you read aloud that have opportunities for students to engage in argumentation. What specific tasks might you develop to use with the books?

- This chapter connected argumentation with children's literature; what other content areas might you connect with argumentation?

Chapter 10 Summary

Children's literature can be a powerful springboard for building toward argumentation. As we saw in Bethany's classroom, students have opportunities to notice, wonder, and imagine in a joyful shared space. Through carefully selected texts and intentional planning, we can open doors of argumentation beyond mathematics! The "Chapter 10 Application Guide" (page 204) can help you connect the ideas in chapter 10 to your classroom.

Chapter 10 Application Guide

Use the following application guide to connect these ideas to your classroom.

Chapter 10 Topics	Connect to Your Classroom
Children's Literature	• Look around your classroom library or search for one of the books recommended in this chapter to use in your classroom. Try to integrate the book across language arts and mathematics. • Prepare some questions to ask as you are reading that will promote argumentation skills shared in this chapter.

Epilogue

Shifting where we put our attention can have a significant impact on how we live, teach, and interact in the world. In this book, we offered ways to think about teaching mathematics to K–2 students, but it goes beyond the elementary mathematics classroom. We hope to inspire a world of wonder and curiosity for all people, starting by nurturing the curiosity that young students bring. Once we start to notice and wonder, we can see things differently, whether we are learners, teachers, or parents. Nurturing students' natural curiosity offers us, as adults, a way to reconnect with the wonder of our world and connect deeply with young students in the world that they live in. We can do this in all places, including the mathematics classroom, by building from what students already do. We shared the example of the ramp throughout the four chapters in part 2 (page 95), allowing you to enter the world of a child playing outside and how she notices, wonders, conjectures, justifies, and extends in a natural environment. Now that we've unpacked the layers in this book, we wonder if you will start to see it everywhere, too!

As explorers of this topic, we noticed that once we oriented ourselves to the mathematical argumentation lens, we started to notice and wonder more about mathematics and our own students, and we became more curious and connected to observations. Through the two-year professional development project with the three K–2 teachers, we anecdotally noted that our language and the teachers' language began shifting so that they would say, "I notice . . ." and "I wonder . . ." as they shared ideas from their own classroom with others. It was so rewarding to see this shift in the teachers' perspectives. We believe that by nurturing curiosity and wonder, we are connecting in a deep way, in both the relationships we have with students and the way we connect knowledge and mathematical ideas.

In one of her final journal entries, a first-grade teacher wrote, "I'm excited to share the process we have been through. I want to pass on how important it is for students to develop language and notice and wonder about things. Noticing and wondering drives motivation for students and being able to verbalize what they see and predict allows students to engage in mathematics on a deeper level."

We believe that teaching in a way that is rooted in both reasoning and curiosity is important in all subjects. Argumentation is not one more thing to check off; it's a way of seeing the world and learning beyond mathematics class. Argumentation can feel like a cumbersome and negative word, but what if we called it *growing wonder* or *nurturing curiosity* instead? Can we grow wonder in our mathematics class, across subjects, and in our everyday lives as we see beauty in the nature and patterns that we are always immersed in? While you picked up this book to learn about argumentation in K–2 classrooms, we hope you can see how to nurture curiosity beyond the mathematics classroom and beyond the school building. We hope you take this way of seeing the world with you into all parts of your life!

APPENDIX A

Instructional Routine Planning Template

This appendix begins with a blank version of the "Instructional Routine Planning Template" for your use. To help you integrate the four layers of mathematical argumentation into instructional routines, we include examples for choral counting, Number of the Day (plus a version with annotations), and true or false.

We've also prepared a video to help you understand ways to use colors when creating class records. Access it by using the following QR code or visiting www.youtube.com/@nurturingmathcuriosity.

Instructional Routine Planning Template

Instructional Routine:

_____

Task:

_____
_____
_____

Content Connections:

_____
_____
_____

Where could argumentation emerge?

_____
_____
_____

Materials:

- Chart paper
- Markers
- _____
- _____
- _____

Anticipate Possible Student Responses

Before trying the instructional routine with students, write out how you will record it with them, and brainstorm ideas that students might come up with as they notice patterns in the routine. Consider how to organize the ideas in a way that could support related patterns to emerge. For example, you could organize related ideas and equations together with the same color. Revisit figure 5.1 (page 100); notice that related equations are recorded in a way that makes patterns visible.

Students Participate in the Routine and Generate Ideas

Once students have participated in the routine and generated ideas, you could pause for the day and regroup after seeing what they came up with and considering how you could reorganize ideas.

Layer 1: Students Notice and Wonder

Invite students to make observations about the instructional routine. Record their ideas on a public record.

Questions to Nudge at Noticing and Wondering	Anticipated Student Responses
• What do you notice? What do you wonder? • What patterns do you see? Will that pattern continue? • What do the equations have in common? • How do the equations relate to other observations? • Who has a related observation? • Where do you see connections?	

Language Supports	Notes for Recording Student Thinking	Supportive Representations
• I notice _____. • I wonder _____. • A pattern is _____.	Use colors, arrows, and placement to connect related ideas.	Possible representations include base ten blocks, number line, two-color counters, and ten-frames.

Layer 2: Students Conjecture

Invite students to make conjectures about what they noticed and wondered. Record ideas on the public record.

Questions to Nudge at Conjecturing	Conjectures That Might Emerge From the Noticings and Wonderings
• Is that observation always true? When will it be true? • What do you believe to always be true about _____? • Will that pattern continue as we keep counting? • How will the pattern continue? • Is that true always, sometimes, or never? How do you know? • Can you draw a visual representation to show what you mean? • How can you use a tool to show what you mean?	

Language Supports	Notes for Recording Student Thinking	Supportive Representations
• My conjecture is _____. • It will always be true that _____. • What do you mean by *it*?	Write conjectures in a color that matches related observations.	Possible representations include base ten blocks, number line, two-color counters, and ten-frames.

Layer 3: Students Justify

Invite students to justify their conjectures. Record their ideas on the public record.

Questions to Nudge at Justifying	Ways That Students Might Justify the Conjecture
• Why do you believe that to be true? • Can you draw a visual representation to show why that works? • How can you convince someone the conjecture is always true? Never true? • Why is that true? Why is it not true?	

Language Supports	Notes for Recording Student Thinking	Supportive Representations
• It is true because _____. • I agree because _____. • I disagree because _____.	Write justification ideas in a color that matches the related conjecture, or parts of the conjecture.	Possible representations include base ten blocks, number line, two-color counters, and ten-frames.

Layer 4: Students Extend

Consider which conjecture would benefit from modifying. Invite students to extend the ideas further to related content.

Questions to Nudge at Extending	Ways the Conjecture May Be Modified and Extended
• Can someone restate _____'s conjecture? • Does anyone have a similar idea or something they'd like to add? • Does anyone have a different idea? • Are there words in the conjecture that anyone has a question about? • How can we rewrite our conjectures to make them more precise? • Are there other things you think might be true now that we've explored this conjecture? • What else might be true?	

Language Supports	Notes for Recording Student Thinking	Supportive Representations
• I think it's also true that _____. • Another idea I have is _____.	Write ideas in a color that matches a related conjecture or parts of the conjecture.	Possible representations include base ten blocks, number line, two-color counters, and ten-frames.

Choral Counting Example

Task:

Count by 10 starting at 3; stop at 93.

Content Connections:

- Place value, adding 10
- Addition within 100

Materials:

- Chart paper
- Markers
- Base ten blocks

Anticipate Possible Student Responses

Before trying the instructional routine with students, write out the choral count, as you will record it with the students and brainstorm ideas as they notice patterns in the sequence. Consider how to organize the ideas in a way that could support related patterns to emerge.

They all have the number 3.	3	13 is 10 and 3.
	13	The 1 in 13 represents 10.
The 3 is three 1s.	23	10 + 3 = 13
	33	
No matter how far you go, there will always be a 3 at the end.	43	The next number would be 103.
	53	
+10, +10, +10 as you go down the column.	63	3 + 10 = 13
	73	13 + 10 = 23
	83	
−10, −10, −10 as you go up the column.	93	The numbers are getting bigger.

Students Count and Generate the Sequence

As a class, invite students to choral count by saying, "Let's count by 10 starting at 3," and record the numbers.

Layer 1: Students Notice and Wonder

Invite the students to make observations about the sequence. Record their ideas on a public record.

Questions to Nudge at Noticing and Wondering	Anticipated Student Responses
- What do you notice? What do you wonder? - What patterns do you see? Will that pattern continue as we keep counting? - How is the sequence growing? - What do the equations have in common? What patterns do you notice in the equations? - How do the equations relate to other observations? - Who has a related observation? - What do you notice about addends within the expressions? - Where do you see addition and where do you see subtraction? - Where do you see connections?	- They all have the number 3. - The 3 is 3 ones. - No matter how far you go, there will always be a 3 on the end. - +10, +10, +10 as you go down. - −10, −10, −10 as you go up. - 13 is 10 and 3. The 1 in 13 represents 10. 10 + 3 = 13. - The next number would be 103. - 3 + 10 = 13 and 13 + 10 = 23.

Language Supports	Notes for Recording Student Thinking	Supportive Representations
- I notice _____. - I wonder _____. - A pattern is _____. - The next number will be _____ because _____.	Use colors, arrows, and placement to connect related ideas.	Base ten blocks (3 ones and 10 rods): add a rod as each 10 is added to the sequence. Hops on a number line: +10 hops from 3, 13, 23, 33, 43, 53, 63

Layer 2: Students Conjecture

Invite students to make conjectures about what they noticed and wondered. Record ideas on the public record.

Questions to Nudge at Conjecturing	Conjectures That Might Emerge From the Noticings and Wonderings
<ul><li>Is that observation always true? When will it be true?</li><li>What do you believe to always be true about _____?</li><li>Will that pattern continue as we keep counting?</li><li>How will the pattern continue?</li><li>What do you predict would come next? Why?</li><li>What do you think will always be true about this sequence of numbers?</li><li>Is that true always, sometimes, or never? How do you know?</li><li>Can you draw a visual representation to show what you mean?</li><li>How can you use a tool to show what you mean?</li></ul>	<ul><li>If you add 10 to a number, it gets bigger.</li><li>If you take 10 away from a number, it gets smaller.</li><li>The tens place goes up by 1 as you go down the column.</li><li>No matter how far you go, there will always be a 3 on the end. (This is followed into the next layers.)</li><li>If you have a number and add 10, the ones place will stay the same.</li></ul>

Language Supports	Notes for Recording Student Thinking	Supportive Representations
<ul><li>My conjecture is _____.</li><li>It will always be true that _____.</li><li>What do you mean by *it*?</li></ul>	Write conjectures in a color that matches related observations.	Base ten blocks, especially tens

Layer 3: Students Justify

Invite students to justify their conjectures. Record their ideas on the public record.

Questions to Nudge at Justifying	Ways That Students Might Justify the Conjecture
• Why do you believe that to be true? • Can you draw a visual representation to show why that works? • How can you convince someone the conjecture is always true? Never true? • Why is that true? Why is it not true?	• Continue the pattern beyond the examples shown. • With the base ten blocks, we can keep adding a ten to the pile and the number of ones (3) stays the same (representation). • When you add 10, the only part of the number that changes is the tens place, or the hundreds, not the ones.

Language Supports	Notes for Recording Student Thinking	Supportive Representations
• It is true because _____. • I agree because _____. • I disagree because _____.	Write justification ideas in a color that matches the related conjecture.	Base ten blocks

Layer 4: Students Extend

Consider which conjecture would benefit from modifying. Invite students to extend the ideas further to related content. (The various type styles will help you connect the questions in the left column with their possible modifications in the right column.)

Questions to Nudge at Extending	Ways the Conjecture May Be Modified and Extended
<ul><li>Can someone restate _____'s conjecture?</li><li>Does anyone have a similar idea or something you'd like to add?</li><li>Does anyone have a different idea?</li><li>Are there words in the conjecture that anyone has a question about?</li><li>How can we rewrite our conjectures to make them more precise?<ul><li>*What do you mean "on the end"?*</li><li>How can you describe the number you start with?</li><li>What do you mean "how far you go"?</li><li>Would it work if you started with a number other than 3? How can we modify the conjecture to say that it works for other numbers besides 3?</li><li>*Would it work if you added a number other than 10? How can we modify the conjecture to say that it works for other numbers besides 10?*</li></ul></li><li>Are there other things you think might be true now that we've explored this conjecture?</li><li>What else might be true?</li></ul>	**Example of an Original Student Conjecture** No matter how far you go, there will always be a 3 on the end. **Possible Modifications**<ul><li>No matter how far you go, there will always be a 3 *in the ones place*.</li><li>When you start with 3, no matter how far you go, there will always be a 3 *in the ones place*.</li><li>When you start with 3, each time you add 10, there will always be a 3 *in the ones place*.</li><li>When you start with a number, each time you add 10, there will always be the same number *in the ones place* that you started with.</li><li>When you start with a number, each time you add 10 or a multiple of 10, there will always be the same number *in the ones place* that you started with.</li></ul>**Possible Extensions** If you have a number and add 10 or a multiple of 10, the ones place will stay the same.

Language Supports	Notes for Recording Student Thinking	Supportive Representations
<ul><li>Ones place, tens place</li><li>Multiple of 10</li><li>Add</li></ul>	Write ideas in a color that matches the related conjecture.	Base ten blocks

Nurturing Math Curiosity © 2024 Solution Tree Press • SolutionTree.com
Visit **go.SolutionTree.com/mathematics** to download this free, full-color reproducible.

Number of the Day Example

Task:

What do you know about 100?

Content Connections:

- Adding and subtracting within 100
- Compensation within addends
- Composing and decomposing numbers

Materials:

- Chart paper
- Markers
- Connecting cubes
- Two large clear zipper bags

Anticipate Possible Student Responses

Before trying the instructional routine with students, brainstorm ideas that students might come up with. Consider how to organize the ideas in a way that could support patterns to emerge, like using writing expressions in an order that shows how addends change. For example, for the equations in Group A (green in the full-color version), the addends shift by one.

Ten groups of 10	Group B	Group C
Three numbers	50 + 50 = 100	100 − 0 = 100
100 is big	40 + 60 = 100	100 − 1 + 1 = 100
Group A	30 + 70 = 100	100 − 2 + 2 = 100
100 + 0 = 100	20 + 80 = 100	101 − 1 = 100
99 + 1 = 100	10 + 90 = 100	102 − 2 = 100
98 + 2 = 100	40 + 50 + 10 = 100	103 − 3 = 100
97 + 3 = 100	It has a 1 in the hundreds place, zeros in the tens and ones.	104 − 4 = 100
96 + 4 = 100		It can be made of tens and ones.
95 + 5 = 100		

Students Explore and Generate Ideas

As a class, invite students to generate ideas related to the number 100. Organize related ideas and equations together with the same color. We have organized them by Group A, B, and C to show which colors would be grouped together.

What do you know about the number _____? Let's write down all of the things we know.

- Is there another way to think about 100 that's related to what _____ shared?
- Can you say more about _____?
- What equations can you come up with that have a sum of 100?
- Can you think of an equation with decade numbers and with a sum of 100?

Layer 1: Students Notice and Wonder

Invite the students to make observations about the ideas they shared. Record their ideas on a public record.

Questions to Nudge at Noticing and Wondering	Anticipated Student Responses
<ul><li>What do you notice? What do you wonder?</li><li>What patterns do you notice in the equations?</li><li>What do they have in common?</li><li>What do you notice about addends within the expressions?</li><li>Where do you see addition and where do you see subtraction?</li><li>What do you wonder about related to the ideas we generated?</li><li>Who has a related observation?</li><li>What connections do you see?</li></ul>	<ul><li>There are lots of ways to get 100.</li><li>The number 100 can be made with tens and ones.</li></ul>**Related to Group A**<ul><li>The numbers go down on the left (100, 99, 98, 97 . . .) and up on the right (0, 1, 2, 3, . . .). But 100 is always the answer.</li><li>As one number (addend) goes up by one, the other number (addend) goes down by one.</li></ul>**Related to Group B**<ul><li>We can add multiples of ten and get 100. There are lots of ways to add multiples of ten.</li><li>As one number (addend) goes up by ten, the other number (addend) goes down by ten.</li></ul>**Related to Group C**<ul><li>When you add or subtract zero, it will still be 100.</li><li>You can add or subtract to get 100 as an answer.</li><li>You can add three numbers together to get 100.</li></ul>

Language Supports	Notes for Recording Student Thinking	Supportive Representations
<ul><li>I notice _____.</li><li>I wonder _____.</li></ul>	Use colors and placement to connect related ideas.	<ul><li>Towers of ten, connecting cubes</li><li>Two clear zipper bags to hold two groups of towers of ten</li></ul>

Layer 2: Students Conjecture

Invite students to make conjectures about what they noticed and wondered. Record ideas on the public record.

Questions to Nudge at Conjecturing	Conjectures That Might Emerge From the Noticings and Wonderings
• Is that observation always true? When will it be true? • What do you believe might be true about _____? (adding multiples of ten to get 100) • Is that true always, sometimes, or never? How do you know? • Does that work with all numbers? • When does the strategy work? • How can you use a tool to show what you mean? • Can you draw a visual representation to show what you mean?	• When one number (addend) goes up by one, the other number (addend) goes down by one. It will always still equal 100. • When one number (addend) goes up by ten, the other number (addend) goes down by ten. It will always still equal 100. • If you add zero to a number, you get the same number again. • If you subtract zero from a number, you get the same number again. • Addition and subtraction are related, opposites.

Language Supports	Notes for Recording Student Thinking	Supportive Representations
• My conjecture is _____. • It will always be true that _____. • Addends and sum	Write conjectures near to where the examples are recorded.	• Towers of ten, connecting cubes • Two clear zipper bags to hold two groups of towers of ten

Layer 3: Students Justify

Invite students to justify their conjectures. Record their ideas on the public record.

Questions to Nudge at Justifying	Ways That Students Might Justify the Conjecture
• Why is that true? Why is it not true? • Why do you believe that is true? • How can you convince someone that the conjecture is true? • How can you justify that the conjecture is true? • Can you use a drawing to show why that works? • Can you use a tool to show why that works? • How can you convince someone the conjecture is always true? Never true?	• Appealing to authority (book, teacher, and so on) • Showing several numerical examples (empirical) • Showing larger numerical examples • Providing a story problem context/example: If we both have 5 candies and I give you one of mine, I'll have 4 and you'll have 6. • If we have two piles, we can take 1 from one addend and share it with the other. • The total amount stays the same. • When one pile goes up and the other pile goes down, it still equals the same. • We still have the same amount. • With the cubes, we can move one group of ten to the other addend.

Language Supports	Notes for Recording Student Thinking	Supportive Representations
• It is true because _____. • I agree because _____. • I disagree because _____.	Show a variety of justifications that are concrete, pictorial, and verbal.	• Connecting cubes • Two clear zipper bags to hold two groups of towers of ten

Layer 4: Students Extend

Consider which conjecture would benefit from modifying. Invite students to extend the ideas further to related content. (The various type styles will help you connect the questions in the left column with their possible modifications in the right column.)

Questions to Nudge at Modifying and Extending	Ways the Conjecture May Be Modified and Extended

• Can someone restate _____'s conjecture?
• Does anyone have a similar idea or something you'd like to add? Does anyone have a different idea?
• Would it still be true if . . . ?
• Are there some words in the conjecture that anyone has a question about?
• Based on what we learned, how can we rewrite our conjecture to make it more precise?
   + *What number do you mean?*
   + *Would it work if the sum was something other than 100? How can we modify the conjecture to say that it works for other sums?*
   + Would it work if you added a number other than 1? How can we modify the conjecture to say that it works for other numbers besides 1?
• Are there other things you think might be true now that we've explored this conjecture?
• What else might be true?
	Example of an Original Student Conjecture
	When one number goes up by 1, the other number goes down by 1. It will always still equal 100.
	
	Possible Modifications to the Original Based on Questions to the Left
	• When one *addend* goes up by 1, the other *addend* goes down by 1. It will always still equal 100.
	• When one *addend* goes up by 1, the other *addend* goes down by 1. It will always still equal *the same total or sum*.
	• When one *addend* goes up by an amount, the other *addend* goes down by the same amount. It will always still equal *the same total or sum*.
	
	Possible Extensions
	When one number goes down by an amount and the other number goes up by the same amount, the total stays the same.

Language Supports	Notes for Recording Student Thinking	Supportive Representations
• Addends • Sum • Group of ten	Continue charting to add to public record.	• Connecting cubes • Images that show labeled boxes to represent the number

Number of the Day Example With Annotations

This version of the "Instructional Routine Planning Template" includes annotations as if we were there with you pointing things out.

Task:

What do you know about 100?

Content Connections:

Where could argumentation emerge?

- Adding and subtracting within 100
- Composing and decomposing numbers
- *Compensating addends*

Materials:

- Chart paper
- Markers
- Base ten blocks
- *Two large clear zipper bags*
- *Connecting cubes*

Anticipate Possible Student Responses

Anticipating helps us to be responsive and intentional. Ch. 3 (Williams, 2022)

Before trying the instructional routine with students, brainstorm ideas that students might come up with. Consider how to organize the ideas in a way that could support patterns to emerge, like using writing expressions in an order that shows how addends change (see green and red in full-color version).

Give credit to students by including their name next to their idea.

Ten groups of 10	Group B	Group C
Three numbers	50 + 50 = 100	100 − 0 = 100
100 is big	40 + 60 = 100	100 − 1 + 1 = 100
Group A	30 + 70 = 100	100 − 2 + 2 = 100
100 + 0 = 100	20 + 80 = 100	101 − 1 = 100
99 + 1 = 100	10 + 90 = 100	102 − 2 = 100
98 + 2 = 100	40 + 50 + 10 = 100	103 − 3 = 100
97 + 3 = 100		104 − 4 = 100
96 + 4 = 100		
95 + 5 = 100	It has a 1 in the hundreds place, zeros in the tens and ones.	It can be made of tens and ones.

These equations have addends that shift by 10.

Even though it's repetitive, the = 100 helps make a pattern obvious.

Subtraction equations might emerge!

These equations make the structure; addends shift by 1.

Possible place value connections

The public record may not look exactly like this! See example record in figure 5.1 (page 100).

Students Explore and Generate Ideas

As a class, invite students to generate ideas related to the number 100. Organize related ideas and equations together with the same color. We have organized them by Group A, B, and C to show which colors would be grouped together.

What do you know about the number _____? Let's write down all of the things we know.

- Is there another way to think about 100 that's related to what _____ shared?
- Can you say more about _____?
- What equations can you come up with that have a sum of 100?
- Can you think of an equation with decade numbers and with a sum of 100?

Layer 1: Students Notice and Wonder

Invite the students to make observations about the ideas they shared. Record their ideas on a public record.

Everyone in the community has ideas to contribute.

May not ask all questions. Just ideas.

Questions to Nudge at Noticing and Wondering	Anticipated Student Responses
• What do you notice? What do you wonder? • What patterns do you notice in the equations? • What do they have in common? • What do you notice about addends within the expressions? • Where do you see addition and where do you see subtraction? • What do you wonder about related to the ideas we generated? • Who has a related observation? • What connections do you see?	• There are lots of ways to get 100. • The number 100 can be made with tens and ones. **Related to Group A** • The numbers go down on the left (100, 99, 98, 97 . . .) and up on the right (0, 1, 2, 3, . . .). But 100 is always the answer. • As one number (addend) goes up by one, the other number (addend) goes down by one. **Related to Group B** • We can add multiples of ten and get 100. There are lots of ways to add multiples of ten. • As one number (addend) goes up by ten, the other number (addend) goes down by ten. **Related to Group C** • When you add or subtract zero, it will still be 100. • You can add or subtract to get 100 as an answer. • You can add three numbers together to get 100.

Open-ended invitation

Helps move toward planned conjectures.

Helps students make connections.

Lots of patterns to leverage.

Questions can impact the discussion in a powerful way.

Which ideas do you hope to leverage? Make sure those questions are included.

No observation is insignificant.

These can be added in colors to match related equations.

Lots of ideas they can share. All students are math knowers.

Related to Group B equations and multiples of 10; clear bags with towers of 10 can help show the two addends.

Language Supports	Notes for Recording Student Thinking	Supportive Representations
• I notice _____ • I wonder _____	Use colors and placement to connect related ideas. *Check our example in figure 5.1 (page 100).*	• Towers of ten, connecting cubes • Two clear zipper bags to hold two groups of towers of ten

These can be put on sentence strips (see figure 5.2, page 100).

Fostering curiosity

Organize in this order even if generated in a different order.

This doesn't all have to happen on the same day. We can pause at this point and regroup if needed.

Layer 2: Students Conjecture

Not all conjectures will be explored today. Save some for another day.

Invite students to make conjectures about what they noticed and wondered. Record ideas on the public record.

Teachers constantly make important decisions in discretionary spaces.

Mistakes are OK.

Can keep representations part of the discussion.

Questions to Nudge at Conjecturing	Conjectures That Might Emerge From the Noticings and Wonderings
• Is that observation always true? When will it be true? • What do you believe might be true about _____? (adding multiples of ten to get 100) • Is that true always, sometimes, or never? How do you know? • Does that work with all numbers? • When does the strategy work? • How can you use a tool to show what you mean? • Can you draw a visual representation to show what you mean?	• *When one number (addend) goes up by one, the other number (addend) goes down by one. It will always still equal 100.* • *When one number (addend) goes up by ten, the other number (addend) goes down by ten. It will always still equal 100.* *Based on the observations of Group A and Group B equations.* • If you add zero to a number, you get the same number again. • If you subtract zero from a number, you get the same number again. *May come up depending on the observations.* • Addition and subtraction are related, opposites. *This conjecture may be harder to justify, but it's an important contribution.*

These don't have to be fully formed conjectures; they are ideas.

Language Supports	Notes for Recording Student Thinking	Supportive Representations
• My conjecture is _____. • It will always be true that _____. *Addends, sum* *These can be written out or modeled verbally.*	Write conjectures near to where the examples are recorded. *Are there ways to push for or add precision to the conjecture?* *Students can revise their thinking to add precision.*	• Towers of ten, connecting cubes • Two clear zipper bags to hold two groups of towers of ten

Layer 3: Students Justify

Invite students to justify their conjectures. Record their ideas on the public record.

These are based on the first two conjectures from Layer 2.

If the teacher is genuinely interested, students will follow.

Questions to Nudge at Justifying	Ways That Students Might Justify the Conjecture
• Why is that true? Why is it not true? • Why do you believe that is true? • How can you convince someone that the conjecture is true? • How can you justify that the conjecture is true? • Can you use a drawing to show why that works? • Can you use a tool to show why that works? • How can you convince someone the conjecture is always true? Never true?	• Appealing to authority (book, teacher, and so on) • Showing several numerical examples (empirical) • Showing larger numerical examples • Providing a story problem context/example: If we both have 5 candies and I give you one of mine, I'll have 4 and you'll have 6. • If we have two piles, we can take 1 from one addend and share it with the other. • The total amount stays the same. • When one pile goes up and the other pile goes down, it still equals the same. • We still have the same amount. • With the cubes, we can move one group of ten to the other addend.

Connect to representations, especially moving toward generic examples.

Different of common justification

Counter-examples come up for false conjectures.

Include talk moves to keep students engaged (page 37).

Listening is part of communication.

Language Supports	Notes for Recording Student Thinking	Supportive Representations
• It is true because _____. • I agree because _____. • I disagree because _____.	Show a variety of justifications that are concrete, pictorial, and verbal. *We learn when we make connections.* Make connections between representations. Try not to label each part of a figure to show how values could shift (see figure 5.1, page 100). *Each tower could be 10, 1, or something else.*	• Connecting cubes • Two clear zipper bags to hold two groups of towers of ten *Exaggerating actions and repeated patterns are helpful.*

Layer 4: Students Extend

Consider which conjecture would benefit from modifying. Invite students to extend the ideas further to related content. (The various type styles will help you connect the questions in the left column with their possible modifications in the right column.)

Questions to Nudge at Modifying and Extending	Ways the Conjecture May Be Modified and Extended

• Can someone restate _____'s conjecture?
• Does anyone have a similar idea or something you'd like to add? Does anyone have a different idea?
• Would it still be true if . . . ?
• Are there words in the conjecture that anyone has a question about?
• Based on what we learned, how can we rewrite our conjecture to make it more precise?
   + *What number do you mean?*
   + Would it work if the sum was something other than 100? How can we modify the conjecture to say that it works for other sums?
   + Would it work if you added a number other than 1? How can we modify the conjecture to say that it works for other numbers besides 1?
• Are there other things you think might be true now that we've explored this conjecture?
• What else might be true?
	Example of an Original Student Conjecture
	When one number goes up by 1, the other number goes down by 1. It will always still equal 100.
	
	Possible Modifications to the Original Based on Questions to the Left
	• When one *addend* goes up by 1, the other *addend* goes down by 1. It will always still equal 100.
	• When one *addend* goes up by 1, the other *addend* goes down by 1. It will always still equal the same total or sum.
	• When one *addend* goes up by an amount, the other *addend* goes down by the same amount. It will always still equal the same total or sum.
	
	Possible Extensions
	When one number goes down by an amount and the other number goes up by the same amount, the total stays the same.

Handwritten annotations:
- *Colors are connected.*
- *We can keep playing with these ideas.*
- *Is there a way to make the conjectures more general?*
- *What are students interested in pursuing?*
- *Do students revisit an earlier conjecture that was put on pause?*
- *It's not just about adding precision but extending ideas.*
- *As they build knowledge, they are growing as mathematicians.*

Language Supports	Notes for Recording Student Thinking	Supportive Representations
• Addends • Sum • Group of ten	Continue charting to add to public record. *Representations help make students' thinking visible.*	• Connecting cubes • Images that show labeled boxes to represent the number

Nurturing Math Curiosity © 2024 Solution Tree Press • SolutionTree.com
Visit **go.SolutionTree.com/mathematics** to download this free, full-color reproducible.

True or False Example

Task:

- 2 + 0 = 2 (T)
- 0 + 5 = 5 (T)
- 3 + 0 = 4 (F)
- 73 + 0 = 82 (F)

Content Connections:

- Adding with zero
- Commutative property of addition may come up, but we'll try to keep the discussion to adding with zero. If a conjecture about the commutative property emerges, keep it aside for another day.

Materials:

- Chart paper
- Markers
- Equation strips
- Counters or blocks

Anticipate Possible Student Responses

Before trying the instructional routine with students, brainstorm ideas that students might come up with. Consider how to organize the ideas in a way that could support patterns to emerge; for example, use colors for zero (red), shown here as italic, and the other addend or sum (blue), shown here as a dotted underline.

Original Set	True Equations
2 + *0* = 2	2 + *0* = 2
0 + 5 = 5	*0* + 2 = 2
3 + *0* ≠ 4	*0* + 5 = 5
73 + *0* ≠ 82	3 + *0* = 3
	4 + *0* = 4
	73 + *0* = 73
	82 + *0* = 82

Students Explore and Generate Ideas

As a class, after deciding whether each equation is true or false, modify the false equations to make them true. Make a new list of true equations on the right. Use colors for zero (red) and the other addend and sum (blue) to highlight the structure.

- How can we modify the false equations to make them true?

Continue to Explore With Manipulatives

Give each student counters or blocks and a paper strip with an equation (created on the next pages). Invite the students to represent an equation with the blocks at their desks and fill in the sum.

- What will go in the blank space to make the equation true?

    1 + 0 = _____

    0 + 1 = _____

    2 + 0 = _____

0 + 2 = _____

3 + 0 = _____

0 + 3 = _____

4 + 0 = _____

0 + 4 = _____

5 + 0 = _____

0 + 5 = _____

6 + 0 = _____

0 + 6 = _____

7 + 0 = _____

0 + 7 = _____

8 + 0 = _____

0 + 8 = _____

9 + 0 = _____

0 + 9 = _____

10 + 0 = _____

0 + 10 = _____

Back at the carpet, have each student share the equation they created. When a student shares, tape their equation to an anchor chart in the following order to highlight the structure, no matter what order the students share in. If students share "out of order," leave spaces for the equations to fill in the pattern as they continue to share. This will help the structure of the equations become more visible.

1 + 0 = 1	0 + 1 = 1
2 + 0 = 2	0 + 2 = 2
3 + 0 = 3	0 + 3 = 3
4 + 0 = 4	0 + 4 = 4
5 + 0 = 5	0 + 5 = 5
6 + 0 = 6	0 + 6 = 6
7 + 0 = 7	0 + 7 = 7
8 + 0 = 8	0 + 8 = 8
9 + 0 = 9	0 + 9 = 9
10 + 0 = 10	0 + 10 = 10

At this point, you could pause for the day or it might make sense to continue to the noticing and wondering layer if time allows and the students are eager to continue.

Layer 1: Students Notice and Wonder

Invite the students to make observations about the set of true statements. Record their ideas on a public record.

Questions to Nudge at Noticing and Wondering	Anticipated Student Responses
• What do you notice? What do you wonder? • What patterns do you notice in our equations? • How might the pattern continue? • What would the next equations be on the paper strips? • What do the equations have in common? • What do you notice about addends in the equations? • Who has a related observation? • What connections do you see?	• All equations have a zero in them. • Zero doesn't add anything. When you add zero, nothing happens. • Some are true, and some are false. • All of the equations have a zero. • We're not adding anything to it, because zero is nothing. • The number you add to zero is the same number it equals. • Sometimes zero is the first number in the equation and sometimes it's second. • You can switch the two numbers that you are adding.

Language Supports	Notes for Recording Student Thinking	Supportive Representations
• I notice _____. • I wonder _____.	• Use colors and placement to connect related ideas. • Write the zeros in red. • Write the matching addend and sum in blue.	• Connecting cubes • Counters (magnetic counters could be helpful so everyone can see) • We could hold the amount for each addend in each hand to show a concrete visual representation of the operation.

Layer 2: Students Conjecture

Invite students to make conjectures about what they noticed and wondered. Record ideas on the public record.

Questions to Nudge at Conjecturing	Conjectures That Might Emerge From the Noticings and Wonderings
• Is that observation always true? When will it be true? • What do you believe might always be true about adding zero? • Does that work with all numbers? • Is that true always, sometimes, or never? How do you know? • How can you use a tool to show what you mean? • Can you draw a visual representation to show what you mean?	• The number you add to zero is the same number it equals. • If you add zero to a number, you get the same number again. • If you have two numbers and one of them is a zero, the sum will be the other number. **Related to the Commutative Property of Addition** (These conjectures can be acknowledged and saved for another day.) • Zero can be the first number or the second number. • You can switch the two numbers that you are adding.

Language Supports	Notes for Recording Student Thinking	Supportive Representations
• My conjecture is _____. • It will always be true that _____.	Write conjectures near to where the examples are recorded.	• Connecting cubes • Counters (magnetic counters could be helpful so everyone can see) • We could hold the amount for each addend in each hand to show a concrete visual representation of the operation.

Layer 3: Students Justify

Invite students to justify their conjectures. Record their ideas on the public record.

Questions to Nudge at Justifying	Ways That Students Might Justify the Conjecture

- Why is that true? Why is it not true?
- Why do you believe that is true?
- How can you convince someone that the conjecture is true?
- How can you justify that the conjecture is true?
- Can you use a drawing to show why that works?
- Can you use a tool to show why that works?
- How can you convince someone the conjecture is always true? Never true?
	- Appealing to authority (book, teacher, and so on)
	- Showing several numerical examples with small numbers
	   $5 + 0; 3 + 0$
	- Showing several numerical examples with large numbers
	   $100 + 0; 999 + 0$
	- Providing a context/example: If I have 4 books and I get 0 more, I still have 4 books.
	- Draw a number of objects and explain something like, "When you add zero, you add nothing. The amount is still the same as what you started with. When you add zero, the amount doesn't change."
	- Show an amount of cubes or counters and use them to explain, "When you add zero, you add nothing. The amount is still the same as what you started with."

Language Supports	Notes for Recording Student Thinking	Supportive Representations
- It is true because _____. - I agree because _____. - I disagree because _____.	Show a variety of justifications that are concrete, pictorial, and verbal.	- Connecting cubes - Counters (magnetic counters could be helpful so everyone can see)

Layer 4: Students Extend

Consider which conjecture would benefit from modifying. Invite students to extend the ideas further to related content. (The various type styles will help you connect the questions in the left column with their possible modifications in the right column.)

Questions to Nudge at Extending	Ways the Conjecture May Be Modified and Extended
<ul><li>Can someone restate _____'s conjecture?</li><li>Does anyone have a similar idea or something you'd like to add?</li><li>Does anyone have a different idea?</li><li>Would it still be true if . . . ?</li><li>Are there words in the conjecture that anyone has a question about?</li><li>How can we rewrite our conjecture to make it more precise?<ul><li>*What numbers do you mean?*</li><li><u>What do you mean total?</u></li></ul></li><li>Are there other things you think might be true now that we've explored this conjecture? What else might be true? (For example, what happens if both numbers or addends are zero?)</li></ul>	**Example of an Original Student Conjecture** If you have two numbers and one of them is a zero, the total will be the other number. **Possible Modifications to the Original Based on Questions to the Left**<ul><li>If you have two *addends* and one of them is a zero, the total will be the other addend.</li><li>If you have two *addends* and one of them is a zero, the <u>sum</u> will be the other addend.</li></ul>**Possible Extensions**<ul><li>If you subtract zero from a number, you get the same number.</li><li>If you add one to a number, you will not get the same number.</li></ul>

Language Supports	Notes for Recording Student Thinking	Supportive Representations
<ul><li>Addend</li><li>Sum</li></ul>	Make connections between different representations by using coordinating colors for the same parts.	<ul><li>Connecting cubes</li><li>Counters (magnetic counters could be helpful so everyone can see)</li></ul>

APPENDIX B

Mathematical Ideas Across Chapters

Mathematical Ideas Across Chapters

This reproducible provides an easy way for you to locate the mathematical ideas in this book.

Chapter	Page	Activity or Context	Mathematical Idea
1	9	Classroom Vignette: Decomposing Tens in a Kindergarten Classroom	Decomposing 10
1	12	Your Turn: Ava's Conjecture	Number of ways to make a number
1	15	Classroom Vignette: Second Graders Conjecture About Even Numbers	Odd and even numbers
1	19	Your Turn: Explore Consecutive Sums	Consecutive sums
2	32	Classroom Vignette: Diego's Kindergarten Conjecture	Subtracting from teen numbers
2	36	Classroom Vignette: Kindergartners Turn and Talk	Skip-counting sequence
3	56	Classroom Vignette: Subtraction With Grade 1	Decomposing when subtracting
4	69	Exploring Number of the Day Instructional Routine	Interpretations of 10
4	71	Classroom Vignette: Ways to Make 64 in First Grade	Number sense—64
4	74	Exploring Choral Counting Instructional Routine	Counting and number sequence
4	77	Classroom Vignette: First Graders Investigate Sarah's Conjecture	Counting by or adding 10
4	83	Exploring True or False Instructional Routine	Understanding equality
4	86	Classroom Vignette: First Graders Make Sense of the Equal Sign	Understanding the equal sign; algebraic thinking
5	99	Classroom Vignette: Number of the Day and Notice and Wonder	Number sense—100
6	119	Your Turn: Decomposing Numbers (figure 6.1)	Decomposing numbers
6	124	Adding With 10 (figure 6.4)	Composing teen numbers
6	133	Tasks for Conjecturing: Which Pictures Represent One-Half? (figure 6.9)	Fractions
7	145	Kindergarten Classroom Example (figure 7.6)	Operating with 0
7	152	Subtraction Card Task	Subtraction from teen numbers
8	163	Classroom Vignette: Number of the Day and Extending	Adding decade numbers
8	169	Making a Ten Task (figure 8.4)	Compositions of 10 and other sums
8	170	Your Turn: Addition Table (figure 8.5)	Properties and sums
9	177	Discovering Opportunities: 9 Plus Game	Adding with nine
9	181	Discovering Opportunities: Even or Odd Card Sort	Odd/even numbers
9	183	Classroom Vignette: Understanding Two-Digit Numbers	Place values and two-digit numbers
10	193	Classroom Vignette: *This Is a Ball* in Kindergarten	Geometric properties

Nurturing Math Curiosity © 2024 Solution Tree Press • SolutionTree.com
Visit **go.SolutionTree.com/mathematics** to download this free reproducible.

References and Resources

Aguirre, J., Mayfield-Ingram, K., & Martin, D. B. (2013). *The impact of identity in K–8 mathematics: Rethinking equity-based practices*. Reston, VA: National Council of Teachers of Mathematics.

Ball, D. L. (1992). Magical hopes: Manipulatives and the reform of math education. *American Educator, 16*(2), 14–18, 46–47.

Ball, D. L., Hill, H. C., & Bass, H. (2005). Knowing mathematics for teaching: Who knows mathematics well enough to teach third grade, and how can we decide? *American Educator, 29*(1), 14–17, 20–22, 43–46.

Blanton, M. L. (2008). *Algebra and the elementary classroom: Transforming thinking, transforming practice*. Portsmouth, NH: Heinemann.

Boaler, J. (2022). *Setting up positive norms in math class*. Accessed at www.youcubed.org/wp-content/uploads/2017/09/Norms-Paper-2022.pdf on October 3, 2023.

Carpenter, T. P., Fennema, E., Franke, M. L., Levi, L., & Empson, S. (2014). *Children's mathematics: Cognitively guided instruction* (2nd ed.). Portsmouth, NH: Heinemann.

Carpenter, T. P., Franke, M. L., & Levi, L. (2003). *Thinking mathematically: Integrating arithmetic & algebra in elementary school*. Portsmouth, NH: Heinemann.

Cervantes-Barraza, J. A., Hernández-Moreno, A., & Rumsey, C. (2020). Promoting mathematical proof from collective argumentation in primary school. *School Science and Mathematics, 120*(1), 4–14.

Chapin, S. H., O'Connor, C., & Anderson, N. C. (2009). *Classroom discussions: Using math talk to help students learn, grades K–6* (2nd ed.). Sausalito, CA: Math Solutions.

Crews, D. (1986). *Ten black dots*. New York: Greenwillow Books.

Delavan, M. G., & Matranga, A. (2020). Culturally and linguistically responsive noticing and wondering: An equity-inducing yet accessible teaching practice. *Journal of Multicultural Affairs, 5*(1), Article 5.

Downton, A., MacDonald, A., Cheeseman, J., Russo, J., & McChesney, J. (2020). Mathematics learning and education from birth to eight years. In J. Way, C. Atttard, J. Anderson, J. Bobis, H. McMaster, & K. Cartwright (Eds.), *Research in mathematics education in Australasia 2016–2019* (pp. 209–244). New York: Springer Nature Singapore.

Empson, S. B., & Jacobs, V. R. (2008). Learning to listen to children's mathematics. In T. Wood & P. Sullivan (Eds.), *International handbook of mathematics teacher education: Volume 2* (pp. 257–281). New York, Springer.

Franke, M. L., Kazemi, E., & Turrou, A. C. (2018). *Choral counting and counting collections: Transforming the preK–5 math classroom*. Portsmouth, NH: Stenhouse.

Franke, M. L., Webb, N. M., Chan, A. G., Ing, M., Freund, D., & Battey, D. (2009). Teacher questioning to elicit students' mathematical thinking in elementary school classrooms. *Journal of Teacher Education, 60*(4), 380–392.

Guarino, J., & Manseau, S. (2023). Identity making in kindergarten: Diego's story. *Mathematics Teacher: Learning and Teaching PK–12, 116*(6), 419–423.

Higgins, T., Russell, S. J., & Schifter, D. (2022). Student-generated conjecture about the behavior of the operations: Four dimensions supporting a structural understanding of arithmetic. *Journal of Educational Research in Mathematics, 32*(3), 183–200.

Huinker, D. (Ed.). (2020). *Catalyzing change in early childhood and elementary mathematics: Initiating critical conversations*. Reston, VA: National Council of Teachers of Mathematics.

Hutchins, P. (1989). *The doorbell rang*. New York: Greenwillow Books.

Illustrative Mathematics. (n.d.a). *Warm-up: Notice and wonder: jumps on the number line*. Accessed at https://im.kendallhunt.com/k5/teachers/grade-1/unit-3/lesson-1/lesson.html on January 23, 2024.

Illustrative Mathematics. (n.d.b). *Activity 1: Number card subtraction with 10-frames*. Accessed at https://im.kendallhunt.com/k5/teachers/grade-1/unit-3/lesson-23/lesson.html on January 23, 2024.

Illustrative Mathematics. (n.d.c). *Warm-up: Notice and wonder: addition table*. Accessed at https://im.kendallhunt.com/k5/teachers/grade-1/unit-3/lesson-1/lesson.html on January 23, 2024.

Illustrative Mathematics. (n.d.d). *Activity 1: The 9 plus game*. Accessed at https://curriculum.illustrativemathematics.org/k5/teachers/grade-1/unit-3/lesson-17/lesson.html on January 19, 2024.

Illustrative Mathematics. (n.d.e). *Activity 2: Card sort: even or odd*. Accessed at https://im.kendallhunt.com/k5/teachers/grade-2/unit-8/lesson-3/lesson.html on January 19, 2024.

Illustrative Mathematics. (n.d.f). *1.4 numbers to 99*. Accessed at https://curriculum.illustrativemathematics.org/k5/teachers/grade-1/unit-4/lessons.html on January 19, 2024.

Illustrative Mathematics. (n.d.g). *Activity 2: Card sort: base-ten representations*. Accessed at https://curriculum.illustrativemathematics.org/k5/teachers/grade-1/unit-4/lesson-8/lesson.html on February 20, 2024.

Jacobs, V. R., & Kusiak, J. (2006). Got tools? Exploring children's use of mathematics tools during problem solving. *Teaching Children Mathematics, 12*(9), 470–477.

Kastberg, S. E., & Frye, R. S. (2013). Norms and mathematical proficiency. *Teaching Children Mathematics, 20*(1), 28–35.

Kazemi, E., & Hintz, A. (2014). *Intentional talk: How to structure and lead productive mathematical discussions*. Grandview Heights, OH: Stenhouse.

Kelly, L. B., Ogden, M. K., & Moses, L. (2019). Collaborative conversations: Speaking and listening in the primary grades. *Young Children, 74*(1), 30–37.

Knudsen, J., Stevens, H. S., Lara-Meloy, T., Kim, H.-J., & Shechtman, N. (2017). *Mathematical argumentation in middle school—The what, why, and how: A step-by-step guide with activities, games, and lesson planning tools*. Thousand Oaks, CA: Corwin Press.

Kroll, V., & O'Neill, P. (2005). *Equal shmequal*. Watertown, MA: Charlesbridge.

Lannin, J., Ellis, A., & Elliott, R. (2011). *Developing essential understanding of mathematical reasoning for teaching mathematics in pre-K–grade 8*. Reston, VA: National Council of Teachers of Mathematics.

Larson, L. C., & Rumsey, C. (2017). Bringing stories to life: Integrating literature and math manipulatives. *The Reading Teacher, 71*(5), 589–596.

Moore, I. (1991). *Six-dinner Sid*. New York: Simon & Schuster Books for Young Readers.

Moss, J., Bruce, C. D., & Bobis, J. (2016). Young children's access to powerful mathematical ideas: A review of current challenges and new developments in the early years. In L. D. English & D. Kirshner (Eds.), *Handbook of international research in mathematics education* (3rd ed., pp. 153–190). New York: Routledge.

National Association for the Education of Young Children & National Council of Teachers of Mathematics. (2002). *Early childhood mathematics: Promoting good beginnings*. Washington, DC: Authors. Accessed at www.naeyc.org/sites/default/files/globally-shared/downloads/PDFs/resources/position-statements/psmath.pdf on October 4, 2023.

National Council of Teachers of Mathematics. (2014). *Principles to actions: Ensuring mathematical success for all*. Reston, VA: Author.

National Governors Association Center for Best Practices & Council of Chief State School Officers. (2010a). *Common Core State Standards for English language arts and literacy in history/social studies, science, and technical subjects*. Washington, DC: Authors. Accessed at https://corestandards.org/wp-content/uploads/2023/09/ELA_Standards1.pdf on January 29, 2024.

National Governors Association Center for Best Practices & Council of Chief State School Officers. (2010b). *Common Core State Standards for mathematics*. Washington, DC: Authors. Accessed at https://corestandards.org/wp-content/uploads/2023/09/Math_Standards1.pdf on January 29, 2024.

NRICH Project. (n.d.). *Summing consecutive numbers*. University of Cambridge Faculty of Mathematics. Accessed at https://nrich.maths.org/summingconsecutive on October 4, 2023.

Parks, A. N. (2015). *Exploring mathematics through play in the early childhood classroom*. New York: Teachers College Press.

Philipp, R. A., Ambrose, R., Lamb, L. L. C., Sowder, J. T., Schappelle, B. P., Sowder, L., et al. (2007). Effects of early field experiences on the mathematical content knowledge and beliefs of prospective elementary school teachers: An experimental study. *Journal for Research in Mathematics Education, 38*(5), 438–476.

Piaget, J. (1952). *The origins of intelligence in children* (M. Cook, Trans.). New York: W. W. Norton

Piaget, J. (1977). *The development of thought: Equilibration of cognitive structures*. New York: Viking Press.

Pinczes, E. J., & MacKain, B. (1999). *One hundred hungry ants*. New York: Clarion Books.

Reiser, L. (1994). *Any kind of dog*. New York: Greenwillow Books.

Ross, D., Fisher, D., & Frey, N. (2009). The art of argumentation. *Science and Children, 47*(3), 28–31.

Rumack, A. M., & Huinker, D. (2019). Capturing mathematical curiosity with notice and wonder. *Mathematics Teaching in the Middle School, 24*(7), 394–399. https://doi.org/10.5951/mathteacmiddscho.24.7.0394

Rumsey, C. (2012). *Advancing fourth-grade students' understanding of arithmetic properties with instruction that promotes mathematical argumentation* [Doctoral dissertation, Illinois State University]. ProQuest Dissertations Publishing. Accessed at www.proquest.com/docview/1033806224 on January 19, 2024.

Rumsey, C., Guarino, J., Gildea, R., Cho, C. Y., & Lockhart, B. (2019). Tools to support K–2 students in mathematical argumentation. *Teaching Children Mathematics, 25*(4), 208–217.

Rumsey, C., Guarino, J., & Sperling, M. (2023). Subtraction, decomposition, and argumentation. *Mathematics Teacher: Learning and Teaching PK–12, 116*(2), 90–98.

Rumsey, C., & Langrall, C. W. (2016). Promoting mathematical argumentation. *Teaching Children Mathematics, 22*(7), 412–419.

Rumsey, C., Whitacre, I., Atabas, S., & Smith, J. L. (2022). Argumentation in the context of elementary grades: The role of participants, tasks, and tools. In K. N. Bieda, A. Conner, K. W. Kosko, & M. Staples. (Eds.), *Conceptions and consequences of argumentation, justification, and proof* (pp. 19–34). Cham, Switzerland: Springer.

Russell, S. J., Schifter, D., & Bastable, V. (2011). *Connecting arithmetic to algebra: Strategies for building algebraic thinking in the elementary grades*. Portsmouth, NH: Heinemann.

Russell, S. J., Schifter, D., Bastable, V., Higgins, T., & Kasman, R. (2017). *But why does it work? Mathematical argument in the elementary classroom*. Portsmouth, NH: Heinemann.

Schifter, D., & Russell, S. J. (2020). A model for teaching mathematical argument at the elementary grades. *Journal of Educational Research in Mathematics, Special Issue*, 15–28.

Seo, K.-H., & Ginsburg, H. P. (2004). What is developmentally appropriate in early childhood mathematics education? Lessons from new research. In D. H. Clements, J. Sarama, & A.-M. DiBiase (Eds.), *Engaging young children in mathematics: Standards for early childhood mathematics education* (pp. 91–104). Hillsdale, NJ: Erlbaum.

Shah, P. E., Weeks, H. M., Richards, B., & Kaciroti, N. (2018). Early childhood curiosity and kindergarten reading and math academic achievement. *Pediatric Research, 84*(3), 380–386. https://doi.org/10.1038/s41390-018-0039-3

Sokolowski, A. (2018). The effects of using representations in elementary mathematics: Meta-analysis of research. *IAFOR Journal of Education, 6*(3), 129–152.

Stanton, B., & Stanton, M. (2015). *This is a ball*. New York: HarperCollins.

Stylianou, D., & Blanton, M. (2018). *Teaching with mathematical argument: Strategies for supporting everyday instruction*. Portsmouth, NH: Heinemann.

Su, F. (2020). *Mathematics for human flourishing*. New Haven, CT: Yale University Press.

Turrou, A. C., Johnson, N. C., & Franke, M. L. (2021). *The young child & mathematics* (3rd ed.). Washington, DC: National Association for the Education of Young Children.

Van de Walle, J. A., Karp, K. S., & Bay-Williams, J. M. (2013). *Elementary and middle school mathematics: teaching developmentally* (8th ed.). Upper Saddle River, NJ: Pearson.

van Es, E. A., & Sherin, M. G. (2006). How different video club designs support teachers in "learning to notice." *Journal of Computing in Teacher Education, 22*(4), 125–135.

Webb, N. M., Franke, M. L., Ing, M., Turrou, A. C., Johnson, N. C., & Zimmerman, J. (2019). Teacher practices that promote productive dialogue and learning in mathematics classrooms. *International Journal of Educational Research, 97*(5), 176–186.

Whitacre, I., & Rumsey, C. (2018). Documenting the process of a prospective elementary teacher's flexibility development: Scaffolded strategy ranges and sociomathematical norms for mental computation. *Cognition and Instruction, 36*(4), 330–360. https://doi.org/10.1080/07370008.2018.1491580

Whitacre, I., & Rumsey, C. (2020). The roles of tools and models in a prospective elementary teachers' developing understanding of multidigit multiplication. *Journal of Mathematical Behavior*, 60, Article 100816. https:// doi.org/10.1016/j.jmathb.2020.100816

Williams, H. J. (2022). *Playful mathematics: For children 3 to 7*. Thousand Oaks, CA: Corwin Press.

Wormeli, R. (2014). Motivating young adolescents. *Educational Leadership, 72*(1), 26–31.

Yackel, E., & Cobb, P. (1996). Sociomathematical norms, argumentation, and autonomy in mathematics. *Journal for Research in Mathematics Education, 27*(4), 458–477.

Yackel, E., Cobb, P., & Wood, T. (1991). Small-group interactions as a source of learning opportunities in second-grade mathematics. *Journal for Research in Mathematics Education, 22*(5), 390–408.

Index

NUMBERS

9 Plus Game, 177–180
100, your turn, 98, 104

A

addition
    addition tables, 107, 109, 169, 170–171
    arithmetic properties and, 130
    behavior of operations and, 131
    mathematical ideas across chapters, 240
    number lines and, 128
    true or false instructional routines and, 83, 85
    your turn: adding and subtracting the same amount, 149
    your turn: justifying addends conjecture, 140–141
Aguirre, J., 34
appealing to authority, 144. *See also* justifying
argumentation. *See* mathematical argumentation
arithmetic properties, 130
artful guidance, 31

B

Ball, D., 48
Bass, H., 48

Bastable, V., 13, 123–124
behavior of operations, 131
Blanton, M., 34, 66

C

card sorts, 181, 182, 183, 184, 185
Carpenter, T., 38, 85, 118, 131
Catalyzing Change in Early Childhood and Elementary Mathematics (Huinker), 31
children's literature. *See* using children's literature to engage in argumentation
choral counting
    choral counting public record, 75, 78
    classroom vignette: first graders investigate Sarah's conjecture, 77–81
    instructional routines for, 74–83
    reproducibles for, 217–221
    your turn: count by 10 starting at 8, 76–77
    your turn: patterns in a choral count, 81–82
classroom communities
    about, 29–30
    classroom vignette: Diego's kindergarten conjecture, 32–34
    classroom vignette: kindergarteners turn and talk, 36–37

connecting the classroom environment and teacher toolbox through routines. *See* routines
making connections to routines, 90
norms and, 35–37
physical classroom space and, 41
playful environments, making, 31–34
questions for further reflection, 42
reproducibles for, 43
summary, 42
talk moves and, 37–40
Cobb, P., 35
communication
asking questions, 55–56
eight effective teaching and learning practices, 45
group structures and, 60
hand signals, 53
language frames, 41, 53, 59–60, 134
norms and, 35–36
supporting precise student languages, 56–59
teacher voices: communication, 40
community roles for teachers, students, and routines, 68
commutative property, 10, 83, 87, 89, 136, 167
comparing and contrasting operations, 14
conjecturing
about, 117–123
add-on conjecture for double-digit numbers, 187
argumentation in the classroom vignettes and, 18
articulating, 14
asking questions and, 55
class conjecture about the order of numbers, 185
classroom vignette: decomposing tens in a kindergarten classroom, 11
classroom vignette: Diego's kindergarten conjecture, 32–34
classroom vignette: first graders investigate Sarah's conjecture, 77–81
classroom vignette: Number of the Day and, 121–123
classroom vignette: second graders conjecture about even numbers, 15–16
conjecture cycle, 165
conjectures chart for grade 1, 123
consecutive sums and, 124–129
examples of, 125, 130–132
justifying and, 150, 151
layers of mathematical argumentation, 14
Number of the Day instructional routines and, 71, 134–136
questions for further reflection, 136
reproducibles for, 137
revised conjecture, 186
summary, 136
teacher voices: conjectures, 125, 135–136
true or false instructional routines and, 85
understanding conjecturing, 123–124
using tasks for, 132–134
your turn: adding and subtracting the same amount, 149
your turn: Ava's conjecture, 12–13

your turn: justifying addends conjecture, 140–141
your turn: previous conjectures, 162
your turn: subtraction conjecture, 58–59
your turn: working with conjectures, 24
connecting cubes, 49, 101, 128
connecting the classroom environment and teacher toolbox through routines. *See* routines
consecutive sums
conjecturing and, 124–129
exploring consecutive sums, 18–25
extending and, 168
justifying and, 143–144
noticing and wondering and, 103–104
reflecting on your experience with, 25
your turn: exploring consecutive sums, 19–23
counterexamples, 148. *See also* examples and justifying; justifying

D

decomposing numbers
charts related to, 11, 120
classroom vignette: decomposing tens in a kindergarten classroom, 9–11
example of, 57, 105
your turn: decomposing numbers, 119–120

E

eight effective teaching and learning practices, 45
Empson, S., 38
equal signs, 83, 85, 86–87, 89, 200
establishing the foundation for mathematical argumentation. *See* foundation for mathematical argumentation
even numbers classroom vignette, 15–16
examples and justifying, 145–146, 146–148. *See also* justifying
exploration, recording sheets for, 79, 126
exploring the first layer: notice, wonder, and beyond. *See* noticing and wondering
exploring the fourth layer: extending. *See* extending
exploring the second layer: conjecturing. *See* conjecturing
exploring the third layer: justifying. *See* justifying
extending
about, 161–164
argumentation in the classroom vignettes and, 18
asking questions, 55–56
classroom vignette: Number of the Day and, 163–164
consecutive sums and, 168
layers of mathematical argumentation, 14
Number of the Day instructional routines and, 71
questions for further reflection, 172
reproducibles for, 174
summary, 173
teacher voices: extending ideas, 168
understanding extending, 164–168
using tasks for, 168–172

F

Fennema, E., 38

Index

finding opportunities for argumentation. *See* opportunities for argumentation

foundation for mathematical argumentation
- about, 9–13
- classroom vignette: decomposing tens in a kindergarten classroom, 9–11
- classroom vignette: second graders conjecture about even numbers, 15–16
- exploring consecutive sums, 18–25
- layers of argumentation in the classroom vignettes, 17–18
- layers of mathematical argumentation, 14–17
- questions for further reflection, 26
- reproducibles for, 27
- summary, 26
- teacher voices: what is mathematical argumentation, 15
- teaching mathematics in grades K-2, 13

Franke, M., 38, 75, 85, 118

G

generating cases, 14

groups, using group structures to encourage conversation, 60

growing our teacher toolbox. *See* teacher toolbox

growing the layers of argumentation. *See* conjecturing; extending; justifying; noticing and wondering

H

hand signals
- classroom vignette: ways to make 64 in first grade, 71–74
- tools for communicating, 53–54

Higgins, T., 14, 118, 123–124, 136

Hill, H., 48

Huinker, D., 31, 97

I

instructional routine planning template reproducible, 212–216. *See also* planning; *specific instructional routines*

introduction
- how do we get started together, 2–4
- K-2 classroom and mathematics, 1–2

J

justifying
- about, 139–143
- argumentation in the classroom vignettes and, 18
- asking questions, 55
- classroom vignette: Number of the Day and, 141–143
- consecutive sums and, 143–144
- examples of K-2 justifications, 150
- layers of mathematical argumentation, 14
- Number of the Day instructional routines and, 71, 156–157
- questions for further reflection, 157
- reproducibles for, 158
- summary, 157
- true or false instructional routines and, 85
- understanding justifying, 143
- using tasks for, 151–155
- ways that students justify, 144–150
- your turn: justifying addends conjecture, 140–141

K

Kaciroti, N., 31
Kasman, R., 123–124
Kazemi, E., 75

L

language. *See also* communication
- language frames, 41, 53, 59–60, 134
- precise language, 56–57, 164

Levi, L., 38, 85, 118

list of children's books for read-alouds, 199–200

listening, 35–36. *See also* norms

M

Martin, D., 34

mathematical argumentation
- children's literature and, 199
- establishing the foundation for. *See* foundation for mathematical argumentation
- finding opportunities for. *See* opportunities for argumentation
- layers of argumentation in the classroom vignettes, 17–18. *See also specific layers of argumentation*
- teacher voices: what is mathematical argumentation, 15
- your turn: identifying argumentation-ready tasks, 181

mathematical ideas across chapters, 240

Mayfield-Ingram, K., 34

minuends, 57, 58, 59, 131, 165

N

nonverbal communication, 53. *See also* communication

norms, 35–36, 53, 66, 102

noticing and wondering
- about, 97–101
- argumentation in the classroom vignettes and, 18
- asking questions, 55
- classroom vignette: Number of the Day and, 99–101
- consecutive sums and, 103–104
- first-grade notice and wonder warm-up, 172
- layers of mathematical argumentation, 14
- notice and wonder public record, 194
- notice and wonder—connecting cubes, 128
- Number of the Day instructional routines and, 71, 110, 112
- questions for further reflection, 112
- reproducibles for, 114
- summary, 113
- teacher voices: notice and wonder, 112
- true or false instructional routines and, 85
- understanding notice and wonder, 101–103
- using tasks for, 105–110

number lines, 49, 128

Number of the Day instructional routines
- classroom vignette: Number of the Day and conjecturing, 121–123

classroom vignette: Number of the Day and extending, 163–164
classroom vignette: Number of the Day and justifying, 141–143
classroom vignette: Number of the Day and notice and wonder, 99–101
classroom vignette: ways to make 64 in first grade, 71–74
conjecturing and, 134–136
example instructional routine planning template, 111
instructional routines for, 69–74
justifying and, 156–157
noticing and wondering and, 110, 112
public record for, 121
reproducibles for, 222–226, 227–231
your turn: 64, 70–71
nurturing a classroom community. *See* classroom communities

O

opportunities for argumentation. *See also* mathematical argumentation
about, 177
classroom vignette: understanding two-digit numbers, 183–187
discovering opportunities, 177–189
questions for further reflection, 189
reproducibles for, 190
summary, 189
teacher voices: instructional materials, 189

P

Parks, A., 117
physical classroom space, 41. *See also* classroom communities
place value, 70, 75, 124, 183
planning
instructional routine planning template reproducible, 212–216
planning read-alouds, 199–202. *See also* using children's literature to engage in argumentation
tools for planning, 46–48
playful environments, 31–32, 66
precise student languages, 56–57. *See also* communication
problem solving, 45
procedures, 130–131
public records
examples of, 52, 72, 75, 78, 100, 121, 180, 194
physical classroom space and, 41
using public records, 51–53

Q

questions, asking, 55–56

R

reasoning, 45, 148. *See also* justifying
recording sheets, 79, 126, 195, 197, 198
reflection teacher voices, 156–157
representations
eight effective teaching and learning practices, 45
examples of, 57, 101, 142, 143, 183, 186
layers of mathematical argumentation, 14
public records and, 51–53
teacher voices: representations, 148

tools for representing mathematical ideas, 48–53
visual and physical representations, 49–51
ways that students justify, 146–148
reproducibles for
chapter 1 application guide, 27
chapter 2 application guide, 43
chapter 3 application guide, 62
chapter 4 application guide, 92
chapter 5 application guide, 114
chapter 6 application guide, 137
chapter 7 application guide, 158
chapter 8 application guide, 174
chapter 9 application guide, 190
chapter 10 application guide, 204
choral counting example, 217–221
instructional routine planning template, 212–216
mathematical ideas across chapters, 240
Number of the Day example, 222–226
Number of the Day example with annotations, 227–231
true or false example, 232–237
Richards, B., 31
roles for teachers, students, and routines, 68
Ross, D., 59
routines
about, 65–66
choral counting instructional routines, 74–83
classroom communities and teacher toolboxes and, 90
classroom vignette: first graders investigate Sarah's conjecture, 77–81
classroom vignette: first graders make sense of the equal sign, 86–87
classroom vignette: ways to make 64 in first grade, 71–74
community roles for teachers, students, and routines, 68
layers of argumentation and, 91
Number of the Day instructional routines, 69–74
questions for further reflection, 90
reproducibles for, 92
summary, 91
teacher voices: instructional routines, 67
true or false instructional routines, 83–89
using instructional routines, 66–69
Russell, S., 13, 14, 118, 123–124, 136, 143

S

Schifter, D., 13, 14, 118, 123–124, 136, 143
sentence frames, 59, 100
Shah, P., 31
speaking and listening, 29, 36, 37, 39–40, 53
students
community roles for, 68
teacher and student opportunities, 67
Stylianou, D., 34, 66
Su, F., 15
subtraction
behavior of operations and, 131

Index

classroom vignette: subtraction with grade 1, 56–58
mathematical ideas across chapters, 240
number lines and, 128
procedures and, 131
subtraction cards tasks, 152
true or false instructional routines and, 83
your turn: adding and subtracting the same amount, 149
your turn: subtraction card task, 153–154
your turn: subtraction conjecture, 58–59

subtrahend, 57, 58, 165

T

talk moves, 37–40, 53. See also turn and talk classroom vignette
tasks
    conjecturing and, 132–134
    extending and, 168–172
    justifying and, 151–155
    noticing and wondering and, 105–110
    your turn: connecting to tasks, 127
    your turn: identifying argumentation-ready tasks, 181
    your turn: subtraction card tasks, 153–154

teacher toolbox
    about, 45–46
    classroom vignette: subtraction with grade 1, 56–57
    connecting the classroom environment and teacher toolbox through routines. See routines
    eight effective teaching and learning practices, 45
    making connections to routines, 90
    questions for further reflection, 60–61
    reproducibles for, 62
    summary, 61
    teacher voices: planning the chart, 51
    tools for communicating, 53–60
    tools for planning, 46–48
    tools for representing mathematical ideas, 48–53
    your turn: subtraction conjecture, 58–59

teachers
    community roles for, 68
    teacher and student opportunities, 67

Thinking Mathematically: Integrating Arithmetic and Algebra in Elementary School (Carpenter, Franke, Levi), 85
This Is a Ball (Stanton and Stanton), 193–199

tools for representing mathematical ideas. See representations
true equations organized to elicit a pattern, 125
true or false instructional routines
    classroom vignette: first graders make sense of the equal sign, 86–87
    instructional routines for, 83–89
    reproducibles for, 232–237
    teacher voices: true or false, 89
    your turn: explore two examples, 84
    your turn: how might students respond, 87–89

turn and talk classroom vignette, 36–37
Turrou, A., 75
two-color counters, 49, 51, 105, 106
types of numbers, 130

U

using children's literature to engage in argumentation. See also mathematical argumentation
    about, 193
    classroom vignette: *This Is a Ball* in kindergarten, 193–199
    mathematical argumentation and, 199
    planning read-alouds, 199–202
    questions for further reflection, 203
    reproducibles for, 204
    summary, 203

W

Weeks, H., 31
Williams, H., 11, 29, 31, 98, 125
Wormeli, R., 98

Y

Yackel, E., 35

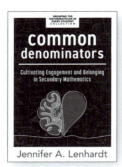

Common Denominators
Jennifer A. Lenhardt
"*Common Denominators* is a collection of stories braided together with research-informed strategies and tools," writes author Jennifer A. Lenhardt. Make sense of student engagement and belonging by using mathematics concepts that illustrate our common humanity and illuminate a clear, sustainable path for honoring and meeting all students' needs.
BKG179

See It, Say It, Symbolize It
Patrick L. Sullivan
Anyone can learn mathematics and stay in the math game for life once they learn key superpowers that can demystify foundational concepts—from whole numbers, fractions, and place value operations to ratios, proportions, and percentages. This book offers teaching methods to develop a dynamic and flexible understanding of numbers and operations in young learners.
BKG187

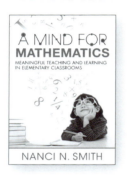

A Mind for Mathematics
Nanci N. Smith
This easy-to-read text combines research, practical strategies, and examples from K–6 classrooms that will inspire and engage mathematical minds.
BKF724

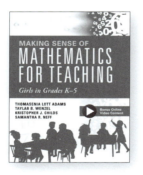

Making Sense of Mathematics for Teaching Girls in Grades K–5
Thomasenia Lott Adams, Taylar B. Wenzel, Kristopher J. Childs, and Samantha R. Neff
Close the gender gap in mathematics. Acquire tools, tips, short exercises, and reflection questions that will help you understand the math and gender stereotypes impacting girls' education and eliminate gender bias through effective elementary school math instruction.
BKF816

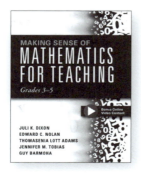

Making Sense of Mathematics for Teaching Grades 3–5
Juli K. Dixon, Edward C. Nolan, Thomasenia Lott Adams, Jennifer M. Tobias, and Guy Barmoha
Explore strategies and techniques to effectively learn and teach mathematics concepts for grades 3–5 and provide all students with the precise, accurate information they need to achieve success.
BKF696

Visit SolutionTree.com or call 800.733.6786 to order.

Quality team learning **from authors you trust**

Global PD Teams is the first-ever **online professional development resource designed to support your entire faculty on your learning journey.** This convenient tool offers daily access to videos, mini-courses, eBooks, articles, and more packed with insights and research-backed strategies you can use immediately.

GET STARTED
SolutionTree.com/**GlobalPDTeams**
800.733.6786